WITNESS OF DECLINE

Albert Camus in 1947

WITNESS OF DECLINE

Albert Camus:
Moralist of the Absurd

Lev Braun

Rutherford • Madison • Teaneck
FAIRLEIGH DICKINSON UNIVERSITY PRESS

© 1974 by Associated University Presses, Inc.

Associated University Presses, Inc.
Cranbury, New Jersey 08512

Library of Congress Cataloging in Publication Data

Braun, Lev.
    Witness of decline.

    Bibliography: p.
    1. Camus, Albert, 1913–1960.   I. Title.
PQ2605.A3734Z553   848'.9'1409   72-11082
ISBN 0-8386-1246-6

Also by Lev Braun:
Winston Churchill: War Speeches 1939-1945 (translated into Czech)

PRINTED IN THE UNITED STATES OF AMERICA

To Micheline

Contents

CONTENTS

Acknowledgments

I wish to thank the following publishers for permission to quote from published works:

Editions Gallimard, for permission to quote from Albert Camus's works, published in *Théâtre, Récits et Nouvelles* (Bibliothèque de la Pléiade, 1962); from *Lettres à un ami allemand*, 1945; from *Actuelles II* and *III*, 1953, 1958, and from *Carnets I*, 1954.

Hamish Hamilton, for permission to quote from Albert Camus's *The Plague*, London, 1948.

Harcourt Brace Jovanovich, Inc., for permission to quote from Milovan Djilas's, *The Unperfect Society: Beyond the New Class*, New York, 1968.

Methuen & Co. Ltd., for permission to quote from Milovan Djilas's, *The Unperfect Society: Beyond the New Class*, London, 1968.

Random House, Inc., Alfred A. Knopf, Inc., New York, for permission to quote various excerpts from Albert Camus's work in translation: from *Lyrical and Critical Essays*, 1969; *Resistance, Rebellion and Death*, 1961; *Caligula and Three Other Plays*, 1958; *The Rebel*, 1954, and *The Stranger*, 1946; also from Chateaubriand, *The Memoirs of Chateaubriand*, 1961.

Walter de Gruyter & Co., for permission to quote from Nicolai Hartmann's *Das Problem des geistigen Seins,* Berlin, 1949.

I also wish to express my thanks to Madame Camus, who has given me two pages of her late husband's manuscripts to be reprinted in this book.

I thank Roger M. Viollet for permission to reproduce the photograph of Albert Camus.

Many thanks are also due to my colleagues Samuel Raphaelides and Dr. Duane Edwards, and to Mrs. Mathilde E. Finch, Editor-in-Chief of Associated University Presses, for their meticulous reading of the manuscript before it went to press.

Special thanks are due to Dr. Lengyel, former chairman of my department at Fairleigh Dickinson University, for his encouragement to continue my work, and to Dr. Charles Angoff, Director of the University's Press, for his keen interest in my book.

Above all, however, I wish to express my profound gratitude to my wife, without whose help and patience I would have been unable to finish this book.

L. B.

Fairleigh Dickinson University
Rutherford, New Jersey

Introduction

Albert Camus is usually regarded as an existential moralist because his ethics are not derived from a preestablished set of values, but are based on a special kind of experience for which he claims universal validity. This experience he sums up in the word absurdity. He describes it in *The Myth of Sisyphus* as a sense of spiritual frustration and dereliction, the result of an incongruity between what we expect from life and what the world actually has to offer: "le divorce entre l'esprit qui désire et le monde qui déçoit."[1]

The deceptive simplicity of this sentence has done Camus much harm since the bulk of his readers, having grasped this piece of thought, have hastily classified Camus among the belated romantics. The feeling of absurdity breeds revolt, and the mechanism is set: having eschewed the temptation of Satanism (*Caligula*) and indifference (*The Stranger*), Camus is supposed to have landed safely in Lamartinien idealism. (Readers of a contrary bent, while accepting the same premises, would deplore Camus's sliding from splendid rebellion into stale humanitarian rhetoric.) It is the purpose of this study to follow the development of Camus's ethics and politics in order to show the fallacy of such simplifications and, having restored Camus to all his complexity and ambiguities, to try and appraise what remains

---

1. *Le Mythe de Sisyphe* (Paris: Gallimard, 1942), p. 71.

valid today—thirteen years after his death and one full generation after *Sisyphus*—in the thought of the man who was called the last French humanist.

A reexamination of Camus's works indicates that he has been unduly imprisoned in the concept of absurdity as expressed in *The Myth of Sisyphus*. It should be realized that Camus's experience of absurdity is not so clear-cut as it seems in the sentence quoted above, and, moreover, that while absurdity is the most conspicuous theme in Camus's life experience, it is not the only one, perhaps not even the most important one, and Camus's unfinished work might have held in reserve surprising developments.

Camus is not an easy writer; his clarity is deceptive and leads to superficial misinterpretations, as we have seen. Conversely, many critics, mainly philosophers, have found his thought woolly and vague—which, unfortunately, is sometimes the case. His emotions, on the other hand, are invariably sharp and compelling. Since Camus is primarily a poet, he expresses these emotions in symbols and rhythm. As an existential—though not an existentialist—thinker, he has conveyed some of his intuitions in philosophical language; some, but not all. For a man of Camus's poetical temper, philosophy is a translation from his native language. It is therefore advisable, for those who wish fully to understand him, to return to the original. The method employed in this study is that of tracing the origin of Camus's ideas back to his initial symbols in order to elucidate both ideas and symbols by comparison and to show his development from experience to ethics and from emotion to values.

WITNESS OF DECLINE

PART I

Camus's Formative Years.

Nuptials And Revolution

1
Emergence of Values

1. Silence and the Desert

In order to trace Camus's conception of values back to its fundamental source, we must turn to the first books he ever published: *L'Envers et l'Endroit* (*The Right Side and the Wrong Side*) in 1937 and *Noces* (*Nuptials*) in 1938. Here we find Camus's experience expressed in all its immediate unity in an atmosphere perceptibly different from that of *The Myth of Sisyphus*. The books contain autobiographical notes that help us obtain a mental picture of Camus in his formative years. When he looked back on those years in his early manhood, he perceived them as wrapped up in silence.

It is well-known that he was born of a poor family; that after his father's death, at the battle of the Marne, his mother made a living as a cleaning woman, and that he was brought up in Algiers' plebeian suburb of Belcourt. It would be a mistake, however, to believe that poverty left ineradicable seeds of revolt in him. When he writes: "Je n'ai pas appris la liberté dans Marx, je l'ai apprise dans la misère,"[1] there is no tinge of class grievance in these words. He bears witness to this in a recent preface to a new edition of a work of his youth:

1. Albert Camus, *Actuelles II* (Paris: Gallimard, 1953), p. 188.

After some soul searching, however, I can testify that among my many weaknesses I have never discovered that most widespread failing, envy, the true cancer of societies and doctrines.[2]

He adds that he is not to be congratulated for such immunity; he owes it to his own people "who lacked almost everything and envied practically nothing. Merely by their silence, their reserve, their natural sober pride, my people who did not even know how to read taught me the most valuable and enduring lessons."[3] Such a sentence may be compared to similar statements by Charles Péguy, another writer whose childhood among the poor has entered literary history. Péguy tells how his mother and his illiterate grandmother had taught him working-class uprightness. The comparison cannot be pursued further, since Camus's childhood in Belcourt was quite different from that of Péguy; however, it remains valid to the extent that both men were impressed by the dignity of the uncomplaining poor, whose acceptance did not come from resignation but from pride.

Silence as a form of dignity is the element in his childhood experience that Camus has chosen to stress in *L'Envers et l'Endroit*. The shrieks of a despotic grandmother, perhaps addicted to self-inflicted martyrdom, were presumably more acutely perceived by Camus the child; but what Camus the man remembers most vividly is his strangely passive, silent mother, who would sit for hours at the window, lost in aimless contemplation. Of the kind of emotional ties that existed between this silent mother and her equally silent son, a conversation quoted in *L'Envers et l'Endroit* conveys a better idea than any analysis could give:

> She is sitting at the foot of the divan, her feet together, her hands together in her lap. He, on his chair, scarcely looks at her and smokes ceaselessly. A silence.
> "You shouldn't smoke so much."
> "I know."
> The whole feeling of the neighborhood rises through the

---

2. *Lyrical and Critical Essays* (New York: A. Knopf, 1969), p. 7.
3. *Ibid.*, p. 7.

window: the accordion from the café next door, the traffic hurrying in the evening, the smell of the skewers of grilled meat eaten between small, springy rolls of bread, a child crying in the road. The mother rises and picks up her knitting. Her fingers are clumsy, twisted with arthritis. She works slowly, taking up the same stitch three or four times or undoing a whole row with a dull ripping sound.

"It's a little cardigan. I'll wear it with a white collar. With this and my black coat, I'll be dressed for the season."

She has risen to turn on the light.

"It gets dark early these days."

It was true. Summer was over and autumn had not yet begun. Swifts were still calling in the gentle sky.

"Will you come back soon?"

"But I haven't left yet. Why do you mention that?"

"Oh, it was just to say something."

A trolley goes by. A car.

"Is it true I look like my father?"

"The spitting image. Of course, you didn't know him. You were six months old when he died. But if you had a little moustache!"

He mentioned his father without conviction. No memory, no emotion. Probably he was very ordinary. Besides, he had been very keen to go to war. His head was split open in the battle of the Marne. Blinded, it took him a week to die; his name is listed on the local war memorial.

"When you think about it," she says, "it was better that way. He would have come back blind or crazy. So, the poor man . . ."

"That's right."

What is it then that keeps him in this room, except the certainty that it's still the best thing to do, the feeling that the whole *absurd* simplicity of the world has sought refuge here.

"Will you be back again?" she says. "I know you have work to do. Just from time to time."[4]

Is that love? An impersonal love, perhaps, "as if she were the immense pity he felt spread out around him made flesh,

---

4. *The Right Side and the Wrong Side of Things* (*L'Envers et l'Endroit*), in *ibid.,* p. 38.

diligently, without pretense, playing the part of a poor old woman whose fate moves men to tears."[5]

This strange vacancy of mind, usually covered by the agitation of life or, in youth, by the frantic search for pleasure, Camus found in most of the simple people he met in his childhood. And it is always ready to reappear—in old age, in sickness, on Sunday, or simply during the summer evenings when the dwellers in poor lodgings sit in their straw chairs on the sidewalks to breathe in the balmy night. All the characters in Camus's world seem to be wrapped in a thin veil of silence and nothingness, insulated, rather than isolated, by it: Meursault— the Stranger, Rieux and Tarrou in *The Plague,* Rieux's mother, the old woman in *Cross Purposes,* Caesonia and Scipio in *Caligula.* This strange aloofness that gives them a kind of transparency and innocence—is it the blessing promised to the poor in spirit? Or is it simply the inner recess of Mediterranean man when the crushing sun has dulled his human restlessness? This impalpable veil, which also wraps Camus's personality, the quietness of his ideas, the coolness of his style, perhaps hides no mystery except the most baffling of all mysteries, that of a blank wall in the sun, of a motionless Mediterranean landscape, of the figures in Greek reliefs with their silent motions and vacant eyes. All this suggests the arrival of consciousness at the extreme point of its course, precariously hanging and flickering between being and nothingness, always on the point of vanishing, yet alive, an immaterial tuning of the absurd man to the "tender indifference of things," as he finds that "at the heart of my revolt, consent is dormant."[6]

This detachment, which Camus observes in himself and calls "une indifférence naturelle,"[7] has nothing to do with resignation, which is acceptance without consent, still less with indifference in the usual sense of the word, which is lack of desire. Nor is it the renunciation of desire; on the contrary, it enhances desire

5. *Ibid.,* p. 36.
6. *Ibid.,* p. 105.
7. *Ibid.,* p. 103.

by the knowledge of the brevity of life. It is the opposite of stoical asceticism, since it involves no contempt for life, or puritan asceticism, which presupposes fear of life. Camus never regarded this kind of detachment he advocates as a shortcoming or as a flight, but as the highest point of wisdom and, indeed, as a religious experience of nothingness as the essence of life.

Camus repeatedly stresses this point in his first two books and expresses it mainly in images connected with *"le désert."* Not the actual Sahara, which begins a hundred miles to the south of Belcourt, but the arid, luminous landscapes of his childhood, the wind at Djemila, the sunbaked ruins at Tipasa merging back into the stony ground, the implacable summer in Algiers, the hills around Florence and, mostly, the metallic glare of the sea. A pantheistic experience of nothingness and desire underlies the most poetical pages of *Noces*. This, not revolt, is Camus's initial experience. However anti-Christian he may be, at the origin of Camus's experience lies a lost paradise. The title *Noces* is revealing enough, as is the recurring image of bathing— nakedness in the sea, nakedness in the sun. It should be stressed that Camus's initial experience is not of a rift between man and the world, but of a tender understanding between "nature without men" and "man delivered from the human."[8]

It is not a comforting experience, for it is, as Camus stresses, inhuman. The facing of it involves two virtues most highly praised by Camus. One is lucidity and the refusal of illusion (mainly of what he regards as the Christian illusion, that of a Providence and of an eternal life). An often-repeated precept of his is: *"ne pas tricher"* (do not cheat). The second virtue involved in acceptance of ultimate nothingness is generosity, the readiness to give up what is most vital, and face utmost *dénuement*. Detachment, however, is a source of strength for those who can sustain it, for it presents man with his ultimate truth, and something in him welcomes it. It brings with itself its inhuman reward: the inner peace of those who *know,* who refuse nothing, hope for nothing and ask for nothing.

---

8. *Ibid.,* p. 120.

When accounting for this experience of detachment, Camus refers not to the Buddhist Nirvana but to the most commonplace experience of his childhood companions, the men and women of Belcourt, who lived exclusively in the present, knowing that it was brief: "Those men have not cheated."[9] Their insight into the human condition and their silent acceptance of it, Camus regards somewhat rashly as the common heritage of the "Mediterranean man,"[10] and his specific contribution to Western thought. He finds a pictorial illustration of it in Florentine painting. Commenting on Piero della Francesca's *Flagellation,* in which Christ and his persecutor have the same vacant look, he observes: "It is because the torment has no sequel. Its lesson ends with the frame around the canvas. Why should a man who expects no tomorrow feel emotion?"[11]

Here, in *Noces,* we have the first intimation of Camus's concept of measure, so basic in his thought and never fully elucidated. "The impassiveness and the greatness that man shows when he has no hope" is the first and probably the main element in *"la pensée de midi"* (Thought at the Meridian), somewhat superficially analyzed in *The Rebel.* This essential silence and consent hide the tragic dialogue of man with an absurd universe.

2. The Absurd as Metaphysical Experience

Thus, the feeling of absurdity is involved in Camus's initial experience of life. Youth, with its desires, is faced with the transparent indifference of the world: the sun and the blue night ("La nuit aux ailes feutrées, la nuit crépitante d'étoiles"), redolent with all the tantalizing magic and the "tender indifference of things." "In the spring, Tipasa is inhabited by gods and the gods speak in the sun and the scent of absinthe leaves. . . . At certain hours in the day the countryside is black with sunlight."[12] The

9. *Ibid.,* p. 91.
10. Camus edited *Jeune Méditerrannée* (1937) and *Rivages, Revue de Culture Méditerranéenne* (1938).
11. *Noces,* p. 94.
12. *Ibid.,* p. 65.

sun is like an invisible wall that isolates man from the feast of
the world and throws him back on his nothingness.

> That is what youth must be like, this harsh confrontation with
> death, this physical terror of the animal who loves the sun.[13]

Other symbols enlarge this counterpoint of life and death: a
broad-hipped dancer in Majorca, whose undulating body stirs
up a despair of life in her entranced audience; a visit to Djemila,
where Roman ruins, reabsorbed into the earth, become stones
again; the contemplation of an Italian landscape: "Plunged deep
in beauty, the mind feeds off nothingness." Nothing in Camus's
experience mitigates the horror of death, neither God nor Providence nor any superior principle. His only certainties are his
lust for life and his despair of it: "a bitterness beneath a flame."[14]

Death is not the only enemy. Old age has to be faced before
death and, in youth, the apprehension of old age is frequently
overwhelming. In *L'Envers et l'Endroit* the feeling of discrepancy
is called, in Kierkegaardian fashion, irony. Three old people are
introduced in succession. They have in common a voracious
hunger for human contact, in order to screen off their inner
void and the inevitability of death, but their relatives reject them
in an unconscious recoiling from the inner void in which they
dread to be engulfed. Both the solitude of the old and the callousness of the young are bathed in the same indifferent splendor
of Mediterranean light.

Even before old age, the whole middle course of life stretches
before young Camus as an arid no-man's-land, which the Mediterranean man fills with miserable pastimes: bowling, the movies,
family routine. Camus does not despise such occupations, for he
knows what lucid hopelessness lies behind them. "Dieu de l'Eté"
(God of Summer), the Mediterranean man has staked everything
on the passions of his brief youth. His life was there to be
squandered and burnt.

Around this basic frustration, feelings appear and disappear

13. *Ibid.,* p. 77.
14. *Ibid.,* pp. 56, 73, 101.

like ripples on a quiet sea: the sight of death and old age evokes a kind of pity, which is not charity but fascinated horror at one's own fate; the sight of the world, a hunger and tenderness that is not love but the agony of unrequited passion; negative feelings too—envy, jealousy, a frenzy of destruction; and underlying all these agitations, the secret homecoming that only poetry can suggest:

> If it is true that the only paradises are those we have lost, I know what name to give the tender and inhuman something that dwells in me today. The emigrant returns to his country. And I remember.[15]

We do not know at what time in Camus's life this obsession with death appeared, but we do know that the concrete possibility of his death hung over him from his late adolescence, ever since he suffered a first attack of tuberculosis (often an incurable disease at that time). The threat of death that overshadowed his youthful years undoubtedly enhanced this passion for life mixed with despair which is the essence of the feeling of absurdity. It was under the sign of his own death that Camus celebrated his symbolic wedding with the earth in *Noces* and looked at human fate in *L'Envers et l'Endroit*; but what he tried to capture in these two works was the feeling of absurdity inherent in the human condition as such, independent of personal circumstances.

Absurdity, as Camus was to explain later,[16] is the result of a discrepancy: life is not absurd in itself, it only appears so to man. The nature of the discrepancy has to be carefully understood. There is no rift between man and nature—at any rate, not in *Noces*. Here on the threshold of Camus's universe lies the promise of finding a home far beyond the regions of frustrated feeling; it neither contradicts nor offsets the absurd but balances it, according to Camus's intuition of measure. The world in *Noces*

---

15. *Between Yes and No,* p. 30.
16. *The Myth of Sisyphus;* see also chapter 3.1 below.

is both enthralling by its beauty and alien. "The tender indifference of things" and "that tender and inhuman something"—these are what Camus experiences. This is much more complex than downright frustration. It is partly unrequited love, love for a sleeping beauty. Thus Camus's experience of nature is not absolutely frustrating but ambivalent. Nature is both frustrating and friendly, and even to frustration, the mind says yes and no.

Is the discrepancy to be found between emotions and the intellect? One would be tempted to believe this, since the feeling of the absurd appears together with consciousness, and the sharper the consciousness, the stronger the feeling of absurdity. This, however, is no valid argument, since there is no trace in Camus of the kind of irrationality that is prevalent in so many modern thinkers. On the contrary, "do not cheat" clearly means do not escape awareness of death; such awareness is regarded in all cases as a positive value.

Where, then, is the discrepancy? To this question only a tentative answer can be offered, derived from Camus's insistence on the value of detachment. It has been seen that his pantheistic relation to nature satisfies both the senses and a secret feeling of harmony before or beyond personal consciousness, while leaving a gaping void in the region of man's nolstagia for understanding and brotherhood. Could it be, then, that the lost paradise—or the promised one—is to be found in an impersonal consciousness, that would be man's awareness of nature's great rhythm of desire and of death. Thus, not consciousness but personal consciousness, would bring about the rift and the discrepancy that are felt as absurdity. "It is to the extent that I cut myself off from the world that I fear death most, to the degree I attach myself to the fate of living men instead of contemplating the unchanging sky."[17] In another moment of pantheistic communion, Camus feels "self-forgotten" (*"oublié de moi-même"*) and writes: "And never have I felt so deeply and at one and the same time so detached from myself and so present to the world."[18]

---

17. *Ibid.*, p. 75.
18. *Ibid.*, p. 78.

Out of this initial experience certain values emerge. Although Camus seems to trace man's unhappiness back to the rift between the personal and the cosmic, to all practical purposes, that is to say, in his ethics and politics, Camus is a convinced individualist. For this individuality, from which man should detach himself in order to unite with the rhythm of life and nature, may not be trampled upon by other individuals or by groups that would inevitably substitute their own purposes for his. Metaphysical freedom is essential to Camus. Any attempt to bring salvation to others must end, according to Camus, in fanaticism. It is for each man to choose his way. From this conviction spring two basic values in Camus's ethics. The first one is life itself, in its tragic sweetness. The other one is happiness understood here as a sense of unity with the sensuous world. (Camus, of course, has other concepts of happiness to offer, but, in his early works, the stress is on sensuous happiness.) The recognition of a man's right to life and happiness was Camus's fundamental ethical demand and always remained so. This made him the enemy of despots and moralists alike. No faith, no duty, no heroic ideal entitle a man to deprive another of his life or happiness. No ethics of submission or sacrifice may be imposed from outside. This is Camus's unflinching conviction.

Out of his initial experience certain duties also emerge: the first one is intellectual lucidity. In contrast to a number of his contemporaries addicted to the irrational, Camus has consistently advocated *more* consciousness as a cure for the wound inflicted by consciousness. "Ne rien éluder" (to eschew nothing) is one of his oft-repeated precepts. The second virtue in Camus's ethics is fervor: enjoying the riches of life to the full, knowing that they will be taken away, is a form of courage in his eyes, since fervor, as seen earlier, implies detachment. The third virtue is compassion—or at least harmlessness—a singularly passive virtue, as pictured in *L'Envers et l'Endroit* (unless one remembers Camus's considerable political activity at that time). As for active kindness or charity, Camus does not mention it. Whether this is a result of his "natural indifference" or of his preference for understatement is impossible to say.

Camus's ethics, as it emerges from his early works, calls for comparison with Gide and Malraux, who also advocated lucidity and fervor. Camus's debt to Malraux will be studied later. What he owes to Gide is, in fact, little. Camus's sensuous outlook on life is similar to that of *Les Nourritures terrestres,* and his early ethics are reminiscent of Gide's *détachment, disponibilité* and *ferveur.* Camus acknowledges this; he feels nevertheless that Gide is painstakingly practicing these virtues out of puritanical asceticism,[19] while he, Camus, has received them as part of his Mediterranean heritage.

Be that as it may, some criticism could be leveled against Camus (and Gide) for presenting as virtues what may be construed as irresponsibility and lack of concern for others. In fact, both writers eventually faced this problem, Gide in *L'Immoraliste* and Camus in *La Chute,* and both failed to harmonize self-expression with duty to others. (It must be admitted, however, that their opponents, the advocates of self-denial, also miss one half of the problem.)

Many readers of Camus's early works will also be disappointed at the purely sensuous character of his early inspirations, which does not square with the prevailing image of Camus as "the last of the humanists." The fact is that neither *Noces* nor *L'Envers* contains any intimation of more lofty pursuits: no intellectual interests—although we know from his *Carnets* that Camus was reading voraciously at that time; no deep human attachment—although Camus was already married, had a child, and was known as a warm-hearted friend; not even any mention of creative work, while he was writing his first prose poems. It may be that Camus's youth was still too vehement for him to accept any compensation for his sensuous frustration by death; or that some men and women of a passionate disposition are so enthralled by the brief feast of life that they feel nothing equal to it—if

19. *Ibid.,* p. 83n.

they are sincere; or it may be simply that young Camus, in spite of his talent and education, was still immersed in the philistine outlook of his surroundings—the illiterate men and women portrayed in *L'Etranger* strangely promoted, in *Noces,* to the status of "gods of the summer." The mature Camus was to discover another universe. *Noces* and *L'Envers* are the testimony of the young man in him, a homage to the senses and a probing into the metaphysics of mortal flesh. This testimony was to be infinitely enlarged, but never revoked.

3. The Absurd as Social Experience

Camus entered the intellectual and political life of France in one of its darkest periods. There are moments in the lives of men when politics become their fate. Such was the case in France for those who entered adult life in the years preceding the Second World War. If ever a time created the impression that the universe was absurd, it was indeed that period. Events seemed beyond control. Men felt trapped, a prey to anonymous forces, unavoidably drawn into a war that nobody wanted to face, that spurred no heroic anticipations, not even an elementary feeling of national solidarity.

> Those men born at the beginning of the First World War who had reached the age of twenty just as Hitler was seizing power and the first revolutionary trials were taking place, who then had to complete their education by facing up to war in Spain, the Second World War, the regime of concentration camps, a Europe of torture and prisons, must today bring their children and their works to maturity in a world threatened with nuclear destruction.[20]

This absurd situation had come about gradually. In more than one sense, France had never recovered from the First World War. The two million dead and the immense material destruction

---

20. Albert Camus, Speech of Acceptance of the Nobel Prize, trans. Justin O'Brien (New York: A Knopf, 1958), p. x.

weighed heavily on the nation's future. The psychological harm was no less serious. To the men who had fought in the front lines, the shock of mechanical warfare had been too dreadful ever to be forgotten. It meant not only four infernal years, but serious misgivings as to the humaneness and sanity of the world—the first collective encounter with the absurd. Perhaps worse than the war itself was the government's handling of it. During the three first years, callousness, incompetence, and senseless sacrifice had reached such proportions that, in the words of Bernanos, there was an unbreakable and disastrous association between the words *Fatherland* and *to die for*. Then came the untenable peace of Versailles, followed by the irreconcilable conflict of nationalists and pacifists, with successive governments zigzagging from one to the other. For all the lofty, humanitarian talk by officials, the world seemed to be ruled by haphazard and violent forces. When a young surrealist of the twenties declared that the simplest surrealist act was to go into the street with a revolver and shoot at random at the crowd, he was applying that secret lesson of the time.

Yet cynicism was not the only outcome of the war. After the armistice, great hopes were entertained for an international order based on good will and equity. In its heyday the French pacifist movement, with its socialist overtones and its insistence on social justice and human brotherhood, summed up the dreams entertained by humanists since the middle of the nineteenth century. But the pacifist movement could not survive the collapse of the Weimar Republic and the rise of Hitler in Germany. By the time Camus's generation had reached manhood, it became obvious that Europe would have to be an armed camp. Equally obvious was the fact that it need not have been so. The peace was lost as a result of disagreements and perfidy among the Allies and, to a large extent, because of the shortsightedness of those French reactionaries who ruled the country immediately after the peace treaty, ordered the occupation of the Ruhr, and provoked economic havoc in Germany. The realization of all these frauds and failures added poison to French national politics.

What remained of the pacifist dream in the thirties was a bitter hangover—the memories of past hopes and the knowledge of what Europe could have been if narrow-mindedness and power politics had not prevailed.

A political rift developed inside France. A negative Left, incensed at the conditions the chauvinists had created during their decade of power, and feeling trapped, with all avenues blocked by the impending war and its own paralysis, merely proclaimed its refusal to cooperate in national defense. A vociferous new Right, with no other aim than to destroy the Left, favored Hitler out of fear and hate of Communism—and of democracy as well. Thus France was not only split into Right and Left as the Third Republic always was, but each party had a pacifist wing and a militant wing. After marching in shirts of various hues, the new Right gave way in 1936 to the Popular Front, in which, for a while, the democratic will of the country revived. After the Popular Front itself collapsed in confusion, nothing remained but to wait for the inevitable.

In Algeria, the political polarization was still more marked than in metropolitan France. There, it was only too obvious that modern society lived by two sets of values. The French schools taught Arabs, Jews, poor whites, and rich whites indiscriminately the Rights of Man and the principles of civic liberty, while big colonists grew fat on Arab labor, and Arab intellectuals were refused naturalization. In a country where the poor are poorer and the rich more insolent, political strife acquires more bitterness than elsewhere. The situation in Algiers when Camus was studying was a magnified image of the trouble that was brewing in the streets of Paris.

A desperate lust for life caught this condemned generation, which knew that each spring could be its last. Life to them meant peace. They desired peace with all their passion for happiness, with all their shattered idealism. They wanted it also as their right, and regarded chauvinists and capitalists as responsible for their predicament. This experience of a generation sentenced to death in full vigor—an experience so similar to that of young

Camus smitten with tuberculosis—was the perfect absurd situation. It was not until the German occupation that Camus named that experience and officially introduced the absurd on the literary scene. But all prewar French literature was permeated by it.

The mood of the absurd had started in Paris in the early twenties with Dada, soon followed by surrealism. To many people, Dada and surrealism seemed but a prank of unruly youth. More perceptive minds detected in both movements deep symptoms of discontent. A sociology of surrealism was written (by Jules Monnerot), and Camus himself, who later studied the movement in *The Rebel,* explained it was an attempt to adjust to absurdity. André Malraux in his youth was also attracted to this movement and took it seriously. Certain demonstrations staged by Dada are revealing, such as their "musical and literary evenings":

> La scène était dans la cave, et toutes les lumières éteintes. . . .
> Il montait par une trappe des gémissements. Un farceur, caché
> derrière une armoire, injuriait les personnalités présentes. . . .
> André Breton croquait des allumettes, Ribemont-Dessaignes
> criait à chaqun instant: "Il pleut sur un crâne." Aragon
> miaulait. . . . Un jeune Dada déposait des bouquets de fleurs
> aux pieds d'un mannequin de couturière . . . pendant que deux
> autres dansaient avec des gloussements de jeunes ours, ou, dans
> un sac, avec un tuyau sur la tête, se dandinaient en un exercice
> appelé "noir cacadou."[21]

Such manifestations cannot be dismissed as insignificant pranks. They had an educational value; their organizers wanted to show by a kind of imitative magic what the world was really like: absurd and frustrating. Fifteen years later Camus's *Caligula* practiced the same kind of imitative magic on a grand scale. Having understood the absurdity of life, Caligula started to act the part of fate and played havoc with all that was held respectable, from the Public Treasury to human lives, feelings, and dignity.

As the political situation deteriorated, the despair of absurdity

---

21. Maurice Nadeau, *Histoire du Surréalisme* (Paris: Seuil, 1945), pp. 41, 49.

pervaded all serious literature. Several revealing themes recurred: that of the man sentenced to death awaiting execution in his cell, a fitting symbol for a trapped generation. Malraux illustrated this theme in *Time of Contempt,* Sartre in *The Wall,* and later on, Camus in *The Stranger.* Stressed in each of these tales is the revolt of healthy flesh against death imposed from outside, relieved neither by the merciful weakness of age or of disease, nor by the intoxication of action, but slow, inescapable death closing in on the trapped victim at the height of his vigor and lucidity. Another recurring theme in prewar French literature is that of madness, from Duhamel's Salavin and Sartre's *The Wall* to Camus's *Caligula.* But by far the most prevalent theme is that of the stranger. The alienation of man from himself and his surroundings is illustrated in the whole of Céline's work. *The Journey to the End of the Night* is a pandemonium of absurdity, a pathetic and impotent protest that grimaces through hundreds of pages. Sartre's first novel was fittingly called *Nausea.* Its hero belongs neither to this world nor to any other—a resentful ghost hunted down by the opacity of things. In a manner more classical than that of Sartre, Louis Guilloux, whose first work was later reedited by Camus, illustrated in *Black Blood* the hopeless alienation of an eccentric professor whose spiritual nostalgia made him a laughing stock to his students and neighbors.

4. Camus's Early Political Activities

For many people in those days, the only hope seemed to lie in revolution—either nihilistic or humanitarian: to do away with meaninglessness by violence, or to make violence meaningful by using it to materialize the old dream of peace and justice. Many intellectuals in the thirties were thus lured to the Communist party, which at that time had donned the humanitarian's immaculate robe. Most of them abandoned the party after a brief time as if they had seen a ghost. They had entered it with half-open eyes, willing to accept "strategic necessities" for the sake of an eventual victory of justice. But they found something they did not expect. It was not the old familiar paradox of doubtful means justified by holy ends. It was something new and unheard of. They expected idealism with teeth in it, perhaps more teeth than were strictly necessary. What they found was idealism used as a bait to swell the ranks of an anonymous power machine, propagating political abstractions. Many were bewildered by the ever-changing party lines, by the political somersaults from left to right. This happened to Camus. He joined the Communist Party in 1934 in order to fight both colonialism and the French fascists. He left it in 1937 (or was expelled); but he seems to have had serious misgivings as early as 1935, when the Soviet Union, having concluded a pact with the French government, dropped the Arab liberation movement in Algeria as a token of good will. It took Camus many years to analyze, as he did in *The Rebel,* the mechanism of Communist dogmatism. But long before the theoretical analysis, instinct warned him, as it warned many others of his generation, that a new threat to human values was developing. Like a large part of the European intelligentsia, he was divided between revolutionary fervor and mistrust of revolutionary parties.

Of Camus's revolutionary fervor, there remains one outstanding testimony. *Révolte dans les Asturies,* a play that was performed in 1936 by the "Théâtre du Travail," which Camus and his friends organized in Algiers.[22] The play was a collective work, although Camus wrote most of it and inspired the whole. It tells of a strike by Spanish miners in Oviedo that ended in bloody repression by the government just a few years before the civil war. This war was particularly painful to Camus, whose mother was Spanish. Since his poor health had prevented him from going to fight in Spain, he thought of the play as a tribute to the ill-fated revolution that was dying out just across the sea, together with the last hopes of socialist Europe.

Contrary to widespread opinion, *Révolte dans les Asturies* is

---

22. The text of this play can be found in Albert Camus, *Théâtre, Récits et Nouvelles,* in *Bibliothèque de la Pléiade,* R. Quillot, ed. (Paris: Gallimard, 1962).

not a propaganda play: both sides are shown practicing summary executions; both are cruel and thoughtless. Nor is the play a historical study. It is a romantic evocation of a revolutionary atmosphere. Its subject is not one particular revolutionary event, located in time and place, but an upsurge of indignation, pride, and hope among the crushed and the poor. It has no future, no precise aim, no strategy; it is just an irresistible urge to stand up and say "No," once in a lifetime, to challenge fate and God and masters, and one's own fears. There are three protagonists: the group of revolutionary miners, the small-town traders and notables poised against them, and, towering over them all, the deafening voice of the Radio, dishing out official truth piecemeal, making history. Various aspects of revolution are suggested in quick succession: the departure of two miners, drawn by lots, to drive a truck loaded with explosives into a barracks wall, the defense of a barricade, executions, defeat. The daily life, too, is implied, with its popular songs and lively streets.

Various characters stand for a few minutes in sharp relief against this background: the illiterate old man who wants education for all, the sadistic officer, the woman whose lover dies on the barricade, the local grocer who explains that his father told him for whom to vote, in good old days, when traditions prevailed. The immemorial dreams of the race are expressed by an inspired, doty old cobbler, whom the revolution passed by:

Et le Père Éternel m'a dit : "Alonso, tu es mon fils, laisse-les, va : eux, y font la révolution, toi tu es mon fils." Alors je sais bien, moi, je peux mourir. Mauvaise tête ne crève jamais. Et quand je serai mort, tous les anges du bon Dieu viendront et ils me diront : "Allons, viens, Alonso, viens, ne fais pas le méchant." Et moi, je dirai "non". Mais c'est pour dire. Parce que j'irai avec eux. Et on montera et puis on montera encore dans le bleu, avec le gros soleil qui monte des champs à midi. En bas, tous ceux de Porcuna seront sous les figuiers à couper leur pain ou à boire et l'alcarazas leur bouchera le ciel. Et Alonso avec. J'irai devant le bon Dieu, tout porté par ses anges et il me dira : "Alonso, tu es mon fils, tu as bien aimé les piments et les tomates et puis les petites montagnes sans arbres

et aussi les murs de pierre avec les lézards." Et Alonso il lui
dira au Père Éternel. Il lui dira : "Oui, j'ai jamais demandé
grandchose—je suis de Porcuna."[23]

All are doomed, all is in vain, and the snow on the Sierra will
cover their bodies and the memory of their brief revolt. There
will remain only a song from the *Mountain of Santander,* to play
on the accordion:

> En el baile nos veremos,
> Esta tarde, morenuca . . .

Perhaps the main message of the play was in its technique, for
actors were mixed with the audience and all were supposed to
participate in a collective perception of the greatness, beastliness,
and frailty of man. Before Camus had worked out his theory of
the absurd man, he felt the need to stage this symbol of rebellion
in an absurd world.

While Camus the artist indulged in revolutionary romanticism,
Camus the journalist was writing serious articles on Arab poverty
for *Alger Républicain.* Again, nothing is further from propaganda
or demagoguery than the series of texts on *Misère de la Kabylie.*[24]
An economic recession produced a near famine situation among
the mountain population of Kabylia. In a sober, controlled style,
Camus describes the lamentable scenes he has witnessed. Personal impressions and carefully checked figures are preferred
to rhetoric, such as wages compared to prices, the amount of
relief wheat for each person, and the location of relief centers
some twenty miles from hungry villages. Camus's precise study
of economic facts shows a man who does not easily resign himself to economic "fatalities." His analysis of political institutions
shows their corruption and inadequacy. The land tenure system
is clearly analyzed (native land owners are no more spared than
are the French settlers, the *colons*). Starvation wages are traced
back to lack of professional education and of union rights. Finally,

---

23. *Ibid.,* p. 418.
24. Reprinted in *Actuelles III.*

a few telling examples show how bureaucratic callousness and obtuseness unnecessarily increase the sufferings due to social injustices and abstract economic laws.

The main features of Camus's future political attitude are already visible in these articles: his soberness and precision of judgment, his concern for human brotherhood, his indignation at the sight of injustice, and his incomprehension of administrative and political inertia that blocks even small reforms that could do much good. The indifference of man to man is more shocking in his eyes than exploitation, just because no interest-motive justifies it. In his controlled indignation, the twenty-five-year-old Camus shows certain convictions that were to rule his future political outlook. One is that there are no fatalities, that intelligence, perseverance, and concern for others are the keys to social improvement. Man is free and, therefore, responsible for whatever injustices he tolerates. Another of Camus's recurring ideas to be found here is that the press has a great and humanitarian part to play by spreading accurate and objective information. (All his life, starting in Algiers with *Soir Républicain,* Camus engaged in noncommercial journalistic ventures.) Finally, Camus is convinced of the basic good will of the poor and simple folk. The tinge of Tolstoian socialism that is present in all his work can be felt here, in his spontaneous sympathy for the people of Kabylia. He might have felt the romantic appeal of revolution. But what he asked for in this series of articles was reform and humaneness in human affairs, guaranteed by the will to understand, sympathize, and act efficiently. By their tone as well as by their aim, the articles on Kabylia read like an early version of *The Plague.*

By 1938, Camus's ethics stand complete: respect for life and happiness as in *Noces;* the call of honor as in *Asturies;* the ethics of justice and brotherhood underlying the articles on Kabylia. Camus's commitment to these principles was proven when he joined the Communist Party as well as when he left it. It was proven by his journalistic activity. It was later confirmed by his participation in the Resistance, and all his political writings after the war reasserted his unwavering commitment to the principles he had reached, so to speak, instinctively in his early works. Yet, Camus was about to enter a period of doubts and produce disquieting works that seem to contradict his earlier insight.

PART II
From Caligula to Sisyphus.
The Cycle of the Absurd

2

The Challenge of Caligula

1. Why Caligula?

On the threshold of Camus's mature work stands *Caligula*. Since
the play was for the most part written in 1938, it belongs to
Camus's formative years. Yet, Caligula's attitude is the negation
of the ethics that were spontaneously taking shape in Camus's
earlier works. Taking as his starting point the portrayal of the
mad Roman emperor by Suetonius, he interprets in his own way
the transformation of an idealistic young man into a self-destructive and life-destructive monster, under the impact of a personal
loss that makes him aware of man's wretched condition. This is
the opposite of Camus's message in his earlier works; in the very
same year that he wrote his first version of the play, he also
published his articles in *Alger Républicain*. In short, Camus was
already the humanitarian thinker he would remain. Then, why
Caligula?

Caligula was conceived and for the most part written in the
intellectual vacuum that followed the defeat of the republicans
in Spain. A period in Camus's life that could be called that of
radical humanism was concluded with *Révolte dans les Asturies*.
Caligula marks the opening of a period of doubts that ends only
after the war, with *Letters to a German Friend,* and leads to the
sober realistic faith of *The Plague*. After the *Révolte,* which

showed the tragedy of faith without hope—that is, of fighting for
honor's sake, *Caligula* introduces the tragicomedy of a world
without hope or faith or honor. Between the two, the objective
situation had changed and so had Camus's conception of absurdity. The victory of fascism in Spain sealed the fate of the
liberal Left for an indefinite period. Caligula is the first—though
not fully conscious—recognition of this fact, an especially painful
recognition, since Camus is questioning his own beliefs in his
radical attempt to understand Caligula not only intellectually
but emotionally as well. It is Camus's determination to see Caligula's point and feel with him to the fullest possible extent in
order to ascertain where exactly their ways part. *Caligula* is a
radical application of the *tabula rasa* method, by which Camus
starts his attempt to reconstruct his shattered ethics. It was
natural enough to choose the subject in 1938, since Caligula was
alive in Nazi circles in which many perverted idealists were to
be found, but the fact that Camus had his play performed in
1945, after the Nazi threat was eliminated, shows that the subject
had more than topical interest for him. In fact, the reappearance
of Caligula in brown shirt presented traditional humanism with
the challenge so aptly phrased by Nietzsche and Dostoevski.[1]
God is dead, everything is permitted. Then, why not Caligula?
And although he was stamped out in 1945, what guarantee was
there that he would not come back? More important still to a
man of Camus's frame of mind, in the name of what was Caligula
to be condemned, if there were no God and no divine law? As
Camus was to say later in *The Rebel,* "in the age of crime, it is
innocence that is called upon to justify itself"—a justification
Camus actually attempted in *The Rebel.* In *Caligula,* however, he
finds no argument to counter the mad emperor's logic—a failure
shown by the self-imposed exile of young Scipio. The only
answer is Cherea's sword—after Cherea refused to be involved
in argument. Similarly, the Allies answered the Nazis with guns

---

1. Camus had read Spengler and Rosenberg, whom he later re-
futed in *The Rebel,* and had been disturbed by their "logic."

and bombers. But Camus still felt that Caligula's intellectual challenge called for an answer.

In a way, the challenge came not so much from Caligula as from the Caligulists. There were quite a few when the play was written, and their number grew among the French intelligentsia. No sooner had the war ended than a rehabilitation of de Sade was under way.[2] Before the war, Montherlant and his admirers, as well as pro-fascist writers, did much to discredit humanitarian values.[3] In the wake of Gide[4] and the surrealists,[5] later joined by Sartre and his protégé, Jean Genet,[6] criminals were deemed more valuable than bourgeois. True, there were criminals and criminals. After proclaiming that the simplest surrealist act as noted above, was to shoot at random into the crowd, André Breton took pains to explain his stand: the crime of interest was, in his view, sordid; only the crime of despair glittered with the dark flame of absolute rebellion. But it did glitter.

This literary background must be taken into account when analyzing Camus's play; for it must be admitted that Camus's *Caligula* bears the stamp of the French literary *avant-garde*. He is more akin to "les grands et les petits satans de l'encrier"[7] than to actual Nazis; and even as a literary figure he falls far short of the infernal grandeur the post-Nietzschean writers were aiming at.

Even cut down to size, Camus's *Caligula* remains an ambiguous play, for Camus repeatedly asserts that his hero must be "understood" in a way quite different from a psychiatrist's understanding of an unsavory case; Caligula was also to be "loved" in a way far beyond Christian charity to the sinner. In fact, Caesonia loves

2. Studies by Paulhan, Bataille, Gide, Beauvoir, and Klostowski, among others, were published in the forties.

3. See Tison-Braun, *La Crise de l'Humanisme,* vol. 2, Part IV.

4. Particularly *Souvenirs de la Cour d'Assises.*

5. Particularly *The Second Surrealist Manifesto.*

6. An ex-convict and novelist, the author of *Journal du Voleur.* Jean-Paul Sartre has written a long essay about him, *Saint-Genet Comédien et Martyr.*

7. According to Paulhan's witty definition in *Les fleurs de Tarbes.*

him unconditionally. Young Scipio, whose father was put to death on Caligula's orders, cannot resist his fascination. Even the level-headed Cherea is attracted to him. In this attraction lies the mystery.

There is, of course, no doubt that Caligula's conduct is abhorrent in Camus's eyes as well as in his own, for Caligula is on the side of his own murderers; and when he falls victim to the conspiracy he has more than encouraged, his last words are his own condemnation: "I have chosen the wrong path, a path that leads to nothing. My freedom isn't the right one. . . ."[8] Yet, it is Camus's contention that Caligula is all of us. The public is invited to identify with him, appreciate his "purity of soul" in the pursuit of evil, reflect on the "logic" of his attitude, and admit that we would all act like him if we had intellectual courage and absolute power.[9] Young Scipio recognizes it, much to his horror; so does Cherea, although he murders him. In the earlier version, Cherea's identification was total: "Si j'avais la puissance de Caligula, j'agirais comme lui parceque j'ai sa passion."[10] It is for the most selfish reasons that he had to kill him. In the 1944 version of the play, Cherea speaks differently:

> Caligula: Then why wish to kill me?
> Cherea: I've told you why; because I regard you as noxious, a constant menace. I like, and need, to feel secure. So do most men. They resent living in a world where the most preposterous fancy may at any moment become a reality, and the absurd transfix their lives, like a dagger in the heart. I feel

---

8. Albert Camus, *Caligula and Three Other Plays* (New York: A. Knopf, 1960), p. 73.

9. In an early outline of the play, after Caligula had been murdered, he was supposed to show his face between the curtains and recite the following words:

Non, Caligula n'est pas mort. Il est là, et là. Il est en chacun de vous. Si le pouvoir vous était donné, si vous aviez du coeur, si'vous aimiez la vie, vous le verriez se déchaîner ce monstre ou cet ange que vous portez en vous.

10. Albert Camus, *Théâtre, Récits, Nouvelles* (Paris: Gallimard, 1962), p. 1763.

as they do; I refuse to live in a topsy-turvy world. I want to know where I stand, and to stand secure.

Caligula: Security and logic don't go together.

Cherea: Quite true. My plan of life may not be logical, but at least it's sound.

Caligula: Go on.

Cherea: There's no more to say. I'll be no party to your logic. I've a very different notion of my duties as a man. And I know that the majority of your subjects share my view. You outrage their deepest feelings. It's only natural that you should . . . disappear.

Caligula: I see your point, and it's legitimate enough. For most men, I grant you, it's obvious. But *you,* I should have thought, would have known better. You're an intelligent man, and given intelligence, one has a choice: either to pay its price or to disown it. Why do you shirk the issue and neither disown it nor consent to pay its price?

Cherea: Because what I want is to live, and to be happy. Neither, to my mind, is possible if one pushes the absurd to its logical conclusions.[11]

This second Cherea is more secure in his ethical beliefs than the first, since he dismisses his temptations as unimportant; yet he (and presumably Camus) takes it for granted that between every man's beastly instincts and Caligula's system, the only difference is that of the actual and the potential. He does not suspect a difference of nature, very similar to Camus's distinction between crimes of passion and crimes of logic.

2. Caligula's Logic

Caligula finds the world unacceptable because "men die and are not happy." He therefore wishes for something not of this world. This wish is expressed by a pun. Camus's Caligula reaches for the moon. On the other hand, the historical Caligula claimed that the moon goddess once visited his couch. Thus, Caligula starts his career as a murderer, with his mind set on obtaining the impossible. From this starting point, Caligula's logic unfurls in several directions, some of which Camus approves—up to a

---

11. *Caligula and Three Other Plays,* p. 51.

point. Caligula's first demand is for absolute lucidity. When
Helicon observes that men adjust quite well and that the thought
of their condition does not spoil their appetite, Caligula answers:
"All this proves that I am surrounded by lies and self-deception.
I've had enough of that. I wish men to live by the light of
truth. . . . They need a teacher."[12] Accordingly, he undertakes
to give the puppet senators a course in the insecurity and absurdity
of life as he plays the part of the gods. ("I wear the foolish,
unintelligible face of a professional god,"[13] or "of the plague."[14]
In this respect, a remarkable progression can be observed in the
play. At the beginning, Camus does not go beyond the commonplace satire of bourgeois mediocrity. Things change in Act II
when Caligula himself poisons one senator, and there is an ugly
suspense on the stage. This is his first murder, and we are suddenly reminded of the many European intellectuals who joined
totalitarian parties because their disorderly hate for the money-
minded and cowardly human type labeled *bourgeois* had made
them receptive to the kind of anti-capitalist propaganda that
was the common platform of Nazis and Communists. Saint-Just
was also led to terrorism by his intolerance of mediocrity, as
Camus later observes in *The Rebel,* but only after he broke away
from the magic circle of anti-bourgeois propaganda.

Another trend in Caligula's "logic" is revealed when, leaving
the senators to care for the Public Treasury, he turns his rage
against more wholesome characters who have either resigned
themselves to relative happiness, like Cherea and Caesonia, or
accepted the bittersweet gifts of life, like young Scipio, the pantheistic poet so similar to young Camus in *Nuptials.* The mad
emperor strangles Caesonia, drives Scipio to despair and spares
Cherea only as his potential murderer. This second trend in
Caligula's madness is supposed to derive "logically" from the
frustration of his desire for happiness. Here Caligula is the uncompromising rebel who accepts only uncompromising rebellion

12. *Ibid.,* pp. 8–9.
13. *Ibid.,* p. 9.
14. *Ibid.,* p. 62.

in others, an advocate of the "all or nothing" attitude that Camus later criticizes in *The Rebel*. Again, this attitude is regarded by Camus as "logical," although he does not approve of it.

Finally, as his madness develops, Caligula identifies with the gods and claims the right to use his absolute power as they use theirs, to make himself as frightening and unpredictable as they are. And here again, no argument is found to counter his logic, except that it is mad and inhuman to wish to play the part of fate, or the plague.

By the standards of *Nuptials* and *Asturies,* Caligula is clearly condemned on two counts. He is wrong in denying any value to life, although, in Camus's experience of the absurd, life is ambivalent. This is what young Scipio maintains in his desperate attempt to save Caligula from his devils. Caligula's second crime is to break the solidarity of men, as victims of fate, and side with the gods against men. At this point, Camus seems to remember Malraux's lesson in *Man's Fate,* which he later developed in *The Rebel*. Crushed by fate like a slave by his master, man can choose either to act as fate and master in relation to other men (which is what Caligula does), or to reject the order of master and slave altogether, and assert the brotherhood of men in the face of an absurd fate. Caligula took the side of the gods, whose "foolish face" he wore. In the name of men, Cherea murders him.

Although Camus saw clearly that Caligula went wrong, he failed to see why this happened. When he took up the question again in *The Rebel,* in the chapters dealing with metaphysical revolt, he came nearer to the solution. He perceived, next to the frustration of man's desire for unity, another element, which he called "resentment," after Max Scheler. This resentment is not the natural anger that results from frustrated desire, but a permanent state of envy and malevolence directed by rebels against their fellowmen; not the logical outcome of their revolt against the human condition, but rather a perversion of this revolt. The nature of perversion appears in *Caligula* as well as in *The Rebel,* although Camus's insight in the play is purely intuitive and somewhat confused.

On the one hand, Camus seems to take for granted that Caligula's revolt proceeds exclusively from his frustrated wish for happiness. Since this wish is innocent and legitimate, it follows that Caligula's conduct must be innocent, too. Accordingly, Camus tries hard to legitimize his monster, against his better judgment. This may be why Caligula has to explain his position too often and why he lacks the simplicity of a living character, while the whole play bears the stamp of a demonstration and sometimes sounds like a court debate with a surfeit of devil's advocates.

On the other hand, Camus is somehow aware that the frustrated desire for happiness is not the *only* element in Caligula's madness. For if it were, then Caesonia's argument would impress him: "At my age one knows that life is a sad business. But why deliberately set out to make it worse?" "No," answers Caligula, "it's no good. You don't understand."[15] What is there to understand except that Caligula's logic is not that of desire, and that something else has been smuggled in, namely insane pride? For if Caligula's supreme aim is not to be happy but to assert his crushed ego, then certain consequences follow. He must naturally reject the gifts of life as so many bribes in a blackmailing game. He denies the very ambivalence of life for fear of yielding to what appears to him as life's whorish allurements. Since he cannot have all, he refuses all, in order to free himself of shameful thralldom. In his determination to break the spell of the absurd, he becomes a life hater and a hater of all life lovers. In contrast to the stoics, who also started with proud refusal of the poisoned gift and often ended in misanthropy, Caligula does not stop at ataractic. Something drives him to active destruction which, indeed, is consistent with the aim of asserting his own injured pride.

Pride, in Camus's eyes, is a virtue. So is revolt, and he cannot blame Caligula on this account. Where did Caligula's pride go astray and become merged with his power instinct? Comparing his outlook to that of Scipio—and of *Nuptials*—one realizes that Caligula failed to identify his enemy correctly. In *Nuptials,* as in

15. *Ibid.,* p. 25.

Scipio's outlook, life and nature, far from being enemies, are victims with whom man identifies. The sinister force at work in the universe, which Camus later called *The Plague,* is not life or nature, but fate, which dooms the nuptials of man and the world with the inevitability of death. Fate, not nature, is the sinister partner in Camus's spontaneous mythology. His revolt is not against nature but against fate—a total revolt of the flesh, of the heart, and of the mind, which vainly look for a reason for the destruction of his fragile happiness. Caligula fails to grasp this difference. He hates life for its very fragility, and identifies with the force that destroys it. In the earlier version of the play, Caligula addresses himself to the dead Drusilla and begs her not to leave him alone: "J'ai peur," he says, "de la solitude des monstres." He is faintly aware of a parting of the ways. He has not been driven by any logic; he freely made an existential choice.

This choice is clearly explained—and condemned—in *The Rebel* (as in Malraux's *Man's Fate*): Man rebels against fate as against a harsh and unjust master. But the value of rebellion must be judged by its aims. If the aim was to expose the harshness and injustice of the master, then rebellion is justified. If, however, the victim was merely attempting to become an executioner himself—in the present case, to use his power in order to emulate fate—then rebellion is unjustified, both logically and ethically. The ethical aspect of the problem cannot be discussed at this stage—we are still in the realm of the absurd. But it is suggested, although not yet explained, that Caligula's conduct was inconsistent with his aims, that his "logic" was faulty.

It is surprising that the flaw in Caligula's—and the Caligulists' —logic does not clearly appear to Camus. Caligula's postulate is not: "if God is dead everything is permitted," but: "if I must die, everything is permitted (to me)." Such a postulate covers a much simpler one: "I have been offended and frustrated, therefore I must revenge myself and get the upper hand." In his futile attempt to emulate fate, Caligula soon regresses to infantile, narcissistic pride and falls a prey to delusions of omnipotence: "My power has no limits," he says. And from the moment he made this discovery, the mirror became the ruling symbol in his life, until he died and crushed it in his fall. In the meantime, he would occasionally realize in a flicker that he had crowned himself a king of carnival, and would act out his grotesque narcissism in impersonating Venus. In his monstrous loneliness, he acted like Prometheus in reverse, a satanic Prometheus who would hear neither the cry of mankind nor the song of the Oceanides, but would engulf them all in his revenge against Zeus.

Between the insight in *Nuptials* and the analysis in *The Rebel,* Camus felt the need to exorcise this monster that challenged both his emotions and his intellect with its deceptive logic.

3

Under the Spell of Sisyphus

1. The Myth of Sisyphus

In his late twenties Camus suffered many misfortunes: a broken marriage, the death of a child, another attack of tuberculosis, and a succession of senseless jobs. His only period of contentment was the year he spent with friends in an apartment near the sea, which he called "la maison devant le monde" (the house in front of the world). This was also the time when Camus and his friend Pascal Pia[1] were editing the financially independent paper, *Soir Républicain.*

However, this short period of recovery was abruptly interrupted by the war. A number of texts bear witness to Camus's distress when it broke out: "So much effort in favor of peace, so much hope in man, resulting in this collapse and this renewed butchery. . . . Trees will bloom again, since the world always prevails over history in the end; but how many men will be present to enjoy the blossoms?"[2] He nevertheless understood how "one can fight

---

1. The future editor of the underground paper *Combat* during the war.
2. From an article in *Soir Républicain* quoted in Albert Camus, *Essais Bibliothèque de la Pléiade* (Paris: Gallimard, 1965), pp. 1376–77.

a war without consenting to it"; but his deferment from the army on grounds of ill health depressed him still more.

Like so many French intellectuals in the prewar years, Camus was a pacifist and believed that good will, and what he obstinately called a sense of fairness to Hitler, could have warded off—and could still stop—the conflict: "Do not humiliate. Try to understand. Grant Hitler what is right while refusing what is unjust. . . . Revise Versailles. . . . Refuse to be carried away by hate." "We believe that this conflict could still be solved to everybody's satisfaction. . . . This has not been tried, but remains possible at every moment."[3] In a letter to an unknown young man, he advocates individual action in favor of peace and later on approves Chamberlain's conciliatory speech of November 1939.[4]

As it frequently happened in the case of French and English pacifists in 1939, the bitterness born of shattered illusions was turned not so much against Hitler as against their own blundering politicians who made the rise of Nazism possible, against Versailles and post-Versailles chauvinist policies. The appeasement policy practiced by England and France after 1930 was to be blamed only for not being radical enough. Camus's confusion reached its peak after Munich, when the shame of the capitulation was added to the despair of the impending war. As a result, his articles in *Soir Républicain* put the blame on Daladier's authoritarian policy during the first year of the war, the introduction of strict censorship, and the breaking of a general strike. Even Daladier's outlawing of the Communist party was blamed, the Ribbentrop-Molotov pact notwithstanding.

As a result of these criticisms, Camus had to leave *Soir Républicain*. He joined Pascal Pia in Paris, where they both edited *Paris Soir* until the invasion in June, 1940. Thereafter, Camus lived precariously, plagued by ill health and depressions. To what extent he could be depressed by northern countries, with their gray skies and their hard-working populations, whom he found

3. *Ibid.*, pp. 1378–80. More will be said about it in chapter 4.
4. *Soir Républicain,* Dec. 3, 1939.

unfriendly and indifferent to nature, Camus has shown in *Cross Purposes*. In this melodrama, Camus hoped to recapture the terror and greatness of Greek tragedy by showing two women who, as innkeepers in a dark Alpine valley, were prompted by their nostalgia for the sun to murder their rich lodgers in order to gather enough money to escape to the South.

Camus's works of this period, *The Myth of Sisyphus* and *The Stranger,* reflect his deep melancholia. He himself regards these two works and *Caligula* as belonging to what he called "the cycle of the absurd." This notion, now inseparably associated with Camus's name in most readers' minds, is clearly present in his first works, but he did not explain it philosophically until *The Myth of Sisyphus,* which became a kind of handbook of existentialist despair in the early postwar years. The subject of the *Myth* is suicide—especially philosophical suicide, like that of Dostoevski's Kyrilov. Having rejected all belief in God or in any superior principle, Camus casts a desperate glance at the inexplicable universe around us, at the meaningless routine of social life, at our mortal fate. Then, reflecting on the impotence of our reason, entangled in its own contradictions, Camus wonders why the most lucid among us do not simply finish it all by suicide. Yet, the wish for happiness and meaning is so strong as to sustain a proud and vital man against his fate, seconded by an unflinching will to live. None of the pantheistic ecstasy of *Nuptials* or the tender irony of *The Wrong Side and the Right Side* has passed into *The Myth*. Man's hopeless predicament is symbolized by Sisyphus, the mythological figure whom the gods had sentenced, for an unknown crime, perpetually to roll his boulder up the hill, then watch it bounce down to the bottom of the valley. It would have been hard to find a more fitting symbol of life in German-occupied Europe, apparently condemned to endless humiliation and war.

Nevertheless, says Camus, Sisyphus must resist the temptation to sit and weep on his rock at the bottom of the valley. He must accept the challenge of fate for the sake of that marvelous minute when he nears the top of the hill and sees the sky—just before the boulder rushes down. "We should picture Sisyphus as happy" is the concluding sentence.

Various styles of life are suggested for the absurd man. One is Don Juan; the Conqueror is another. Still other figures are outlined in *The Myth*: even a small clerk, a part-time helper at the post office. This cannot fail to suggest Meursault in *The Stranger,* who is trying to find his modest happiness in a world he has long felt to be absurd.

2. "Sisyphus Happy"

As far as involvement in human affairs is concerned, *The Stranger* stands exactly at the opposite pole from *Caligula* in Camus's work, the story of the destructive emperor being at the zenith of the absurd, while the nadir—or "point zero" as Camus calls it—is occupied by the story of a detached, quietly asocial character. Meursault's challenge to socially accepted patterns of feeling and behavior is evident in the first paragraph of the book:

> Mother died today. Or, maybe, yesterday; I can't be sure. The telegram from the Home says: Your mother passed away. Funeral tomorrow. Deep sympathy. Which leaves the matter doubtful; it could have been yesterday.
> The Home for Aged Persons is at Marengo, some fifty miles from Algiers. With the two-o'clock bus I should get there well before nightfall. Then I can spend the night there, keeping the usual vigil beside the body, and be back here by tomorrow evening. I have fixed up with my employer for two days' leave; obviously, under the circumstances, he couldn't refuse. Still, I had an idea he looked annoyed, and I said, without thinking: "Sorry, sir, but it's not my fault, you know."
> Afterwards it struck me I needn't have said that. I had no reason to excuse myself; it was up to him to express his sympathy.[1]

1. Albert Camus, *The Stranger* (New York: Vintage Books, 1954), p. 1.

Then come details of Meursault's journey: "I took the two o'clock bus . . . ," "It was blazing sun . . . I had to run . . . I was a little dizzy . . . I slept most of the way."[2] During the vigil, every concrete detail is described accurately. Meursault was slightly disturbed by the crying and sniffling of his mother's friend, but greatly comforted by a cup of *café au lait,* for he "was very partial to *café au lait.*" The next morning, he noticed that the screws on the coffin lid had been driven in, and that the hearse looked like a pencil box. Finally he reflected on the weather and what a glorious day it would have been for bathing "if it had not been for Mother."

Modern novels offer a rich variety of family hatreds, of monstrous feelings between parents and children. This is obviously not the case in *The Stranger.* One could not even say that Meursault did not like his mother. He speaks very affectionately about her, calling her *Maman*; he frequently quotes her or recalls her habits. But "they had nothing to tell each other any more"; their lives had quietly drifted apart. A frequent occurrence, no doubt, but rarely admitted.

After this initial shock treatment, the reader is informed of Meursault's love life—another important element in any social code. On the morrow of his mother's funeral—by a mere coincidence—Meursault starts an affair with Marie at the beach. Everything is innocent and simple between them:

> While I was helping her to climb on to a raft, I let my hand stray over her breasts. Then she lay flat on the raft, while I trod water. After a moment she turned and looked at me. Her hair was over her eyes and she was laughing. I clambered up on to the raft, beside her. The air was pleasantly warm, and, half jokingly, I let my head sink back upon her lap. She didn't seem to mind, so I let it stay there. I had the sky full in my eyes, all blue and gold, and I could feel Marie's stomach rising and falling gently under my head. We must have stayed a good half-hour on the raft, both of us half asleep. When the sun got too hot she dived off and I followed her.[3]

2. *Ibid.,* p. 14.
3. *Ibid.,* p. 23.

Upon learning that his mother died the day before, Marie "shrinks away a little," but by the evening "she had forgotten all about it" and accompanies Meursault to his room.

A few weeks later, however:

> Marie came that evening and asked me if I'd marry her. I said I didn't mind; if she was keen on it, we'd get married.
> Then she asked me again if I loved her. I replied, much as before, that her question meant nothing or next to nothing— but I supposed I didn't.
> "If that's how you feel," she said, "why marry me?"
> I explained that it had no importance really, but, if it would give her pleasure, we could get married right away. I pointed out that, anyhow, the suggestion came from her; as for me, I'd merely said, "Yes."
> Then she remarked that marriage was a serious matter.
> To which I answered: "No."
> She kept silent after that, staring at me in a curious way. Then she asked:
> "Suppose another girl had asked you to marry her—I mean, a girl you liked in the same way as you like me—would you have said 'Yes' to her, too?"
> "Naturally."[4]

Most unromantic behavior, to be sure yet the odds are that if marriages were investigated, the majority of them would turn out to have been initiated that way; but it should not be admitted. All of Meursault's relations follow the same pattern. He becomes acquainted with his neighbor, Raymond Sintes—a pimp, by the way, but who cares?

> He slapped me on the shoulder and said: "So, now, we are pals, ain't we?" I kept silent and he said it again. I did not care one way or the other, but as he seemed so set on it, I nodded and said "Yes."

Here again, Meursault's behavior appears to be perfectly normal. Upon learning that Raymond had some difficulties with his

---

4. *Ibid.,* pp. 52–53.

girl friend, who would not "work," Meursault immediately agrees to write a letter that will lure the girl back to Raymond's rooms, where she would be "taught a lesson." It may seem strange for Meursault to get involved in somebody else's business to that extent, but "I wanted to satisfy Raymond, as I had no reason not to satisfy him."[5] A few days later, when the shrieks of the beaten woman drag the whole houseful onto the landing, Marie is so upset that "she hadn't any appetite and I ate nearly all myself. She left at once, and then I had a nap."[6]

Thus, Meursault's detachment covers a variety of attitudes, ranging from indifference to downright callousness. It would be rash, however, to call him a monster—that is to say, an abnormal creature—considering that he is neither better nor worse than most human beings, but only less addicted to pretense. The readiness with which simple people accept him confirms the fact that Meursault is perfectly ordinary, "just like everyone else," as he (and Camus) often points out; in fact, an indifferent, shallow, and perfectly boorish young man. The key to his character might well be found in *Nuptials,* in the portrayal of the Mediterranean man.

Intelligence does not occupy the place here that it does in Italy. This race is indifferent to the mind. It worships and admires the body. From this comes its strength, its naïve cynicism, and a puerile vanity that leads it to be severely criticized. People commonly reproach its "mentality," that is to say, its particular mode of life and set of values. And it is true that a certain intensity of living involves some injustice. Yet here are a people with no past, with no traditions, though not without poetry. Their poetry has a hard, sensual quality I know very well; it is far from tender, even from the tenderness of the Algerian sky; it is the only poetry, in fact, that moves me and restores me. The opposite of a civilized people is a creative one. These barbarians lounging on the beaches give me the foolish hope that, perhaps without knowing it, they are modeling the face of a culture where man's greatness will

---

5. *Ibid.,* p. 41.
6. *Ibid.,* p. 46.

finally discover its true visage. These people, wholly engaged
in the present, live with neither myths nor consolation. Investing
all their assets on this earth, they are left defenseless against
death. The gifts of physical beauty have been heaped upon
them. And, also the strange greediness that always goes along
with wealth that has no future. Everything people do in
Algiers reveals a distaste for stability and a lack of regard for
the future. People are in a hurry to live.[7]

Nevertheless, the reader feels mystified. What is it that makes
Meursault so peculiar? Camus himself admitted that his character
was built deliberately ("très concerté").[8] Of course, he does
not reveal the gimmick, but there is a gimmick. By now, the
reader discovers that what makes Meursault so peculiar is a lack.
In fact, one essential but undisclosed nerve center has been
skillfully severed from him, with the result that his conduct
appears as both unpredictable and perfectly coherent.

Although he is intelligent—everybody says so, including his
boss, he lacks a principle of unity and continuity, and the power
of integration that is usually called personality. This integrative
power is not lacking in him in the same way as in a psychotic,
but it does not operate above the level of pragmatic and bodily
needs. Accordingly, Meursault has desires and emotions, but
lacks sentiment, which would presuppose memory and projection
into the future. He registers facts with accuracy, and Camus
chooses them with a view to conveying a certain meaning, but
Meursault himself seems indifferent to meaning. He never expresses any opinion; he refrains from interpreting or extrapolating
in any field. He has been disconnected from this specifically
human, though mysterious, capacity of giving meaning to the
world. The "meaning endowing act," in Husserl's words, is absent
from Meursault's conduct. There is no doubt that this amputation
was deliberately performed by Camus. If, indeed, the world is
absurd, that is, devoid of meaning, the absurd man, if he is

---

7. Albert Camus, *Lyrical and Critical Essays* (New York: Alfred
Knopf, 1969), p. 89.
8. Camus, *Essais,* p. 1931.

lucid and logical, should recognize that he cannot find meaning in it. He should therefore refrain from trying, and refuse the pretense the majority of men want to impose. Although less overtly proclaimed, Meursault's logic is, in Camus's eyes, as compelling as that of Caligula.

Two main aims seem to have been pursued by Camus in writing the novel—one theoretical, the other perhaps personal. Camus's aim in *The Stranger* is to dissociate the real, or, one might say, natural man from the conventional image society superimposes on him. In this respect, Meursault, like Voltaire's Huron, acts as an acid test, laying bare social pretense and irrationality. This, however, is not Camus's only aim. Next to this satirical intention, Camus's characters, including those in *The Plague,* bear witness to their creator's phobia of value judgments, especially ethical judgments, so that his main concern in *The Stranger* seems to be to assert Meursault's innocence (even after he has committed murder) and deny anyone the right to judge another (apart from his own merciless condemnation of judges). Thus a novel that started as a psychological study develops in its second part as a *roman à thèse* of a most peculiar kind.

In the second part Meursault is tried and executed for having committed an absurd crime. As a result of his involvement in Monsieur Raymond's sentimental affair with an Arab girl, Meursault took part in a brawl with the girl's brother and his two friends. Meursault's handling of the situation was praiseworthy: he avoided the worst by confiscating Raymond's gun and brought the fight to a speedy end. A few hours later, however, as Meursault went strolling on his own in order to dispel the effects of a copious lunch, he came upon the girl's brother, who threatened him with a knife. Blinded by sun and heat, with perspiration running into his eyes, Meursault lost his head, shot at the man, and killed him. According to his usual pattern of discontinuous perception, Meursault did not think: I killed a man. He perceived the deafening shot and sensed that he had disrupted the "miraculous harmony of a beach where [he] had been happy." Then, for no reason whatsoever—except, perhaps, this fascination with the worst, which also caught Caligula faced with his murderers—Meursault fired four more shots into the prostrate body, "like four knocks at the door of fate." Fate answered the call, in the shape of Meursault's arrest and trial.

In the second part, not nearly so good as the first, the trial shows the absurd man as a victim of those who refuse to acknowledge the absurdity of the human condition. Simple people— Meursault's friends—accept as a matter of course the existence of unmotivated acts, including crimes—hence Celeste's somewhat solemn testimony that, in his opinion, it was not murder but misfortune ("C'est pas un crime, c'est un malheur"). And indeed, Meursault could have benefited from extenuating circumstances. But the court and jury refused to admit the possibility of an absurd crime, because it ruined their belief in rational ethics, self-control and, eventually, the whole system of moral accountability. Yet, however compelling their clinging to psychological security, they did not let the emotion pass the threshold of consciousness for fear of having to face unpleasant truth. In the resulting haze, Meursault was condemned, not for having committed murder, but because the murder was inexplicable. For want of clear-cut motivations, he was indicted on the basis of his socially unacceptable behavior: he did not cry at his mother's burial, he led an immoral life with Marie, he did not disapprove of old Salamano's mistreatment of his dog; he associated with a pimp, and so on. In a series of skillful flashbacks, the slim episodes of Meursault's life since his mother's burial are related anew, this time as seen by the public prosecutor and jury. Events are accurately repeated but their meaning is distorted beyond recognition, the resulting confusion being aptly summarized by Meursault's counsel: is he accused of having killed a man or of having gone to his mother's burial? This produces a peculiar kind of polarization: while the court and public regard Meursault as a fiend, he becomes, in Camus's eyes, an uncomprehending

Christ, whose innocence shows off his persecutors' hypocrisy. Camus is singularly obdurate in this respect, as shown by his preface to the American edition of *The Stranger*:

I summarized *The Stranger*—a long time ago, with a remark that I admit was highly paradoxical: "In our society any man who does not weep at his mother's funeral runs the risk of being sentenced to death." I only meant that the hero of my book is condemned because he does not play the game. In this respect, he is foreign to the society in which he lives; he wanders, on the fringe, in the suburbs of private, solitary, sensual life. And this is why some readers have been tempted to look upon him as a piece of social wreckage. A much more accurate idea of the character, at least, one much closer to the author's intentions, will emerge if one asks just *how* Meursault doesn't play the game. The reply is a simple one: he refuses to lie. To lie is not only to say what isn't true. It is also and above all, to say *more* than is true, and, as far as the human heart is concerned, to express more than one feels. This is what we all do, every day, to simplify life. He says what he is, he refuses to hide his feelings, and immediately society feels threatened. He is asked, for example, to say that he regrets his crime, in the approved manner. He replies that what he feels is annoyance rather than real regret. And this shade of meaning condemns him.

For me, therefore, Meursault is not a piece of social wreckage, but a poor and naked man enamored of a sun that leaves no shadows. Far from being bereft of all feeling, he is animated by a passion that is deep because it is stubborn, a passion for the absolute and for truth. This truth is still a negative one, the truth of what we are and what we feel, but without it no conquest of ourselves or of the world will ever be possible.

One would therefore not be much mistaken to read *The Stranger* as the story of a man who, without any heroics, agrees to die for the truth. I also happened to say, again paradoxically, that I had tried to draw in my character the only Christ we deserve. It will be understood, after my explanations, that I said this with no blasphemous intent, and only with the slightly ironic affection an artist has the right to feel for the characters he has created.

January 8, 1955[9]

9. *Lyrical and Critical Essays,* pp. 335–37.

It would, of course, be absurd to read into this page an apology
for crime; what Camus definitely condemns is "l'univers du
procès" (the world of trial)—a condemnation that had appeared
earlier:

> Ce qui est attaqué ici ce n'est pas la morale, c'est le monde
> du procès, qui est aussi bourgeois que nazi et que communiste
> et qui, en un mot, est le chancre contemporain.[10]

Although it is not clear how he wants to protect human rights
and safety, Camus, no less than the surrealists, tends to condemn
the repressive functions of the state.

At this point, a real fight is waged by Camus against his reader;
while recognizing that Meursault is right in refusing to lie about
his feelings, most readers will insist that sincere feelings are
possible and are superior to Meursault's aloofness. Camus, on
the other hand, wants the reader to regard his own attitude as
hypocritical and recognize Meursault's attitude as not only honest
but logical. For there is a logic in Meursault's attitude as well
as in Caligula's, and both are supposed to be compelling. For
what does a mother's death matter or the shooting of a man,
since we are all bound to die anyway? What does even the desire
for a woman matter, if we are sentenced to death? In the last
days of his imprisonment, Meursault forgets Marie; her image
has melted away into an impersonal desire for the elusive beauty
of the world.

Since the beginning of the trial, another suspicion has developed
in the reader's mind, prompted by the use of the first person:
to what extent is Meursault's aloofness a genuine attitude, or a
demonstration of Camus's own defensive reaction. It is in this
second part that the reader becomes aware of some inconsistencies
in Meursault's character.

In spite of his deliberately neutral tone, Meursault occasionally
uses a poetic style inconsistent with his matter of fact view of
the world. In the second part, he wields legal language with

---

10. *Carnets,* 2:172.

surprising skill, considering his ignorance of public affairs. In the whole novel, an odd remark here and there suggests that there has been another, less detached, Meursault. "When I was a student . . . In the course of my travels . . . When I lived in Paris . . ." This leads to the suspicion that Meursault's aloofness was not natural but induced, that Camus intended to portray a man—perhaps himself—who tried to escape the painful awareness of absurdity by returning to the kind of sleep described in Sisyphus, before "backdrops fall" and the absurdity of life is perceived. Meursault knew all the while that the backdrops had fallen, as is shown by the recurring phrase, "Ça m'est égal" (This is of no importance; I do not care either way). Having read about Camus's "natural indifference," we easily recognize the silent world of his childhood and his Belcourt friends, and understand Meursault's temptation to take shelter in this uncomplicated, undemanding world.

It would, of course, be as absurd to assimilate Camus to Meursault as to Caligula, although he stated that in creating *The Stranger,* he used "two men (including myself) and one woman";[11] yet, it is surely Camus's "natural indifference" that is portrayed in Meursault and, moreover, Camus openly stands by his hero and repeatedly assumes a defensive or even militant attitude on his behalf. From the beginning, Meursault's non-involvement shows traces of militancy in his insistence on telling absolute truth, and in his rebuttal of any invitation to show feelings. In the second part, this militancy increases to the limits of credibility. Camus's use of the phrase "jouer le jeu" (playing the game) implies that everybody has agreed to pretend certain feelings: to cry for one's mother, marry Marie, love dogs, and so on, and that "society" ruthlessly liquidates the outsider who refuses to take part in this hypocrisy.

There is no doubt, in view of Camus's own comments and the excessive praise elicited by his novel, that he was answering an emotional and intellectual need of his time. In creating a character whose aim was to refrain from thinking, feeling, and

11. *Essais* (Pléiade), p. 1934.

judging beyond the realm of physical pleasure, he was following, among others, Céline's example and expressing the tired amoralism of part of the prewar generation. But, in contrast to Céline, he gave his character heroic stature by letting him fall undaunted in defense of his right to feel and think nothing.

How much more authentic was the young Camus who wrote in his *Carnets:* "Et les voilà qui meuglent: Je suis immoraliste. Traduction: J'ai besoin de me donner une morale. Mais avoue-le donc, imbécile! Moi aussi!"[12] Meursault's social conduct, however, has not yet been probed to the end. Why did he get involved, after all, contrary to all his habits, and why was his involvement so contrary to his usual harmlessness? For Meursault's complicity with his neighbour Raymond was an ugly one: by writing a letter for Raymond, he helped him to lure his girl friend to his apartment in order to inflict on her the punishment she supposedly deserved. When, on the following Sunday, the whole tenement house was roused by the shrieks of the beaten woman, Marie suggested that Meursault should fetch a policeman. "I don't like policemen," was his answer. After one came, brought by someone else, and assigned the pimp to the police station, Meursault gave false testimony to the effect that the woman had let Raymond down.

Meursault not only got involved, but his involvement followed a recognizable pattern. During Meursault's trial, one of his witnesses stated that Meursault was "a real man." When asked to specify, he merely answered that every one understood what that meant. It could mean, of course, that Meursault was level-headed and unsentimental. But Camus gave a more detailed explanation of this phrase in *Nuptials*. In his native place, Camus explains, no one has a clear notion of "virtue"; however, there are things one does not do, such as fail to pay due regard to one's mother, or allow one's wife to be insulted, or fight two against one. He who does not abide by these "elementary imperatives" is "not a man." This "code of the street," as Camus calls it, seems to him

----

12. P. 41.

"just and strong."[13] Meursault, while refusing the ethics advocated by the public prosecutor and jury, never failed to respect the "street code," the straightforwardness of which was congenial to his personality.

However, this seemingly praiseworthy code of the streets, which was imprinted on Camus's mind during his youth in Belcourt, easily merges into another one, not expressly formulated but prevailing in marginal characters in most Western cities. This second aspect of the street code clearly prevails in the behavior of Meursault and his friends. The first unwritten law in the code is that everybody should mind his own business and not be nosy. It is bad taste to intervene for beaten women or beaten dogs. Morality is for the bourgeois. The rule is: no demands and no interference. The second law is that disagreements should be settled privately, without calling the police. The third is that male solidarity is holy: Meursault accepts Raymond's account of his disagreement with the girl at its face value. Later on, during his trial, he acknowledged Raymond as his "pal," knowing what a bad impression this would make on the jury. This was a code of honor and Meursault abided by it. He felt free in it because no sentimental demands were made on him. Meursault was not an immoralist: he accepted the code of Belcourt and rejected that of the residential districts. But the code of Belcourt had two faces—the second one unproclaimed—and Meursault accepted both.

Again, it would be a gross exaggeration to assume that Camus's ethics is that of his hero. He certainly does not approve of his callousness. But he refuses to blame it, according to the code of Belcourt. This dual code is not identical with working-class ethics. It prevails on the uncertain borderline of the underworld, where semi-demoralized proletarians merge with semi-respectable hoodlums; it is followed by the kind of people with whom,

---

13. *Lyrical and Critical Essays*, p. 87. The same presentation of Belcourt ethics can be found in an article in *Combat*, reprinted in *Essais*, p. 1544.

presumably, Camus's grandmother did not like him to associate, people to whom Meursault is socially superior (he is regularly employed, more educated, more refined), but whom he prefers because they make no demands on him. In this respect, Camus's novel responds to another contemporary trend: the intellectual fascination with the underworld that was to culminate in Sartre's eulogy of Genet. This predilection is ostensibly motivated by a dislike of bourgeois hypocritical virtue, sentimentality, and good manners. But it is hard to tell how much tiredness, how much abdication of self-control it conceals in old countries threatened with decadence, where flirtation with amoral characters is the first sign of a decaying will. Here, Camus's firsthand experience, in contrast to that of writers of bourgeois origins, enables him to offer a strikingly realistic picture of a milieu he knew well. His remarkable talent in this respect distracts attention from the central paradox of the novel: the reader is invited to accept an indictment of "bourgeois" values conducted in the name of so-called values of the absurd, which are, in fact, values of socially marginal characters enthusiastically taken up by tired intellectuals.

This uneasy confusion is made still more complicated by the insertion of a third set of values, genuinely humanitarian, which appear in connection with Meursault's trial. Camus's campaigns against the death penalty are well known. He argued that, in view of the shortcomings of human justice, no group has the right to kill. Thus, *The Stranger* conveys another lesson, not unlike that of Gide's *Souvenirs de la Cour d'Assises:* the highhanded routine of the court isolates the defendant and crushes him even before he is convicted. On the other hand, whenever the accused's personality is taken into account, abstract patterns of ethics are imposed on living reality, so that personal human elements, which should help the defendant, often work against him.

Even as the dying Caligula recognized that his freedom was not the right one, so Meursault experienced two awakenings in the last days of his life: the first one took place when he under-

stood that he was going to die, and the second when he bullied
the prison's chaplain. Meursault's reaction after he understood
his sentence was one of fear. The word is not pronounced, for
according to his usual techniques, Meursault simply notes what
he feels and thinks: perspiration, the need to keep his mind
occupied, frantic listening at the door every morning. Only a
few pages later he would note: "I was frightened; this was quite
natural." The second reaction was the anger the priest touched
off by announcing that he would pray for him. Neither fear
nor anger leads Meursault to the kind of humanitarian feelings
Camus advocated in his later works. The awakening Meursault
experiences brought him a greater awareness of his condition:
he had always been sentenced to death, although it was not
imminent. From this fact, he deduced that nothing mattered,
neither his mother's death nor that of the man he killed; unlike
Caligula, he did not wish to increase suffering, but if he did so
inadvertently, it did not matter too much. One thing mattered,
however, and that was his own death. In the masterful pages that
show how Meursault became aware of his imminent death in
spite of his efforts at suppression, an existential attitude took
shape, although it was not completed until the confrontation with
the priest.

This attitude may well seem surprising, but it is in keeping
with Camus's conception of the world as absurd: Meursault does
not find—as a humanitarian would—that other people's lives
are as important as his own, but, on the contrary, that his life
is as unimportant as that of anyone else's. He thus reaches the
state of self-detachment, coupled with love of life, advocated in
Sisyphus, and becomes a true hero of the absurd, conscious of
being an outsider, the hate-free target of everybody's cries of
hate. Again, the last sentences of the novel suggest a fleeting
comparison of *The Stranger* with Christ, "the only Christ we
deserve."

As shown by the preface quoted above, which is dated January
8, 1955, Camus never revoked his contention that Meursault was
a fighter for truth, a sort of hero of the absurd. In spite of the

ambiguities of their characters, Caligula and Meursault, as well as
the other type outlined in *Sisyphus* and also the characters in
Cross Purposes, are figures of despair. They appear with unusual
frequency at the time of *The Stranger.* This, however, does not
authorize us to localize the "cycle of the absurd" in time as a
passing mood in Camus's life. As we have seen, *Caligula* was
performed in 1945, *Cross Purposes* one year earlier. The militant
preface to *The Stranger* was written as late as 1955. Camus's
frenzy of negation coincided with the development of his humanitarian vein. There are memories of *The Stranger* in *The
Plague.* Nor is Camus's pessimism to be explained away by personal unhappiness: *Sisyphus* was written in the year of his second
marriage. The obsession with the absurd is a permanent feature
in his life—offset to a lesser or greater extent by solidarity. All
his life, he had to grapple with Caligula and was tempted by
Meursault's indifference. In his later works, strange figures appear: the penitent judge, the renegade, the fallen artist. There is
no way to decide which trend was prevalent in Camus: all seem
to have been present and competing in him at the same time.

It is nevertheless true that the year 1943 opened a new cycle
in Camus's life.

PART III

Camus's Mature Years
1. The Cycle of *The Plague*

4
Farewell to Caligula

1. Letters to a German Friend

Even during Camus's most nihilistic period, when he was writing *Sisyphus,* he was aware of the possibility of overcoming despair by fighting. Among the possible types of conduct for the absurd man, which he mentions in *Sisyphus,* is that of the Conqueror. But Camus gave this character a peculiar twist. It would have been surprising indeed if Camus had written a eulogy of Caesar or Napoleon: no human type is more alien to him. In fact, what he calls a conqueror is a fighter for freedom even if his cause is lost. Camus's conqueror, as his argument develops, comes closer and closer to the resistance fighter hopelessly protesting against "what crushes him." "Hitherto, the greatness of a conqueror was geographical. . . . There is a reason why the word has changed its meaning and has ceased to signify the victorious general. The greatness has changed camp. It lies in protest and the blind-alley sacrifice."[1]

When the Resistance actively began in France, Camus was in a sanatorium, recovering from a new attack of tuberculosis. It was not until 1943 that he started to write for the underground paper *Combat.* That was again a time of great personal unhappi-

---

1. *The Myth of Sisyphus and Other Essays* (New York: A. Knopf, 1967), p. 87.

73

ness for him: his wife and children were in North Africa when the Allied invasion took place, separating the family for an indefinite period. Yet, this was the time when Camus's ethics underwent a major change, and when he propagated the values that made him—much to his annoyance—a symbol of humanitarian virtue and won him the Nobel Prize.

Camus's war articles have not been collected, except for four particularly important ones, published under the title: *Letters to a German Friend*. In many respects, the *Letters* read like a settling of accounts with Caligula. It is very unlikely that an actual German friend of Camus ever existed. But Camus was admittedly influenced by Nietzsche and perturbed by some German post-Nietzscheans, such as Karl Juergens, Rosenberg, and Spengler, whose pessimism or cult of violence had been instrumental in the development of the Nazi ideology. We have seen, in the chapter on *Caligula,* that Camus shared their experience of nihilism and the breakdown of traditional values—what he calls the European tragedy of intelligence[2]—and that he found no answer to Caligula's "logic." After the war, his distaste for Caligula grew to positive horror. He did not know the answer yet, but he was groping toward the solution. The question, it will be remembered, was the following: If we start from the notion that the world is absurd, and that neither God nor any transcendent principle dictates our conduct, how then are we to escape the conclusion that our actions are morally indifferent and that, therefore, everything is permitted? In the play, Caligula said: my solution was wrong. Here, in the letters, Camus's answers are not yet conclusive, but they are "more assured."

> Qu'est-ce que la vérité, disiez-vous? Sans doute. Mais nous savons au moins ce qu'est le mensonge. Qu'est-ce que l'esprit? Nous connaissons son contraire, qui est le meurtre. Qu'est-ce que l'homme? Mais là je vous arrête, car nous le savons. Il est cette force qui finit toujours par balancer les tyrans et les dieux. Il est la force de l'évidence.[3]

2. *Lettres à un ami allemand* (Paris: Gallimard, 1948), p. 78.
3. *Ibid.,* p. 39.

This is Camus's first renunciation of the absurd as a global philosophy. A human order is clearly opposed to the disorder of the world. From the postulate of the absurd, according to this sentence a choice is still possible, while according to Caligula's logic there was no choice. Here, the choice is put in terms of unusual beauty:

> "Où était la différence? . . . C'est que vous admettiez assez l'injustice de notre condition pour vous résoudre à y ajouter, tandis qu'il m'aparaissait au contraire que l'homme devait affirmer la justice pour lutter contre l'injustice éternelle, créer un bonheur pour protester contre l'univers du malheur. Parceque vous avez fait de votre désespoir une ivresse, parceque vous vous en êtes délivrés en l'érigeant en principe, vous avez accepté de détruire les oeuvres de l'homme et de lutter contre lui pour achever sa misère essentielle. Et moi, refusant d'admettre ce désespoir et ce monde torturé, je voulais seulement que les hommes retrouvent leur solidarité pour entrer en lutte contre leur destin révoltant.
>
> Pour tout dire, vous avez choisi l'injustice. Vous vous êtes mis avec les dieux. Votre logique n'était qu'apparente. J'ai choisi la justice au contraire, pour rester fidèle à la terre. Je continue à croire que ce monde n'a pas de sens supérieur. Mais je sais que quelquechose en lui a du sens et c'est l'homme, parcequ'il est le seul être à exiger d'en avoir."[4]

We know that, in Camus's personal mythology, Fate or the gods symbolize the forces of arbitrariness and chaos, while the earth is both a mother symbol of perennial wisdom and harmlessness and an erotic symbol of pantheistic ecstasy at the sight of threatened beauty. As for Camus's proclaimed "faithfulness," it is reminiscent of Malraux's famous observation that a man who is both active and pessimistic is bound to become a Fascist unless he is held back by "faithfulness." Camus's faithfulness is not exactly that of Malraux, and the opposition later appeared clearly in *State of Siege*. But faithfulness there was, and it sprang from the midst of the absurd as a force that opposed the absurd.

This "something that makes sense" ("quelque chose qui a

---

4. *Ibid.,* pp. 72–74.

un sens") in the absurd universe is identified as "man, friendship, happiness and our desire for justice." The whole of the letters—and, in fact, most of Camus's works—consists of a definition of these words. Man, for Camus, is "that force which opposes tyrants and gods"; in other words, the fighter for freedom and the creator of meaning. Happiness, of which friendship is a part, is the state of communion between nature and human beings, so beautifully illustrated in Camus's early works. As for justice, it is the wish to remove natural or social obstacles that stand in the way of man's happiness. Here we have Camus's unswerving ideal reasserted against both ideological and natural barbarism. First of all against all glorification of hate and violence, all power ideologies. Especially hateful in Camus's eyes is nationalism, whether French, German, or any other. We are reminded in the preface that the letters do not contrast France and Germany but Nazis and free men in both camps; that the most urgent task is the construction of Europe. And Camus specifies that he loves his country too much to be a nationalist. This is Camus's first condition—a negative condition—for the emergence of a human world: the end of national egotism, bent on conquest; the end of national short-sightedness that prevents nations from seeing any light beyond their boundaries.

Camus's second precondition for the creation of a civilized world is respect for intelligence and rationality. Here Camus not only condemns the Nazi cult of the irrational, but recalls with shame that not a few French intellectuals had sought the comforts of unreason: "Car nous imaginons parfois quelque heureuse barbarie ou la vérité serait sans effort."[5] It is clear that here *we* means the French. But it also means we men, especially modern men, plagued with doubts, deprived of traditional certainties, and faced with the task of rebuilding a world in ruins. To go the way of the irrational in the hope of discovering "effortless truth" is another way of taking the part of Fate or the gods—of betraying the human. This is the essence of that "tragedy of

5. *Ibid.*, pp. 23–24.

intelligence" common to the whole of Europe, the result of which was the war.[6]

With this positive and negative ideal in view, Camus had something to offer to a weakened France on the eve of its liberation: a return to the true sources of its real greatness. But something else had to be said. A painful admission was necessary before the evil ghosts of the past could be laid to rest. Besides bidding farewell to Caligula, the letters contain a reappraisal of French prewar pacifism, or rather of the anti-patriotism which, by undermining the national instinct for self-preservation, had made Hitler's rise possible. "You do not love your country," the German friend was supposed to have told Camus before the war. In 1944, when the nightmare of German occupation was receding and the Resistance fighters could look with pride at their achievements, the reproaching sentence comes back to Camus's mind with nagging persistence: "You do not love your country." Camus notes that five years had passed and those words remained on his mind all that time.[7]

It cannot be denied that Camus's answer to this reproach is feeble and borders on self-complacency. After the often heroic years of the Resistance, the prewar appeasement policy must have seemed as incomprehensible as the existence of French collaborationists was shocking, and it is noteworthy that Camus does not squarely face the fact of prewar anti-patriotism.

This prewar anti-patriotism was the result of a sort of conditioned reflex, helped by propaganda on the one hand and political blunders on the other. The reflex dated back to 1917 when, due to criminal incompetence on the part of the military command and an orgy of chauvinistic propaganda in the press, the French soldiers came to regard the Fatherland, *la Patrie,* as a voracious idol demanding human sacrifices. Skillful propaganda —first by the Communists who feared another intervention by Western powers against Russia, then by the developing Nazi Party—exploited this basic resentment. Political blundering did

---

6. *Ibid.,* p. 78.
7. *Ibid.,* p. 20.

the rest: the senseless crushing of Weimar Germany at Versailles and the persistent refusal by the French Right to abandon any part of its economic privileges led to the conviction that the blood of the people was being used in defense of economic interests. So strong was anti-patriotic feeling in the thirties, when the country was faced with another senseless war, that few people perceived how the situation had changed, and that the former German underdog was now up and biting. French paralysis in the late thirties was the result of a four-pronged pacifist offensive—a pacifism of the Right that said: better Hitler than Stalin; a pacifism of the Left that believed war was a greater evil than whatever evil it was supposed to remove; supporting this, a general weariness of people who did not want to hear about the possibility of having to go to war again; finally, a form of pacifism with high ethical overtones that condemned violence altogether. This is the attitude that Camus claims not only for himself but for the whole of France. As far as Camus's own pacifism was concerned, it might have been idealistic, but it certainly did not spring from a commitment to nonviolence. *Révolte dans les Asturies,* to say nothing of Camus's previous joining the communist party, shows clearly that the commitment to nonviolence was a selective one. Revolutionary violence was serving justice and man's dignity. But the use of force by the national community, even in self-defense, as at the time of Hitler's rise to power, was regarded as unjust, the result of chauvinism and pressure by vested interests. It is probable that Camus's pacifism was the direct outcome of such propaganda: he writes in his notebooks that he remained a pacifist until 1942 and several earlier entries in his *Carnets* bear witness to the fact. In 1939, answering a distressed young man, he states that European nations have not done all they could to prevent the war, and each person should today try to spread conciliatory ideas.[8]

So much for Camus's pacifism. As far as the pacifism of prewar France was concerned, perhaps it was not advisable to recall it in 1944 just when the nation was about to rise to its feet.

---

8. *Carnets,* 1:180–81.

What Camus does, in fact, is recall France's specific contribution to civilization while warning her that the spirit without the sword is powerless. France's contribution to the history of civilization was a regard for happiness, a predilection for a peaceful destiny. It was not easy to give up this "passion for friendship," knowing that no victory pays and that any human loss is irreparable.[9] Yet, the realities of a power-ridden world had to be faced. To civilized nations forced into the war by the conquering spirit of others, Camus offers the most difficult of all tasks: "Se battre en méprisant la guerre. . . . accepter de tout perdre en gardant le goût du bonheur . . . courir à la destruction avec l'idée d'une civilisation supérieure."[10] It is Camus's belief that, although the spirit is powerless against the sword, "the spirit with sword is stronger than the sword by itself." The letters, as well as his subsequent articles, published under the title: *Actuelles I,* sometimes convey the hope of an incipient renaissance.

Thus, on the eve of a victory to which France contributed more by the heroic example of the Resistance fighters than by its military strength, Camus reasserts France's spiritual mission, which is to perpetuate the values she helped create. If read by the victorious giants of the war, these letters might help to remind them of the importance of the values without which their victory would be meaningless. Addressed to a prostrate nation about to rise to its feet, the letters were apt to restore the national self-confidence. However, Camus was careful to remind his fellow citizens that France is part of Europe and means nothing without it. Fearing, perhaps, the perpetuation of old hatreds, he never tires of repeating that civilization is a common creation, and that, after the collapse of Hitler's Europe, the true humanist Europe must be rebuilt.

Unexpectedly, Camus emerged from the war as a fully committed man, and for the next few years he devoted his time and thoughts to politics, although the elated optimism expressed in the letters was of short duration.

---

9. *Ibid.,* pp. 28, 26, 25.
10. *Ibid.,* p. 23.

2. The Lessons of Combat

Combat was the title of the underground paper for which Camus worked during the Resistence. After the war, *Combat* came out as one of the leading newspapers to replace the prewar press compromised in collaboration. It was fully independent of private or party interests. Most of the writers and thinkers of the time wrote in *Combat* (Sartre and Raymond Aron being among the most prominent.) Camus and Pascal Pia were on the editing board and remained there until the paper, plagued by financial difficulties, was taken over by a new, more conventional team, after the departure of its founders (1946).

A selection of Camus's editorials has been published in *Actuelles I*; M. Roger Quillot, in his monumental edition of Camus's works[11] added a number of significant articles, not yet reedited, which complete the picture of Camus's political opinions at that time. As far as internal politics were concerned, Camus regarded himself a socialist, although he did not always see eye to eye with the reconstructed Socialist Party. During the war, Léon Blum was in prison and many prewar socialist personalities lived in exile. After the liberation, some differences developed between the old guard and the militants of the Resistance, who wanted to have their say. These differences were given vent at two successive socialist congresses. Apart from Léon Blum, whom he always admired, Camus had little esteem for prewar socialist parliamentarians who, according to him, had sunk the Popular Front, betrayed the Spanish republicans, stumbled into the war and "left Paris when they should have stayed." Camus's hopes were for a rejuvenated Socialist Party, including Resistance fighters and a few—very few—former politicians.

Camus's position in *Combat* editorials can be summed up in his formula: "We want a combination of justice and freedom," or, more precisely, "a collectivized economy with political freedom." He was thus fighting on two fronts: against the capitalists

---

11. Albert Camus, *Essais,* in *Bibliothèque de la Pléiade* (Paris: Gallimard, 1962).

who were rebuilding their shattered power, and against the Communists, whose popular appeal was steadily growing. Meanwhile, the Socialist Party was in power, but once more headed by the old guard. Although some industries were nationalized, no radical change of structure occurred and Camus was soon disappointed.

In September 1944, he wrote: "The human face can be seen again. Politics is no longer dissociated from the individual. It is a direct appeal from one man to another. It has its own accent."[12] In place of the old order "which was not democracy but its caricature," he hoped to watch "one unanimous people" born of the Resistance and the working class, whose "unformulated thought . . . hides the germs of a Renaissance." He defined his aims as: "Justice plus freedom." Justice, to him, meant equality of opportunity, a state of affairs in which the majority is not kept in an undignified condition by a privileged minority. Freedom meant respect for persons, their private lives and political rights. He summed up his aims as collectivization of the economy together with political liberalism, and regarded liberal socialism as the only regime that could ensure that man is free and responsible for his own fate and happiness—the only regime that does not add iniquities of a purely human origin to the unavoidable misery of our condition.[13]

Camus seemed to put his trust in humanitarian rather than in Marxist socialism (although, surprisingly, he mentioned Jules Guesde in connection with the first group.)[14] On the whole, his conception of socialism was not devoid of romanticism. He loved the feeling of human brotherhood and hoped that the working class ("which is the ruling class of tomorrow") would not settle down to a petit bourgeois existence ("bowling clubs, Galeries Barbès furniture") but would go on fighting for "two or three great ideas."[15] To this body of generous but in no way novel ideas, Camus added a very high conception of the mission and

---

12. *Ibid.,* p. 1524.
13. *Ibid.,* pp. 1525, 1527, 1528.
14. *Ibid.,* p. 1547.
15. *Ibid.,* pp. 1546, 1545.

duty of writers and journalists, and the necessity for a sincere and independent press.

In November 1944, Camus wrote that "a social doctrine is taking shape in large segments of public opinion." Three months later he spoke of the technique by which one can undermine a revolution.[16] Camus's thoughts and hopes oscillated between these two poles, like those of a man who had lived through great moments during the Resistance and liberation, and who had seen the initial enthusiasm gradually, irrevocably subside into dull political routine. Camus's political ideas, on the whole, appear sound and idealistic, but somewhat vague, sustained by no solid notions either of economics or of political skill. They were a nostalgic but hardly original blend of humanitarian socialism, with little chance of survival in the postwar jungle.

Camus's relations with the Communist Party deteriorated steadily during the post-war years. The common fight in the Resistance, as well as his friendship with the poet Francis Ponge, brought him nearer to the Party, in spite of his earlier break with it before the war. No sooner was peace restored, however, than the familiar pattern of intellectual independence versus party dogmatism reappeared. At first, the conflict was literary. Then Camus realized that the Communist Party was using the trials of pro-Nazi writers in order to dispose of their enemies. Most of all, Camus was repelled by Stalin's dictatorship and terror. This was the time when an important group of anti-Communist left-wing intellectuals was being constituted. Camus knew Koestler and Manès Sperber.[17] He maintained less close but cordial relations with Richard Wright, Silone, and Gide, who were soon to give an account of their break with Communism in *The God that Failed* (1950). Camus was already the object of attacks by Communist magazines, particularly *Action* and *Lettres françaises*. David Rousset, the author of world-famous books about Nazi

16. *Ibid.,* pp. 281, 154.
17. In *Carnets,* 2, he relates a conversation among these writers, himself, and Sartre.

concentration camps, soon raised a protest against the existence of similar camps in Russia. Camus also protested against that, as well as against the putsch in Prague and the Communist domination of half of Europe. This attitude was responsible for his break with Merleau-Ponty, whose *Humanisme et Terreur* was interpreted by Camus as a defense of Stalinist terror.

However, in spite of Camus's hostility to Communist methods and dogmatism, he avoided any clear denunciation of them until *The Rebel,* so that his hostility appears between the lines rather than in open pronouncements (as in the case of *The Plague*). The first reason for this restraint was, of course, the shocking sight of social inequality in France, in spite of social welfare and economic recovery as the noncommunist left reverted to the kind of immobility that had undermined its popularity before the war. The second and more serious reason was Camus's understanding of the international situation. Like most French intellectuals, Camus started from the axiom that Americans and Russians were equally guilty of imperialism and that, in view of the existence of the atom bomb, any conflict would lead to the extinction of the world. When the United States and the USSR fell apart in two hostile blocs, Camus's attitude was reminiscent of what he had said and done ten years earlier concerning Hitler: he deplored the lack of conciliatory spirit. To those who accused him of utopianism, he answered that the choice was between Utopia and the Apocalypse, an argument with more appeal in the West than in the East. Finally, having watched the failure of the European third force, he had no remedy but to back Garry Davis's romantic undertaking, which collapsed, despite the help of such distinguished writers as R. Wright and Emmanuel Mounier.

During all this period of considerable intellectual confusion, many illusions vanished. Final decisions were still far away. And Camus's novel and plays of the forties, while showing traces of political skepticism, invariably reflected relative optimism in human affairs. A new cycle had opened in Camus's life; the cycle of *The Plague*. In contrast with the cycle of *Sisyphus*, it is characterized by an upright, assertive attitude in the face of crushing forces. Camus now united the moderation of a mature man in determining his aims and demands with a fighting spirit that was absent from his early works and from the cycle of the absurd. At the same time, thanks to his slow, obstinate meditation on moral problems, his new ethics was starting to take shape around the new symbol of *The Plague*.

5
History as the Plague

1. The Unassuming Fighters

The symbol of the plague is complex and open to interpretation on several levels. In the most general sense the plague is, of course, a symbol of man's metaphysical condition. Man is seen as a prisoner sentenced to a cruel death for a crime of which he knows nothing. A fitting symbol of the absurdity of his fate is that of the plague-stricken actor who collapses on the stage as he sings the part of *Orpheus in Hades* for the hundredth time. This is another type of absurdity than that of Sisyphus, more akin to that felt by Caligula, but unrelieved by Caligula's delusions of all-powerfulness. At the same time, the beleaguered city of Oran is an obvious allegory of the Resistance in occupied Europe.[1] Camus incorporated into the novel his own experience of the war years: fear, claustrophobia, separation, the tyranny of material life, the endless waiting, the torture of unending time. In a broader sense, the plague is the war, or Nazism (or any totalitarian government), or, generally speaking, any kind of social or political upheaval. Here lies the root of Camus's subsequent conflict with his Marxist friends, especially Sartre and the *Temps Modernes* group.

---

1. As Camus confirmed. See *Lyrical and Critical Essays,* p. 339.

These Marxists, whether or not they agreed with Stalin's rule, believed that history had a meaning, complete with causality, finality, and dialectic. Hitler was the latest incarnation of capitalist imperialism; therefore, history had worked against him: after his defeat it would be the task of the working class and Marxist intellectuals to bring peace and justice to the world by establishing the classless society. Nothing of the kind is found in *The Plague*. The mixture of scientific analysis and prophecy known as historicism is totally alien to Camus, whose conception is at the same time much more profound and considerably hazy.

Historical messianism is not only alien but frankly abhorrent to Camus. In his view history lacks any discernible meaning; it is as absurd as it is atrocious: it is absurdity itself, unredeemed by any hope—except the hope that the furies will subside for a while and life will become tolerable again. Camus's characters do not dream of a glorious future for mankind. They simply fight an intolerable present, struggling in a tunnel for a little more air and light. No human fulfillment is to be achieved through history: such is Camus's conviction. Individual man has no worse enemy than history; it degrades and crushes him, separates him from all that is precious to him, reduces him to his trembling body. Communities of men are also the victims of history: "les peuples heureux n'ont pas d'histoire." History is the curse of mankind: It is the plague.

History is not only meaningless to individuals. It destroys collective creations. When it rolls on, civilizations are tossed about like pebbles, and in the tumult of historical forces the voice of the spirit is not heard. "History is a sterile earth where heather does not grow." "History has no eyes." It is, indeed, the scourge of God, a *fléau*.[2]

History seen under the guise of the plague is stripped of all romantic glamour. Every spark of flamboyance or pathos has been quenched in Camus's deliberately tuned down narrative. Meticulous observations of material details pile up like a heap of ashes; the tragic features of the situation are pushed into the

---

2. *Lyrical and Critical Essays*, pp. 140, 141.

background by the necessity of waiting in long lines for food. Identification with characters is discouraged by the constant use of clinical or administrative style. This deliberate monotony is a reminder of the humbleness of the human condition, a warning against Caligula's pride. It is also an effort to demystify, to deromanticize, history by stripping it of its aura of glory and exposing it as a dull routine of suppression and death: "Nothing is less sensational than pestilence." "Great misfortunes are monotonous . . . a slow, deliberate progress of some monstrous thing." "A long night's slumber." "No one was capable any longer of exalted emotions; all had trite, monotonous feelings."[3]

The old French phrase *fléau de Dieu* suggests richer images than pestilence or the scourge of God, inasmuch as *fléau* is not a whip but a flail that purifies as it punishes, separating the wheat from the chaff. Throughout *The Plague* a faint whistling sound is heard above the street lamps at night, reminiscent of that of a flail at work. The *fléaux* were part of medieval life, a proof of God's wrath and concern. The plague, the Huns, hail, and floods were *fléaux*. As everyone knows, the plague has disappeared from the Western world, together with the Inquisition, witch burning, hundred years' wars, and other medieval atrocities. Belief in the *fléaux* has disappeared together with belief in God, with the result that when a new *fléau* rises from the medieval past, it masquerades as socio-historical causality.

Faced with a *fléau* in modern garb, the modern rationalists invariably fail to recognize it, which is the reason why "the humanists" (as Camus calls those who believe everything to be on a human scale) are always hit harder than others "because they have not taken their precautions."[4] The people of Oran belonged to this category:

---

3. Albert Camus, *The Plague* (Hamish Hamilton, London: 1948), pp. 168, 171, 169.
4. *Ibid.*, p. 37.

Our citizens work hard, but solely with the object of getting rich. Their chief interest is in commerce, and their chief aim in life is, as they call it, "doing business." Naturally they don't eschew such simpler pleasures as love-making, sea-bathing, going to the pictures. But, very sensibly, they reserve these pastimes for Saturday afternoons and Sundays, and employ the rest of the week in making money, as much as possible. In the evening, on leaving office, they forgather, at an hour that never varies, in the cafés, stroll the same boulevard, or take the air on their balconies. The passions of the young are violent and short-lived; the vices of older men seldom range beyond an addiction to games of bowls, to banquets and "socials," or clubs where large sums change hands on the fall of a card.

It will be said, no doubt, that these habits are not peculiar to our town; really all our contemporaries are much the same. Certainly nothing is commoner nowadays than to see people working from morn till night and then proceeding to fritter away at card-tables, in cafés and in small-talk what time is left for living. Nevertheless, there still exist towns and countries where people have now and again an inkling of something different. In general it doesn't change their lives. Still, they have had an intimation, and that's so much to the good. Oran, however, seems to be a town without intimations; in other words, completely modern.[5]

When the plague hit them, they had no suspicion of anything. Even Dr. Rieux, who was later to organize the resistance, absent-mindedly pushed aside the dead rat on his landing. Only on second thought did he realize that a dead rat was out of place there; but, after all, this was the caretaker's business. Even when dead rats had to be cleared away by the truckload, local authorities went on denying that anything unusual had happened. This could not be the plague, they argued, since, as everybody knew, the plague had disappeared from the Western world, etcetera.

But it was the plague all right, and it soon exhibited all the characteristics of the *fléau,* particularly its unpredictability. It started and ended without reason, struck or spared at random, and followed its own unpredictable rhythm. And while the earth

---

5. *Ibid.,* p. 6.

was being "purged of its secreted humours" and the sea, in the background, "told of the unrest, the precariousness of all things in this world," the victims gradually settled down to a "new order,"[6] that of death and separation.

The preposterous return of the Plague eroded modern rationalist mythology without altering modern phraseology and style of life. In accounting for this ambiguous experience, Camus's grim humor is reminiscent of Chateaubriand's description of the cholera epidemic in 1835:

If this scourge had fallen upon us in a religious age, if it had spread in the midst of poetic manners and popular beliefs, it would have created a striking picture. Imagine a pall flying by way of a flag from the towers of Notre-Dame; the cannon firing single shots at intervals to warn the imprudent traveller to turn back; a cordon of troops surrounding the city and allowing no one to enter or leave it; the churches filled with a groaning multitude; the priests chanting day and night the prayers of a perpetual death-agony; the Viaticum carried from house to house with bell and candle; the church bells constantly tolling the funeral knell; the monks at the cross-roads, crucifix in hand, summoning the people to repentance and preaching the wrath and judgment of God, made manifest in the corpses already blackened by hellfire.

Then the closed shops; the pontiff, surrounded by his clergy, going, with every curé at the head of his parish, to fetch the shrine of St. Geneviève; the sacred carried round the city, preceded by the long procession of the different religious orders, guilds, corporations, congregations of penitents, groups of veiled women, scholars of the university, ministers of the alms-houses, and soldiers marching along without arms or with pikes reversed; the *Miserere* chanted by the priests mingling with the hymns of the girls and children; and all, at certain signals, prostrating themselves in silence and rising to utter fresh complaints.

There is nothing of this today; the cholera has come to us in an age of philanthropy, incredulity, newspapers and material administration. This unimaginative scourge found no old cloisters awaiting it, no monks, no vaults, no Gothic tombs; like the Terror of 1793, it wandered about with a mocking air, in broad daylight, in a new and unfamiliar world, accompanied by its

6. *Ibid.*, pp. 17, 40, 167.

bulletin, which recited the remedies which had been used against
it, the number of victims it had claimed, the progress it had
made, the hopes which were entertained of seeing it come to
an end, the precautions which had to be taken to guard against
it, what one should eat, how one should dress. And everyone
continued to attend to his business, and the theatres were full.
I have seen drunkards at the city gates, sitting drinking at a
little wooden table outside a pot-house, saying as they raised
their glasses:

"Here's to your health, Morbus!"

Morbus, out of gratitude, came running up, and they fell dead
under the table. The children played at cholera, calling it
"Nicholas Morbus" and "Morbus the Rascal". And yet the
cholera had its terrifying side: the bright sunshine, the indifference of the crowd, the ordinary course of life, which went on
everywhere, invested these days of pestilence with a new character and a different sort of horror. You felt aches and pains in
every limb; your mouth was parched by a cold, dry north wind;
the air had a certain metallic quality which took you by the
throat. In the Rue du Cherche-Midi, wagons from the artillery
depot were used to cart away the dead bodies. In the Rue de
Sèvres, which was particularly affected, especially on one side,
the hearses came and went from door to door; there were not
enough of them to satisfy the demand and people shouted from
the windows:

"Over here, hearse!"

The driver answered that he was full up and could not attend
to everybody.[7]

Similarly, in Camus's *The Plague,* Morbus walks around carrying a statistical bulletin. Everything is caught in a web of red tape,
from rat control to the disposal of dead bodies. Strict regulations
govern the black market and the sanitary units as well, and "flee-
carriers" are to report to the next prophylactic center. The pitiful
inadequacy of official measures is another illustration of the establishment's cowardice and lack of imagination. The social resentment in *The Stranger* had not subsided: "Insist on social criticism,"
writes Camus in his *Carnets.*[8]

7. Alphonse de Chateaubriand, *Memoirs* (New York: A. Knopf,
1961), pp. 308–9.
8. 2:68–69.

It is not known whether Camus had read Chateaubriand's *Memoirs* and borrowed from him the idea of the *fléau sans imagination*. Unlike his Catholic predecessor, however, Camus does not regret the age of faith, but launches his most violent onslaughts on the Christian religion. You have sinned, you are punished: such is the central theme of Father Paneloux's sermon. The plague was sent by God to remind the lukewarm believers of His existence. He had no other means; the plague was a proof of His love, so to speak. Let us listen to God and mend our ways, and He might spare us. This sermon was suggested to Camus by actual sermons preached during great plagues of the past. It summarized, in Camus's eyes, Catholic beliefs concerning sin and the avenging God. Suffering is beneficial in calling the sinner to repent. In a subtly ironical way, Father Paneloux's sermon recalled the penitent style of the Vichy Government calling on the public devoutly to bear with Nazi occupation in atonement for their past sins of individualism and disobedience.

This submissive attitude was all the more repugnant to Camus since it invited a gloomy fatalism and permeated the people with a sense of guilt. Characteristically, Paneloux's sermon was most warmly applauded by Judge Othon, whose narrow, punitive, authoritarian mentality made him for Camus a representative of Vichy's ideology.

Subsequently, Father Paneloux felt less sure: the indiscriminate ravage of the Plague, especially the death of children, shattered his faith. His second sermon was less assertive than the first. He did not say "you" any longer, but "we." We should accept the will of God, even uncomprehendingly. Blind faith should follow blind obedience. Pride of spirit and pride of life—the two assets of Prometheus—were the chief enemies of the Christian. His faith shattered, Paneloux finally died of an illness that might have been the plague but need not have been. On his card they wrote *Dubious case*.

Camus's indictment of Catholicism in *The Plague* is the most radical he ever made. It involves ethics, politics, and metaphysics. Christian ethics repels Camus by its identification of sensuous

enjoyment with sin and its belief in purification by suffering.
Camus always regarded sensuous pleasure as innocent and, in a
way, holy, one of the surest paths to communion with nature and
human beings. "I do not refuse communion with Being, Camus
writes, but not if the path takes me away from beings." On the
other hand, Camus does not seem to believe that sin—if one means
by this the wish to inflict pain on others—is a basic disposition in
man. On the contrary, it is man's reaction to his wretchedness and
dereliction. (And such is Camus's indignation at the sight of human
misery that he is ready to understand even Caligula's reaction.)
Fate is the aggressor. The Christian error—or perhaps Camus
would say betrayal—consists in regarding man as guilty and justly
punished, and not as the victim of an incomprehensible curse. The
result of this wrong pedagogy is a kind of degradation of man:
"Man tries naturally to resemble the best image of himself. . . . For
two thousand years, the image of himself offered to him has been
that of a humiliated creature." In politics, Camus views the
Catholics as the natural allies of those who want to crush and
humiliate man—of judges, for instance, and other figures of repressive power.[9] Camus's ideas on this point are far from clear, but,
considering that we are unjustly and inexplicably punished for no
crime, he often seems to believe that we are basically innocent
and should not be condemned for reacting with hate and violence
to this initial injustice. And why, of all punishments, should we
suffer more deprivation of the very things the lack of which makes
us frantic? Indeed, Camus's chief reproach to Christianity, and
especially Catholicism, is that of having sided with fate and
betrayed the suffering man.

Since Camus blames the rationalists for not believing in *fléaux*
but rejects Christian explanations and remedies for them, what,
then, does he suggest on his own account? Surprisingly, Camus's
own explanation is not very far from the Christian one. Several

---

9. *Carnets,* 2:97, 16.

critics have wondered why Camus had chosen a disease, an act of fate, to symbolize such obviously man-made evils as war, Nazism, and other social monstrosities.[11] In fact, Camus was adequately expressing his idea of the relation between man and historical forces. History in his view was indeed made by man, and his main disagreement with the simple-minded Marxists came from the fact that he did not believe in economic determinism. Man was a free agent in the making of history. Since man did not realize this, however, history hit him as an external force (in proper Marxist terminology, a case of alienation). Yet, man himself was the germ-carrier. Hence Camus's choice of the plague as an allegory and not, for instance, an earthquake, as suggested at the beginning of the novel when a street sweeper, at the sight of the rats, predicts "a catastrophe like an earthquake."

Thus Camus believes in sin, though not in original sin: the sin is the result of ignorance, and unenlightened choice. He believes also that men are punished for their wrong choice, not by an avenging God but by a natural process, half psychological, half metaphysical, akin to the Greek concept of *nemesis*. The curse of history, in Camus's opinion, seems to consist in man's propensity to react to one excess with another one, without ever finding proper limits or balance. Thus, one evil breeds another, in an endless chain. The real curse of mankind, in Camus's opinion, is not so much history as historicism; for the worshipers of history —whether they relish the dark forces unleashed by the multitude or believe in salvation through historical change—are apt to produce fanatical ideologies, in the name of which they become self-righteous murderers. We have seen how Camus watched with growing distress his former comrades of the Resistance falling under the spell of another tyranny. Hence his fear that the plague fighters would become enamored with their fight to the point of creating another plague led him to stress, sometimes to the point of dullness, the values of restraint and relativism. Camus's determination to discredit fanaticism led him to tone down both hope

11. See letter to R. Barthes, in *Lyrical and Critical Essays,* p. 338.

and indignation. The fighters tend to underrate their chances of success, knowing that "the plague bacillus never dies," and its behavior is unpredictable. On the other hand, while being fully committed to the fight, they refuse to blame those who are not, and even to restrain those who break the rules. This is part of the prophylaxis, to avoid propagating the *fléau*. Finally, in view of these beliefs, his cure for the plague is not atonement, humiliation, and more suffering, but the traditional humanistic remedies for social evils: lucidity and sympathy. To this, Camus adds the indispensable material remedies, for it had been the lesson of the war that idealism was not enough. ("The spirit without the sword is powerless.") Without the spirit, however, the plague could not be warded off at all; it would merely give way to cholera, leprosy, or any other pestilence.

The analysis of Camus's main characters in *The Plague* seems to confirm this interpretation of sin and purification. If we want to know about the kind of sin that unleashes the plague, we can look at two characters who are like geniuses of the plague: Cottard and the asthmatic old man. Cottard is a realistic but somewhat enigmatic figure. Wanted for an unspecified offense, he had attempted suicide before the plague broke out and then thrived on the epidemic that stayed judicial pursuits, making a fortune on the black market while enjoying the sight of death, to which he himself felt immune. When his reprieve came to an end with the ebbing of the plague, he ended by shooting into the crowd in a frenzy of hate and despair. Camus could not express more clearly that the plague was lack of love and solidarity. Cottard might be a midget Caligula.

Another character conveys the same idea in a deeper and more obscure symbolism. An asthmatic old man, shut off from life but apparently immortal, has no other pastime in his bed than measuring time by transferring dry peas one by one from one tank to another. ("Watches are expensive and they don't work," he says.) He knows about the rats before anyone else: "They're coming out! They're coming out!" he cries excitedly. In this powerful though episodic sketch of a realistic and allegorical character, Camus has portrayed the perfect nihilist, who experiences the essence of empty time and relishes evil as one privileged form of vitality. He is the true genius of the plague: "What does that mean: plague? Just life, no more than that."[12]

Facing these two figures of misanthropy and dereliction, the people who fight and finally conquer the plague are men of good will, with a gift of sympathy: Rieux and Tarrou and, in a less prominent way, Rambert and Grant. The first one is a doctor, who fights the plague by purely pragmatic means: vaccines, sanitation, organization. A realist, he nevertheless believes in love and friendship as positive remedies against pestilence; and, although fully committed in the fight, he does not feel he has the right to blame those who remain outsiders. As a preventive remedy, he advocates modesty. He never raises his voice; he believes "the thing [is] to do your job as it should be done."[13] He obstinately refuses to assert more than he knows, refuses theories and—as one can gather—illustrates Camus's utter dislike and mistrust of ideologies. Tarrou was originally more ambitious. He wanted to create absolute good, to eliminate legal murder—from war to the death penalty. He tried to practice absolute nonviolence. But experience made him modest and, after joining a political party, which made him an accomplice to murder, his final aim was to do "as little evil as possible." Between the doctor "who cannot resign himself to the fact of death" and the opponent of the death penalty, a warm friendship is joined, since their aims are complementary.

When it comes to Rambert and Grant, the connection between their life aims and the fight against the plague is less apparent: the former, a stranger to the quarantined town, has only one aim: to escape and join his wife in Paris; the latter, a modest office clerk, has the preposterous ambition of writing the perfect novel and has been laboring on the first sentence for many years. Both of them interrupt their pursuits in order to fight the plague, Grant as a matter of course, and Rambert after a long resistance, when

---

12. *The Plague,* p. 283. This character seems to have a model in reality, since he is mentioned in *Carnets,* 2:18.

13. *Ibid.,* p. 41.

he discovers that "the plague is everybody's concern." It is clear, however, that their personal aims, love for Rambert and artistic perfection for Grant, although fated to destruction in an absurd world, had in themselves the power to keep the plague at bay. Both are saved. Both have conquered absurdity—for a while.

It should be obvious by now that Camus's remedy against the plague—that is, against the man-made evil of history—is the positive assertion of man's powers of creation and sympathy in whatever field they manifest themselves—be it in art or personal relations, or knowledge, science, or action. All creative personalities are one. Rieux, the man of duty, does not blame Rambert for trying to escape the closed city. Tarrou, the pacifist, does not protest if those who try to escape are shot at the gates. This may seem contradictory; the reason is that, indeed, human values are contradictory, and only by keeping both extremes together can man escape the danger of fanaticism. Thus, the main lesson to emerge from *The Plague* is an unassuming Promethean spirit. The spirit is Promethean: a human order is to be substituted for chaos. The main point is not to submit; "a fight must be put up, in this way or that, and there must be no bowing down."[14] Revolt, therefore, is the main value, for it is directed against chaos, which is at once injustice and disorder and a scandal against reason. With Aeschylean pride, Camus contrasts man-created justice with the haphazard injustice of the gods. He quietly asserts in his *Carnets* that we, not the gods, are creators and that our only opportunity to have gods is to create them ourselves. This is the deeper meaning of revolt.[15]

What should be avoided at all costs, however, is making revolt an absolute value, either through romanticism or fanatical belief: loving the fight for its own sake, and putting its aims above everything else are equally dangerous. Camus's horror of ideology, or what he calls "abstractions," is the second lesson of *The Plague*. The plague-fighters must practice honesty as a prophylactic mea-

---

14. *Ibid.,* p. 128.
15. *Carnets,* 2:127.

sure: to do one's job as well as possible, while knowing that it has only relative value; to be honest with oneself and others, not to pretend more or less than one feels; above all (as in *The Stranger*) to refrain from judging and from prescribing their duties to other people. Here Camus's familiar phobia against judges and trials is shown again. In his *Carnets,* contemporary with the preparation of *The Plague,* he reasserts that all attitudes are basically similar when men are faced with the plague, and that nothing should be affirmed since everything can be denied. Here, Rieux and Tarrou judge no one, blame no one (except the judge, a malevolent and dogmatic character called Othon). "Everybody is right" is Camus's repeated warning, and he goes so far as to assert that one should forgive the plague!

Here again, as in *The Stranger*, this phobia against system tends to become a system. It might be a reaction against the excess of political moralizing Camus saw and heard around him. To fanatics and breeders of abstractions—the genuine plague-carriers in his eyes—Camus repeats that the main anti-plague virtue is regard for happiness and love as the only values grounded in nature that will prevail in the end: ". . . A loveless world is a dead world, and always there comes an hour when one is weary of prisons, of one's work and of devotion to duty and all one craves for is a loved face, the warmth and wonder of a loving heart."[16] This is why Camus tends persistently to regard heroism and sainthood as secondary virtues. Tarrou, who once belonged to a party for the improvement of mankind, feels that he has thereby made himself an accomplice of fanaticism and murder. Rieux also observes: "I have seen enough of people dying for an idea. I don't believe in heroism. I know it's easy and I have learned it can be murderous. What interests me is living and dying for what one loves." This subtle balance between necessary heroism and preference for happiness, between respect for other people's choices and persuasion by example, seems to be Camus's last word on how to fight pestilence without spreading it.

---

16. *Ibid.,* p. 243.

Nevertheless, in the end the reader is reminded that "the plague bacillus never dies or disappears for good; that it can lie dormant for years and years in furniture and linen-chests . . . and that perhaps the day would come when, for the bane and enlightening of men, it roused up its rats again and sent them forth to die in a happy city."[17]

2. The Heroic Fighters

In *The State of Siege*, the allegory of the plague is maintained, but the tone is different and the setting more spectacular: a walled city by the sea, with medieval undertones, replaces the "entirely modern" town of Oran. The pestilence is announced not by rats, but by a comet. Stage setting and a chorus ensure a kind of audience participation reminiscent of *Révolte dans les Asturies* and in contrast with the chilling tone of *The Plague*. Moreover, the plague itself is impersonated by a man in uniform, who is courteous and even jovial, but ruthless, accompanied by a correct secretary. It is questionable that this new presentation of the *fléau* was a happy innovation. But what is studied here is not Camus's art but his ideas. The first part pictures the old order in the city of Cadiz. After the arrival of The Plague (impersonated by the man in uniform), the old order is replaced by the new, which, however, turns out to be a more systematic version of the old one. In the old order, the government was despotic, the people went hungry while the rich were hoarding; the clergy and the magistrates lorded it over the people. Nevertheless, ordinary folk enjoyed the sweet summer and believed that winter would never come. The love scene between Diego—a young doctor, like Rieux—and his fiancée, Victoria, sums up the dreams and ecstasies of youth.

This life routine went on even after the comet was seen. The authorities had forbidden mentioning it, anyway; everything was supposed to remain exactly as before: "I like my habits," says the Governor, and "change is the thing I detest." "Nothing new is

17. *Ibid.*, pp. 284–85.

good." "I stand for immobility." Accordingly, things remain as usual—although whistling and rumbling sounds are heard—until the first death occurs (that of an actor, as in *The Plague,* and as in *The Seventh Seal*). Old remedies are tried: the priest organizes public confessions and the chorus proclaims, contrary to his previous words, that nothing is true but death and "nothing endures but misery."

When the Plague enters and takes over, it soon appears that the new order is just a stiffening of the old, with the help of all modern methods. The powerful ones agree to collaborate with the Plague, in order to safeguard their lives "in the people's own interests." The priest preaches submission to the new order and the judge enforces the new law because law enforcing is his life passion. The new order involves imprisonment, compulsory denunciation, silence, separation, and death. Contaminated houses are marked with a star and obscure decrees are issued: "The less people understand, the better they behave." The *fléau,* in keeping with its modern character "hates difference and unreason." "I do not rule," says the Plague; "I function." Accordingly, love and beauty are forbidden, as are greatness and emotion, since the Plague's intention is to humiliate as it crushes and produce submissiveness through guilt. This aim is achieved by the persistent use of arbitrariness.

Just as in the novel, there is a genius of the plague. Characteristically, he is called Nada (Nothing). An invalid and a drunkard, he wishes nothing, fears nothing—not God or Law or Comet. His contempt for men equals that of Caligula and, like him, he would enjoy having the whole of mankind before him like one panting bull, plunging his sword into the beast's neck, and watching it "fall through the abyss of space and time until the crack of doom."[18]

The moment of truth is the moment of the kill.

In Part Two, something changes. (This change was already indicated in Part One, when Diego, the young doctor, avoided

---

18. Albert Camus, *Caligula and Three Other Plays* (New York: A. Knopf, 1968), pp. 142–70.

the sight of his beloved because he felt ashamed of himself.)
The element of separation, so prevalent in the novel, assumes a
new meaning here: inner necessity, not external fate, causes it.
A sharp difference appears between the men and the women.
The men, like Diego, want to fight for honor's sake. The women
want to preserve life and love. Both groups have a tragic status,
as eternal principles conflicting and yet united in their fight
against the plague.

Resistance gathers momentum through the second part. It
starts with the common-sense obstinacy of an illiterate fisherman
who defends his private life against official questioning and
declares that he respects established order only if it is reasonable.
The second challenge comes from the chorus of women who
assert that justice means bread for all. The real duel between
man and the *fléau* then occupies the center of the scene. It is
profoundly different from what it is in the novel. Since the *fléau*
is no longer pictured as an evil we all carry within ourselves but
as a force external to us, innocence appears as natural, primary,
but at the same time more threatened, because there is a choice.
For Rieux and Tarrou, even for Rambert, there was *no* choice.
They were *in* the plague. Diego has a choice, or so he believes.
His first movement is to run away, but whoever takes to flight
belongs to the Plague as an accomplice, and Diego is warned by
the Plague for the first time. When honor deserts the town, contradictory concepts of it clash in a wild family scene in the judge's
house: the judge's honor is to apply the law and demand his
rights; his wife's honor is to defend her illegitimate child; his
daughter's honor is to keep the family's honor; all the forms of
infection break loose as Diego's panic drives him on. The last
word remains with the adulteress, who proclaims that "honor is
on the side of the sufferers, the afflicted, those who live by hope
alone." In the relaxation that follows this wild outburst, Diego
finds his beloved and expresses the wish to sink with her into
endless sleep. He is immediately branded by the Plague for the
second time, and shrinks away from his love in self-disgust.

Now Diego is alone—"each of us is alone because of the cowardice of others." But gradually he gathers enough courage to challenge the Plague. The Plague's law is all or nothing. Whoever challenges the Plague conquers it: "for there is in man an innate power . . . that you will never vanquish, a gay madness born of mingled fear and courage, unreasoning yet victorious through all time. One day this power will surge up and you will learn that all your glory is but dust before the wind."[19] Then the marks of the plague disappear from Diego's body and the wind rises.

One more trial awaits the plague fighters. In Part Three, some men in the crowd get hold of the Plague's list of victims, and begin to act like the Plague: they kill their own enemies, and then they kill for fun. "They are doing the work themselves, observes the Plague. . . . When they are frightened, their fear is for themselves, but their hatred is for others." And he heaps sarcasm on Diego, showing him for what worthless people he has risked his life. "The madman dies . . . the rest are saved. And they don't deserve to be saved." Diego finally wins all the trials and conquers the Plague. He has lost his fear ("neither fear nor hate, herein lies our victory"). He refuses to be saved alone, out of solidarity with others. He rejects the temptation of contempt: "I reserve my scorn for the oppressors." He is willing to forgive the victims their cowardice and mediocrity: "why scoff at their bowed heads when for so many generations the comets of fear have been roaming the skies above them? . . . The worst of their crimes has always an excuse. But I find no excuse for the harm that has been done them since the dawn of time."

Until now, in spite of considerable differences, the message of *State of Siege* coincides with that of *The Plague*. Diego has reached the human level by conquering his fear, and refuses to rule by despising others. ("Bien faire l'homme," said Rieux, after Montaigne.) In the last scenes of the play, Diego surprisingly piles up heroism and sainthood, sacrificing his life to save Vic-

19. *Ibid.*, pp. 177–206.

toria's, in a symbolic, somewhat obscure end in which pessimism seems to prevail. The separation between the two groups of men and women is not healed, but both ways are condemned: the women, who have chosen to preserve lives and show themselves fearless in love, have helped the plague by not fighting it, while the men have also helped it by relishing the fight. ("Men go whoring after ideas.") Both sexes have sinned. Both have transgressed, for "there is no justice, but there are limits," as the chorus proclaims. And since those limits are always overstepped, at the end of the play, even before Nada, the genius of the plague, has drowned himself, the old masters are seen coming back "blind as ever to the wounds of others, sodden with inertia and forgetfulness of the lessons of the past. And when you see stupidity getting the upper hand again without a struggle, you will lose heart." This provides a very fitting image of the way French affairs appeared to Camus in 1948. However, the last word remains with the small angry man who calls upon the sea to flood the evil cities of men: "O mighty mother whose bosom is the homeland of all rebels, behold thy people who will never yield! Soon, a great tidal wave, nourished in the dark of underseas will sweep away our loathsome cities."[20]

"Why Spain?" asked Gabriel Marcel in a review of the play.[21] Why? Because it was at the sight of Spain's fate that the twenty-five-year-old Camus had understood the meaning of totalitarian government. And no doubt a gust of wind from the Asturies gives *State of Siege* its heroic overtones. Nevertheless, Camus makes it quite clear both in his answer to Marcel and, after *The Plague,* in his *Letter to Roland Barthes,* that what he meant to attack was all forms of tyranny, whether of the right or of the left. And indeed, it had become increasingly clear in his journalistic writings that his last illusions regarding Communist-inspired regimes had

---

20. *Ibid.,* pp. 216–32.
21. See *Actuelles II, Pourquoi l'Espagne?*

vanished, and he was about to enter a new cycle in his thought, culminating with *The Rebel*. It seems, however, that this conviction penetrated his intellect but not his heart. Instinctively, he felt that political tyranny meant Fascism, although rationally he knew it could mean other regimes as well. Only in *The Rebel* did he get rid of all lingering illusions.

6
Revolt And Values

The Rebel presents Albert Camus's defense of ethical values together with an analysis of their perversion. The book, which Camus worked on for almost four years, is actually a collection of previously published essays, upon which a structure was superimposed later. This explains the unwieldy and rather confused sequence of ideas in this work. The arrangement of the book does not give a clear account of the genesis of Camus's thought. Indeed, some disappointment is felt when, after the first impact of Camus's often impassioned eloquence, one probes the intellectual solidity of the various components.

Moreover, in trying to trace the development of Camus's ideas, it might be well to remember that he is not a systematic philosopher. There is ample proof in *The Myth of Sisyphus* and in *The Rebel,* as well as in his *Notebooks,* of his relative indifference to fundamental methodological problems of ethics. About *The Rebel,* Camus has stressed that it should be regarded as a personal confession of a writer trying to clarify his own ideas. Although

The Rebel is, among other things, an inquiry into the logical and phenomenological foundations of ethics, and although Camus proceeds from metaphysics to ethics in his exposition of this problem, nevertheless his arguments are not deduced from a metaphysical view of the universe but spring from an emotional shock at the sight of human affairs.

Accordingly, in the following analysis of *The Rebel,* we shall not necessarily follow Camus's sequence of ideas but first analyze the chapters containing his main thesis and then proceed to the monographs illustrating what Camus regards as their perversion.[1]

1. Logical Crime

"Murder is the problem today," writes Camus in the opening chapter of *The Rebel.* For anyone who has witnessed the rise of Hitler, the Second World War, and the transformation of humanitarian socialism into a totalitarian empire, this statement does not require further elaboration. However, Camus's problem is not murder as such, but a kind of murder peculiar to our time, that which he calls *crime de logique*—a premediated crime which its perpetrators regard as necessary and legitimate. To clarify this point Camus gives the following example:

> Heathcliff, in *Wuthering Heights,* would kill everyone on earth in order to possess Cathy, but it would never occur to him to say that murder is reasonable or theoretically defensible. He would commit it, and there his convictions end. This implies the power of love, and also strength of character. Since intense love is rare, murder remains an exception and preserves its aspect of infraction. But as soon as a man, through lack of character, takes refuge in doctrine, as soon as crime reasons about itself, it multiplies like reason itself and assumes all the aspects of the syllogism. Once crime was as solitary as a cry

---

1. The present chapter deals with the parts of *The Rebel* entitled *Introduction, The Rebel, Rebellion and Murder,* and *Beyond Nihilism.*

of protest; now it is as universal as science. Yesterday it was put on trial; today it determines the law.[2]

This, however, is an elliptical argument. Not all legitimized murder is a "crime of logic" in Camus's sense. Heathcliff's crime is an outburst of individual passion, an admitted infringement on an established system of values. But not all criminals would plainly admit to have broken the moral code. Attempts at the moral justification of crime are almost as old as crime itself. The vendetta or crime of honor has long been regarded as high virtue. Raskolnikov upset this pharisaic pattern. He did not justify his crime by reference to any set of higher values; on the contrary he denied the existence of such values. He merely asserted a claim to individual imperialism, in the absence of any higher law. Nevertheless, he still felt the necessity to justify himself. And since he did not want to resort to ethical values, which he had discarded, he had to find something else: he invoked logic—the logic of nihilism. So did Camus's own Martha in *Cross Purposes*. Are we to understand that Camus has quietly dropped Martha's claim to unlimited freedom?

If we now move from the individual to the social plane, we find the same evolution. For centuries the moral justification of crime had been part of the cultural pattern. Christian nations that honored the Mosaic law and the Gospel nevertheless felt justified in killing and stealing, ·in the name first of God, then of national expansion; similarly the Jacobins found ethical reasons to guillotine their political enemies. Imperialists and Jacobins were Macchiavellian in their conduct, not in their principles.

Socialist moralists had been at great pains to explode this pharisaic structure. From the eighteenth-century philosophers

---

2. Albert Camus, *The Rebel: An Essay on Man in Revolt,* with a foreword by Sir Herbert Read. Revised and complete translation of *L'Homme Revolté* by Anthony Bowen. (New York: Vintage Books, 1956), p.3. Because of substantial improvements in the translation of the original text, the revised American paperback edition is used in this essay instead of the first translation by Bowen, (New York: Alfred A. Knopf, 1954).

and humanitarian romantics to the pacifists of 1920, all denounced barbarian conduct perpetrated under the cloak of patriotism.

With Hitler, a new kind of self-righteousness appeared in social conduct akin to that of Raskolnikov in private affairs. Like him, the theoreticians of the totalitarian state discarded all former ethical values and proclaimed their right to unlimited expansion. Like him, nevertheless, they are obsessed with the need to justify themselves on grounds other than ethical.

What the pacifists had done against the moral pharisees of Jacobinism and nationalism, Camus is trying to do against the "logical" pharisees of our time:

> The purpose of this essay is once again to face the reality of the present, which is logical crime, and to examine meticulously the arguments by which it is justified; it is an attempt to understand the times in which we live. One might think that a period which, in a space of fifty years, uproots, enslaves, or kills seventy million human beings should be condemned out of hand. But its culpability must still be understood.

In this new universe of crime, Camus is struck by "a curious transposition peculiar to our times," namely, that if crime is regarded as legitimate, "it is innocence that is called to justify itself."[3]

By these introductory pages Camus plunges into one of the thorniest thickets of modern nihilistic theology, a thicket in which he is partly caught, so that *The Rebel* seems in parts as if Dr. Rieux had undertaken to refute the diehard ghost of Caligula, with Tarrou supplying the philosophical argument. When Camus proclaims his intention to defend "innocence," the very use of this term shows that he is instinctively arguing from the traditional standpoint of *la morale laïque*. His indignation at the crimes of our times springs from an unsophisticated belief in the value of human life, dignity, and happiness—*la morale des honnêtes*

---

3. *The Rebel,* pp. 3, 4.

gens, so deeply ingrained in our civilization that there seemed to be no need to justify it, even after the destruction of religious values.

When faced with "logical" justification of these crimes, he is as sincerely bewildered as Cherea when he first hears the nagging voice of Caligula, and calls it a "strange challenge." Camus's own compulsion to take it up is no less strange. Who bothered to discuss with Hitler? He had to be destroyed either with one blow, as Caligula was killed by Cherea, or by perseverance, as Rieux fought the plague. But neither Cherea nor Rieux was a metaphysician. They were simple men, men of duty, both of them atheists, no doubt, and convinced of the absurdity of the world, while regarding humanistic values as axiomatic. When challenged to defend their standpoint, both Cherea and Rieux implied that, in the silence of the universe, "happiness" was the supreme value, and that general happiness demanded the elimination of Caligula, or the plague. But why happiness? and whose happiness—or satisfaction? Pushed to the wall, they both assumed that their feeling was "natural" and that of Caligula "abnormal," mad. But what is the criterion of normalcy in matters of ethics? Is not this concept dangerously similar to that of the natural kindness of man? This is the problem. In the absence of any transcendental or divine sanction, what can be the attitude of those who still feel ethics to be both necessary and valid? Either God or Sade. *Le Diable et le Bon Dieu,* Sartre said, with his usual sense for striking formulations.

Outside these two alternatives nothing was in sight, except good nature, Rousseau's "conscience as divine instinct," and utilitarian philosophy, with its sense of personal and general well-being. All these notions were already wearing thin at the end of the eighteenth century, when they were intellectually challenged by Sade. After Hitler challenged them in fact, and proved their total inefficiency, something more convincing had to be found.

Thus, at the time of totalitarian revolution and logical crime, Camus found himself—*mutatis mutandis*—in the same situation as Kant between the Marquis de Sade[4] and the Terror. A fundamental inquiry into the nature of ethics was imperative. It had to be conducted by the method of *tabula rasa*. This is what Camus undertook in *The Rebel*.

However, there was more on Camus's mind than the philosophical problem of ethical foundation. *The Rebel* has its roots in the political situation. Therefore, before analyzing Camus's argument, it might be useful to ask ourselves exactly against whom he was arguing. Who was committing logical crimes in 1951, murdering with good conscience? The war had been over for six years, but the traumatic shock was still felt: it had been shown that the barbarian in man was not dead. And although Fascism had lost international importance, Spain's fate was still weighing heavily on Camus's heart. This, however, was not the main cause that prompted Camus to write his plea against crimes of logic. The obvious offender was Stalin's Russia. Camus's indictment of the Soviet totalitarian system is spelled out in Part III of *The Rebel* (State Terrorism and rational Terror), and also underlies both the plea for peace and tolerance in chapter 1 and the concept of restraint in the concluding part. This being Camus's main preoccupation, why did. he resort to such abstract, roundabout methods? One explanation may be found in the kind of public to whom Camus addressed himself: essentially, European intellectuals whose emotional and mental confusion led them to back an ideology of which they could not really approve. *The Rebel* reads like a last appeal to moderation and common sense, in order to ward off the polarization that was taking place between the profit-seeking technocratic society and an alienated group of intellectuals dragged to Communism for lack of an alternative. While Camus was addressing himself to the general reading public, very much like Koestler or Orwell, he was particularly aiming

---

4. He had never read the works of the Marquis. However, such ideas were rampant, as in Hume's remark that *reason* in no way dissuades us from destroying the whole world in order to stop an itch in our little finger.

his arguments at the *Temps Modernes* team,[5] whose philosophical knowledge and skill he could not hope to emulate. Much that is confused in *The Rebel* can be ascribed to an ill-advised wish to counter these philosophers on their own ground.

By announcing in the introductory chapter of *The Rebel* his determination to take up the "strange challenge" of having to defend innocence, Camus reveals at first the limited and negative purpose of his study, namely, the attempt to refute pseudo-philosophical justifications of murder. And, indeed, the main part of his book is devoted to the undermining of these philosophical fetishes by retracing their psychological origins and development on the metaphysical plane: from Rousseau and Saint-Just to the Nazis and Stalinists *via* Hegel, Stirner, Marx, Nietzsche, and Lenin. Here, the intention is to discredit the opponent by uncovering his real, partly neurotic motives, and stripping the superstructure under which they masquerade—an original and efficient method that Camus applies with great skill. At the same time, Camus's analysis involves refutation of the arguments used for the pseudo-philosophical justification of murder, and in so doing he is led to justify his own ethical standpoint. This is the second, positive aspect of his argument.

Camus maintains that the modern philosophical justification of murder, in contrast to the natural human propensity for self-righteous violence, has its origin in philosophical nihilism, which has gradually pervaded the human mind since the second half of the Eighteenth Century. When the waning of Christianity left man faced with an absurd universe bereft of meaning and values— a world similar to that of *Sisyphus*—a few radical thinkers and writers were led to believe that "if God is dead, everything is permitted." According to this line of argument, philosophical nihilism must lead to crime. It is this logical necessity of crime which Camus tries to refute in *The Rebel,* while acknowledging the death of God. For although nihilism may lead to an apology

---

5. Although most of *The Rebel*'s chapters had been published in *Temps Modernes.*

for murder, the theory that it necessarily leads there is, in Camus's opinion, a logical fallacy. In his refutation of this fallacy, Camus departs from the traditional humanitarian standpoint, in that he starts at precisely the same point as his opponents: the absurd universe of Sisyphus.

In the absence of any transcendent ground, ethics must be rooted in our limited and relative human experience. After the decline of Christianity, this problem has confronted all empiricists, because they try to ground ethics in universally valid human experience. In this respect, some of the modern philosophers of existence could be called empiricists of a kind, although they are far from sharing the classical empiricists' glib optimism about the possibility of harmonizing general and private interests thanks to the rationality and goodness of human nature. In fact, most philosophers of existence have discarded the concept of human nature altogether and rejected psychology in the classical sense. What they do instead is select certain experiences they consider basic, insofar as they reveal a fundamental mode of man's existence. The selected experience varies from one philosopher to another: Kierkegaard's conflict between the temporal and the eternal, Nietzsche's will to power, Unamuno's tragic sense of life, Jasper's Kantian reaction to man's sense of shipwreck, and Scheler's belief in sympathy. To Camus, the crucial experience is revolt. It is from his analysis of revolt as an existential mode that Camus intends to derive arguments against the spurious logic of logical crime. His introductory chapter indicates his determination to expel the still unquiet ghost of Caligula from his mind as he had expelled him from his heart.

2. Revolt and Values

Revolt, as analyzed in *The Rebel,* differs profoundly from the argument presented in *The Myth of Sisyphus* ten years earlier. Although Camus had chosen to put his first philosophical essay under the sign of Sisyphus, as a fitting symbol of the human condition during the desperate years of the war, he nevertheless maintained, as in *Noces,* that love of life could balance such despair, and insisted, somewhat unconvincingly, that we should imagine Sisyphus happy. But, as we have seen, *The Myth* was a pre-Resistance essay; it can be assumed that the common experience of fighting tyranny made the rock lighter. Unlike *The Myth, The Rebel* does not start with the lonely experience of metaphysical absurdity. Rather, it takes it for granted, and instead of discussing at length the problem of suicide, it advocates the right to live and centers on the condemnation of murder.

The difference between *The Myth of Sisyphus* and *The Rebel* was clearly outlined by Camus himself. The first book, he said, belonged to "the time of negation," the other to "the time of ideologies,"[6] the first one naturally dealing with suicide and the second with murder. Perhaps the chronology implied in this passage should not be taken too strictly. The fact that both nihilism and ideology worked hand in hand in 1942 as well as in 1951 is stressed in the whole of *The Rebel*. So is the idea that both nihilism and ideology lead to suicide and murder, or rather to a suicidal-murderous apocalypse of the Hitlerian kind. It is possible, however, that Camus regarded as "negative" the decade dominated by Hitler, during which *Sisyphus* was written, while he called the following decade the "age of ideologies." It was at this juncture that French intellectuals accepted Communism in large numbers. However, the passage could also mean that he was personally more receptive to nihilism at the time of Sisyphus —and Caligula—than in the fifties, when he had recovered from such nihilism and was ready to offer a positive message. He was particularly shocked by the spread of totalitarian ideologies among his fellow-intellectuals. However that may be, Camus was aware that a momentous development had taken place, both in himself and in others, when they discovered during the Resistance years that their rebellion implied something called values.

Herein lies the great novelty of Camus's book. After almost two thousand years of Christianity, obedience, resignation, and self-effacement were regarded as cardinal virtues. The century-old

---

6. *The Rebel*, pp. 4ff.

feudal tradition in France, the prestige of which still kindled
reactionary imaginations in the thirties, had left a strong imprint
on authoritarian minds. Nor was this attitude confined to the
political Right, for no sooner had the great Revolution disposed
of theocrats and tyrants than it built a new system of allegiance
and borrowed from the world of antiquity its superstitious respect
for the City and the "General Will." Individualism was a late
child of Western civilization, and it grew up with a bad conscience.
And although the nineteenth century was a time of revolutions—
culminating in 1917, they were supposed to derive their value
from loyalty to "the people." Individualism, the great discovery
of the eighteenth century, was forgotten, in spite of romantic
efforts, and only in the first half of the twentieth century did it
gain a new audience, against the demands of both right and
left-wing parties.[7] Camus's originality was not only to show that
all progress started with revolt—in the name of individual dignity
—but that revolt itself was creative of values. He tried to establish
a modern basis for ethics, individualistic and critical. Not obedience and devotion but revolt was, in his view, the source of
genuine virtue, including devotion (but without obedience, conformity, and self-abasement).

In his analysis of "genuine revolt," that is, "revolt based on
values," Camus takes great care to distinguish it from mere anger
and the more permanent phenomenon of resentment.[8] This dis-
crimination, however, appears only *after* the analysis of the values
implied in revolt, and is meant to show, after Scheler and Nietzsche,
how Western values became vitiated by envy and resentment.
However, Camus's point can be grasped only by reversing the
order of his argument, since Camus does mean—and say—that
when the slave rebels and says "no," this "no" does not merely
express the protest of his crushed and resentful ego, but implies
the conviction that a right, vested in something individual but

---

7. See Micheline Tison-Braun, *La Crise de l'Humanisme* (*Le
conflit de l'Individu et de la Société* [*1890–1939*]), vol. 2 (Paris:
Nizet, 1967).
8. He even reproaches Scheler for confusing revolt and resentment.

higher than this ego, should not be violated. This personalist, in contrast to the egotistic, aspect of revolt is basic to Camus:[9]

> Rebellion cannot exist without the feeling that, somewhere and somehow, one is right. . . . He [the rebel] demonstrates, with obstinacy, that there is something in him which "is worthwhile. . . ." Every act of rebellion tacitly invokes a value.[10]

This fundamental value is human dignity. The slave who rebels has somewhere in his mind, however confusedly, the conviction that man ought to be valued for himself, that he should not be regarded as a tool or a plaything by another man, by society, or even by fate or the gods.

Still other values can be discovered in the act of rebellion. The rebellious slave feels that the dignity he is defending "does not belong to him alone" but is "the common ground where all men . . . have a natural community."[11] Thus, in the act of revolt the rebel transcends his own ego, and together with the defense of his own dignity, he discovers human solidarity.

A third value is implicit in revolt as understood by Camus, although it is not clearly spelled out in the theoretical chapters but underlies the case analysis that follows. It is to be understood that when the slave rebels he does so not as slave but as man, so that the solidarity of rebels should be extended to include even the former oppressors, if and when they become cured of their tyrannical impulse. A resentful Spartacus who wants to crucify his master in order to rule in his place merely perpetuates the karma of persecution and vendetta. Only a humanitarian Spartacus—a genuine rebel in Camus's sense—will extend solidarity to his master, not as master but as man.

Thus, when all the values implicit in revolt have been brought to light, the whole construction of Camus's ethics unfolds into

---

9. Personalism in the 40s was mainly Catholic (E. Mounier was an outstanding case); but nonreligious personalist ethics had existed before (as illustrated, for instance, by Renouvier).

10. *The Rebel*, pp. 13–14.

11. *Ibid.*, p. 16.

a romantic and humanitarian pattern: the sense of universal brotherhood, coupled with the demand for happiness through a passionate and tragic existence, supplies the positive content of humanitarian ethics toward which Camus had been groping since his early works. It is tragic humanism and heroic humanism too, in a world where nothing is given or explained, where every bit of happiness has to be wrenched from a harsh fate and every value created in darkness and suffering as a source of order in an absurd world. In this perspective, life becomes indeed meaningful. Imperceptibly, the imagery has changed from Sisyphus and his rock to Spartacus, whose image gradually grows from that of a victorious gladiator who is unable to shake off his earlier submissiveness, to that of an eternal champion of mankind against gods and fate—Prometheus. While it was not easy to imagine Sisyphus happy, as Camus invites us to do at the end of *The Myth,* there is no difficulty in imagining Prometheus proudly dying on the Caucasus for the noble man-made values that he, alone in the mute universe, discovered and practiced, while the Oceanids sing to him of the doomed beauty of the world.

Yet, the logical snag remains: whence values? and why should man, alone in the whole universe, have acquired the strange ability to conceive them?

3. Values without Transcendence

Camus's analysis of the values implicit in revolt leaves one important question unanswered: that of the nature and the origin of the values involved in the act of revolt, whether the question is psychological—how are these values discovered?—or metaphysical—what are they, where do they come from?

A superficial reading might lead to the belief that Camus is merely deducing the highest values of dignity, solidarity, and universality from the simpler and more common experience of revolt, according to the well-known reductive pattern of materialist philosophers. But what he does, in fact, is just the opposite. Values are gradually unveiled in the process of revolt. There are Hegelian undertones in Camus's analysis of the rebel's unfolding consciousness. As in the *Phenomenology of Mind,* Camus's rebel seems gradually to discover what had always been there, unperceived, so that the discovery appears either as an unveiling or as a deduction, according to whether it is observed in process or as completed. However, the Hegelian analogy is purely superficial and there is nothing in Camus of the impeccably reversible dialectic apparent in the unfolding of Hegel's Notion. In the initial chapter of *The Rebel,* the fundamental values implied in revolt are related to each other and to revolt in different fashions. Thus, the initial value of human dignity—the idea that men should be treated not as means but as ends in themselves—is in no way deduced from the experience of revolt but discovered in the course of this experience, as existing before it and the hidden motive in the name of which it was conducted. Not so the solidarity of rebels, which looks like a natural and even pragmatic consequence of revolt. As for the third value implied in revolt, the solidarity of all men, including repentant enemies, it also appears as a motivation of revolt, like the sense of human dignity; however, solidarity shows still another kind of relation to the central experience of revolt, since it is neither the cause nor the consequence of it. Rather, it is the result of a complex intellectual operation, merging the rebels' solidarity with the intuition of the dignity common to all men. One feeling is, to a large extent, natural, while the other requires something of a spiritual mutation; one does not progress in one straight line from the solidarity of rebels to the solidarity of men.

Camus insists that his development from the "negative" *Sisyphus* to the "positive" *Rebel* was of the nature of an unfolding, not a conversion. His insistence on this point, as unnecessary as it is unconvincing, is not motivated by a vain desire to appear consistent at all cost, but by a determination to reassert the validity of his initial experience of the absurd and lack of transcendence. As a result, the question of Camus's consistency appears in a different light when examined from the logical or the lyrical point of view.

Camus was led by his experience in the Resistance to endow all values connected with revolt with the same metaphysical status, for the simple reason that all were dormant in him and discovered at the same time in action. Indeed, the experience of solidarity against fate was already implicit in Camus's early works, such as *The Right and the Wrong Side of Things,* but pushed into the background by the total revolt of flesh and spirit against death. It survived the nihilistic temptations expressed in *Caligula, The Stranger, Cross-Purposes* and *Sisyphus,* and steadily asserted itself from *Letters to a German Friend* through the postwar articles to *The Plague.* It had always been there, waiting for intellectual recognition. Thus Camus was right in asserting that there was no conversion in his case, no turning away from an absurd universe to meaningful solidarity. Both attitudes had always been present at the same time, but on two different levels. Objectively, the world was still absurd, but Camus knew that something in it has meaning and that was man, because man alone demanded that there be meaning.[12] Camus was right subjectively, that is, lyrically, for he always rebelled in the name of meaning, although admittedly not knowing what that meaning was. From *Nuptials* and *The Stranger* to *The Plague* and *The Rebel,* Camus's notion of meaning evolved as he added to his search for personal happiness a sense of mission to mankind. In all these cases, a somewhat illicit intellectual operation was performed to express a valid emotional experience.

We have seen that Camus's theory of values has a metaphysical as well as a psychological aspect, the question being not only how values are discovered but what their nature and origin are. The difficulty starts when Camus proceeds from a subjective perception of these values to the assertion of their objective validity. He says, quoting Lalande's *Vocabulaire philosophique,* that

---

12. *Letters to a German Friend*, p. 74.

Values, according to good authorities, "most often represent a transition from fact to rights, from what is desired to what is desirable (usually through the intermediary of what is generally considered desirable)." The transition from facts to rights is manifest, as we have seen, in rebellion.[13]

This is a purely empiricist definition. But then, if metaphysical foundations of ethics have been discarded, with what right does Camus assert that certain human aspirations can be regarded as ethical to the exclusion of others—especially when he does not recognize as valid such trite pragmatic criteria as the greatest possible happiness for the greatest possible number? In Camus's own framework, why should dignity, solidarity, and measure be more ethical than, say, greed or the will to power, or André Gide's "ferveur," or any other general innate disposition? Faced with this question, Gide frankly admitted that his values were not ethical but aesthetic. In some cases Camus does the same. He exhibits an aesthetic partiality for the tragic, heroic, rebellious attitude.

The question of the origin of these values is no clearer than that of their nature, since Camus rules out all transcendence. As to the origin of the rebel's sense of dignity, nothing is said clearly, although a lyrical passage of great beauty suggests the dawn of spiritual awakening.

Awareness, no matter how confused it may be, develops from every act of rebellion: the sudden, dazzling perception that there is something in man with which he can identify himself, even if only for a moment. Up to now this identification was never really experienced. Before he rebelled, the slave accepted all the demands made upon him. Very often he even took orders, without reacting against them, which were far more conducive to insurrection than the one at which he balks. . . . But with loss of patience . . . a reaction begins which can extend to everything that he previously accepted. . . . The very moment the slave refuses to obey the humiliating orders of his master, he simultaneously rejects the condition of slavery. . . . He exceeds the bounds that he fixed for his

13. *The Rebel*, p. 15.

antagonist, and now demands to be treated as an equal. . . .
The part of himself that he wanted to be respected he proceeds
to place above everything else and proclaims it preferable to
everything, even to life itself. It becomes to him the supreme
good. Having up to now been willing to compromise, the slave
suddenly adopts . . . an attitude of All or Nothing. With
rebellion, awareness is born.[14]

Although the content of this insight coincides with one of
Kant's criteria of the ethical act, namely, that man should be
regarded as end and not as means, the lyrical, almost mystical
tone of the passage sounds like an echo of a long-lost, perhaps
undiscovered faith, the desiccated rationalization of which is found
in Kant's criterion. However, Camus firmly rejects any intimation
of transcendence.

The same applies to the value of solidarity. The slave is not
defending his dignity as an individual but as man: "in his person
and in that of others," as Kant would say, here again echoing a
Christian concept, that of legitimate self-love.[15] However, here
again Camus rejects any kind of transcendence, either rational
or mystical. He is determined to root his own ethics exclusively
in experience. Unity for Camus is but a human aspiration. As
mentioned before, Camus's experience of rebellion and solidarity,
like Malraux's experience in *Man's Fate,* was born of action and
of observation of the fight against tyranny all over the world. In
order to show that it is in the movement of revolt that the individual sacrifices himself for others, Camus uses the example of
prisoners in the Chinese revolution of the thirties and those in
the Siberian salt mines, who committed suicide in protest against
the beating of fellow prisoners:

It is in revolt that man goes beyond himself and discovers

14. *The Rebel*, pp. 14–15.
15. These analogies between the ethics of Kant and Camus have
been studied by the German scholar Otto Bolnow. Cf. "Existen-
zionalismus und Ethik," *Die Sammlung* 4 (Jahrgang, 1949): pp. 321–
35.

other people, and from this point of view, human solidarity is a metaphysical certainty.[16]

Revolt thus understood provides a means of transcending utter loneliness and frustration in an absurd universe:

There is something beyond anguish, which is outside the solution of religions; it is revolt.[17]

With the third and last value implied in revolt, that of the solidarity of all men, including strangers or enemies, we enter one of the most intricate parts in Camus's thought, the one most open to reproaches of contradiction and confusion. The notion of self-restraint in the exercise of revenge is, of course, the cornerstone of every humanitarian, indeed, civilized ethics. How is it to be achieved? How can the victor be persuaded to refrain from logical crime?

In Kant's cool, rational universe, the whole problem is encompassed in a syllogism: The concept of man as an end in himself applies to friends and foes alike. But Camus's ethics rests on something more concrete than syllogisms. Moreover, passing from the solidarity of rebels to that of all men, including enemies, seems to require a rational mutation. Camus insists, however, that it is an existential experience. The personalist belief in a community of men, based on freedom and respect for others, is very much alive in Camus and probably represents the deepest message in his essay.

All the values Camus has unveiled in revolt are borrowed from the Christian-humanitarian tradition. Their emotional appeal both to Camus and idealistic socialists is undeniable. Whether they can be logically founded without recourse to any form of transcendence seems highly dubious. If we try to assess the logical value of Camus's argument, we should admit that it has little. The initial

---

16. Camus *et al.*, "Remarques sur la révolte," in *L'Existence*, ed. Jean Grenier (Paris: Gallimard, 1945), p. 11.

17. *Ibid.*, p. 22.

facts are correct: All men protest. A few of them rebel. A handful of those rebel in the name of human values and still fewer
maintain them after victory. This is why revolutions usually end
in dictatorship and terror, as Camus was painfully aware. So
much for the question of facts. As far as logic is concerned, once
it has been asserted—as Camus unequivocally does assert—that
the universe is absurd and that nothing in it betrays the presence
of a transcendent or even an immanent God, then all logic collapses like a sand castle and Sartre is right: Whether you become
master of the world or whether you get drunk all by yourself
in a bar is absolutely indifferent. In quiet, happy times, most
people will behave decently. In times of trouble and decay, the
barbarians will rule; there will be kings with the souls of slaves;
philosophers and prophets will preach the gospel of nothingness,
and perhaps a handful of desperate humanists, exiles from the
Absolute, will go on serving mankind out of sheer generosity, or
nostalgia—or habit. If Camus's romantic, pantheistic, and humanitarian vision is to be maintained, a substitute has to be found
for transcendent values of the Christian type.

4. On Human Nature

In view of Camus's efforts to preserve all the values of traditional Christian humanism without the transcendence vouchsafed
them, not a few commentators[18] have regarded Camus as a
transcendentalist unaware of having this tendency, and even as a
potential Christian who refused to hear the voice of grace. Such
extrapolations seem to be encouraged by Camus himself, who, at
times, recognizes man's tendency to transcend himself: "Man is
the only creature who refuses to be what he is,"[19] and there is
indeed something peculiar—strangely obstinate perhaps—in keeping this exclusively human ability of transcendence hanging in the
air. This refusal of any God or extramundane power or entity to

18. See Jean Onimus, *Camus (Les écrivains devant Dieu)*, and E.
Mounier, *L'Espoir des Désésperés*.
19. *The Rebel*, p. 11.

explain man's ability to transcend himself is not the only peculiar feature in Camus's philosophy. There is also his insistence on the total absurdity of the world, his unwillingness or inability to detect any root of transcendence in the pre-human world—in short, his unawareness of evolutionist philosophies which, while leaving man still bereft of God, nevertheless link his adventure with trends perceptible in the cosmos. Camus the poet, the lover of nature, regarded nature as totally alien to the humanist part of man, actually demanding its elimination, though it is poignantly akin to "something tender *and inhuman*" in him. Thus, the paradox of Camus's deeply felt humanism is not only his lack of faith in a transcendent God, but his failure to discover any mediation in the natural universe.

If man's ability to transcend himself is vested neither in God nor in the universe, it must be grounded in something peculiar to man, and we are thrown back to the old problem of human nature, which Malraux once formulated with great lucidity in the following way:

> Existe-t-il une donnée sur quoi puisse se fonder la notion d'homme? . . . La vérité, c'est l'animal. . . . La notion d'homme, a-t-elle un sens? Autrement dit: Sous les croyances, les mythes, et surtout sous la multiplicité des structures mentales, peut-on isoler une donnée permanente, valable à travers les lieux, valable à travers l'histoire, sur quoi puisse se fonder la notion d'homme?[20]

To this question, Camus answers unequivocally "yes", not once but several times in *The Rebel*. To quote but a few examples, he writes:

> Rebellion, in man, is the refusal to be treated as an object and to be reduced to simple historical terms. It is the affirmation of a nature common to all men, which eludes the world of power.[21]

---

20. *André Malraux, Les Noyers de l'Altenburg* (Paris: Gallimard, 1948), pp. 130, 146, 150.
21. *The Rebel*, p. 250.

Rebellion at grips with history adds that instead of killing and dying in order to produce the being that we are not, we have to live and let live in order to create what we are.[22]

And, conversely:

The triumphant revolution must prove by means of its police, its trials, and its excommunications that there is no such thing as a human nature.[23]

No doubt it is this conviction which prompted Camus to declare: "I am not an existentialist."[24]

In the preceding sentences, human nature is contrasted with "history." It is clear, however, from the context, that "history" means the dogmatic ideologies that deny man's freedom in order to turn him into a tool for the community, or its leaders. Ruling out such manipulations, the question arises: what is this human nature, where does it tend? Here, Camus offers a variety of answers more often implicit than explicit, until we reach the last part of *The Rebel.* One thing, however, is obvious: that human nature is ambivalent to the world, that it says both "yes" and "no." It craves happiness, beauty, and friendship, and refuses their opposites. Both unity and revolt are in the nature of man. Such ambivalence is nothing unusual in Camus's works. During the period between *Letters to a German Friend* and *The Plague,* Camus's conception of human nature is not only confused but borders on sentimentality. The author of *The Rebel* sometimes seems to follow the shallow conception of human nature propagated by the anarchists, believing in the intrinsic goodness of man and in salvation by the idea of human brotherhood. Such a doctrine is especially attractive in times of crises and catastrophes. In all this we may detect Camus's quietism mentioned earlier and his desperate nostalgia for peace, love, and unity in an "Age of

---

22. *Ibid.,* p. 252.
23. *Ibid.,* p. 250.
24. Televised interview (see: *Les Nouvelles Littéraires,* Nov. 15, 1945, p. 1).

Fear." In *The Rebel,* Camus seems to have rejected this facile optimism, while maintaining a Christian notion of man as an evil but redeemable creature; the idea of human brotherhood is repeatedly mentioned and obviously constitutes the center of Camus's message.

However, as we have seen in the previous section, the Christian element in Camus's thought is not the most convincing. He abandons it in the last part of the essay, *Thought at the Meridian,* and, apart from occasional references to it, Camus's conception of a human nature opposed to history and ideologies is borrowed from the Greeks.

According to classical Greek philosophy, human nature was characterized by reason, understood as *logos* or ability to create an intelligible world out of the chaos of appearances. This is also one of Camus's underlying ideas, but one on which he does not elaborate. In earlier works (especially the *Letters* and *The Plague*) man was characterized by his need for "meaning"; this demand is at the heart of *The Myth.* Obviously reason for Camus means something other than the intellect; not the ability to deduce and argue logically about cause, effect, and identity, but rather the ability to discover purpose and a principle of unity in the chain of events, and of imposing them on human affairs. In his appeal to Greek thought, Camus tends to leave out the intellectualistic tradition as represented by Aristotle and perhaps the late Plato and borrow from the pre-Socratic philosophers and poets. For these, reason was concerned with conduct rather than with epistemology. Reason meant measure, the respect for limits, and the practice of self-restraint. It was the opposite of *hubris.* It seems ironical that in a work advocating universal brotherhood and protesting against the master-slave relationship Camus should have borrowed one of his main ideas from a civilization that admitted slavery and professed the superiority of the Greeks over the barbarians. However, the argument that the Greeks used to rationalize their practice was noteworthy: slaves and barbarians were deemed incapable of the precious virtue of self-restraint, the pride of human nature. And whoever lost it and allowed himself

to be ruled by his passions—even if he was born free and a
Greek, even if he was a prince like Sophocles' Creon—unavoidably
fell to the subhuman level that was attributed to slaves and barbarians. Measure, then, was the supreme virtue, and it is not
without justification that Camus appealed to it when trying to
solve the problem of values without transcendence. Prometheus
in his fight against the gods is a hero after Camus's heart, and
the evolution from Sisyphus to Prometheus sums up the evolution
of Camus's ethics and politics, not only because Prometheus
"stands up to Gods and Tyrants"[25] but because even Prometheus
has to be reminded of his limits. Just like the very humane Rieux
and Tarrou, Aeschylus's hero has to know his limits. Zeus, Fate,
the gods, and The Plague are man's limits. To recognize necessity
while fighting it is the sign of a noble and mature mind. Joining
modesty with courage, such is the double duty allotted to man
in Camus's view.

Camus's argument is, of course, valid. But is it sufficient as a
basis for *all* the values propounded in *The Rebel*? This is doubtful. By no stretch of imagination can such values as brotherhood,
charity, and the total giving-up of power relations be deduced
from the virtue of self-restraint or discovered in the exercise of
this virtue. These are values of religious origin partly transmitted
through the Stoics to modern humanism but absolutely irreducible
to the values of ancient classical civilizations. How far the Greek
virtue of clemency was from the Christian notion of forgiveness
and charity can be illustrated by the simple example of Achilles
giving back Hector's body to his father.

Acutely conscious as they were of the dangers of savage pride,
the Greeks took a more realistic view of human nature than did
the Christians in their appeal to clemency. By the institution of
supplicants, they managed to fan both the tiny trembling flame
of compassion in the victor and the enormous blaze of his pride.
"You are so great and I so humble," repeated Priam, catering to
Achilles' pride, adding only once: "remember your old father."

---

25. As Man in *Letters to a German Friend*, p. 39.

Manuscript page of *Carnets I*
(pp. 27 and 28 in the Gallimard edition)

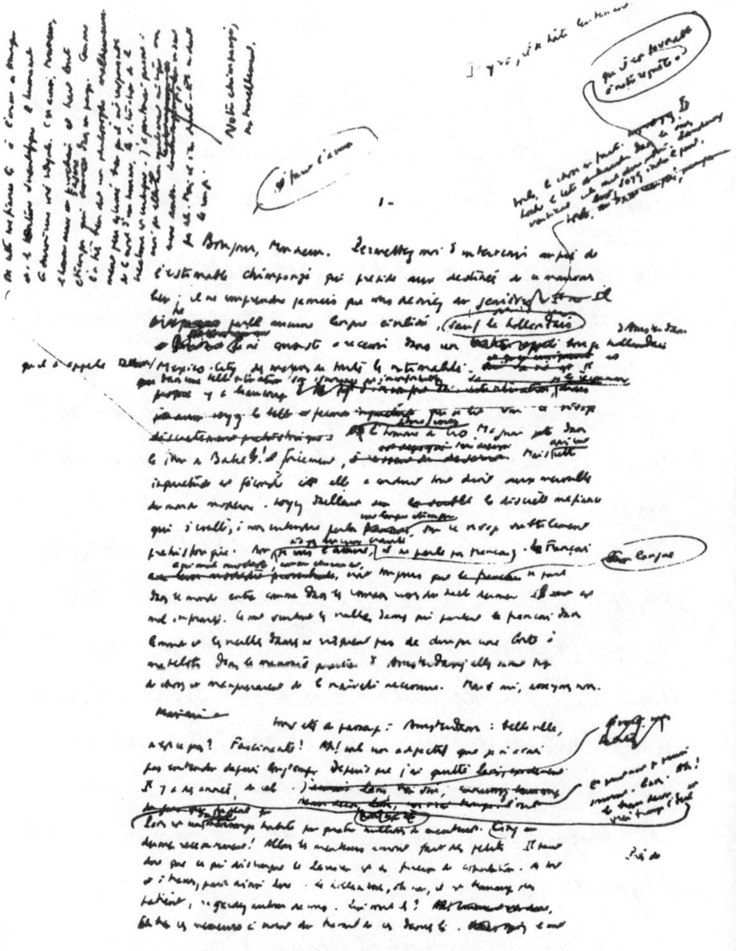

Manuscript page of *La Chute*
(first page of the first version)

It was from the towering height of his power that Achilles yielded to compassion and gave back Hector's body; such generosity was fitting for a victorious king. So fierce was his inner fight, however, and so glorious his victory over himself, that this act of generosity made him the complete hero in Homer's eyes, one who could accept a premature death in the certainty of his immortal glory. Camus probably concurred with this sober view of human nature. But, then, if generosity required such an effort from a prince, was a slave expected not to get drunk with power and victory?

In attempting to overcome this difficulty, Camus does not appeal to generosity but to logic. Revolt properly understood, he said, implies measure. By his revolt the slave reminds his master that certain limits must not be transgressed. The principle of reciprocity demands that he himself should not violate them, though he may have the power to do so. Only by the practice of restraint does the solidarity involved in the act of revolt become truly universal.

However, Camus feels the need to borrow yet another argument from the realistic Greeks who, while admiring Achilles' generosity, thought it safer to put supplicants and the defeated under the direct protection of the gods. Priam mentions this and Aeschylus does not fail to warn Prometheus—and Zeus—against *hubris*. So important was this notion in their eyes that even before belief in the gods had started to wane, philosophers took over from the poets, and Nemesis became an objective law of the cosmos; excess was self-destructive, and thus after excess, balance was restored by a natural process.

> The real madness of excess dies or creates its own moderation. . . . In its most extreme manifestations, it finds its limit.[26]

It is known that during his studies in Algiers with the philosopher Jean Grenier, who later became his friend and to whom *The Rebel* is dedicated, Camus was much impressed by Empedocles' conception of a regulating principle between excesses

---

26. *The Rebel*, p. 301.

of love and hate, strife and harmony. Elsewhere in *The Rebel*
Camus speaks of Heraclitus and the regulating function of the
goddess Nemesis:

> Heraclitus, the discoverer of the constant change of things,
> nevertheless set a limit to this perpetual process. This limit
> was symbolized by Nemesis, the goddess of moderation and
> the implacable enemy of the immoderate.[27]

However, there is nothing here indicative of a benevolent
Providence. The law of balance works in a purely automatic way,
and once more Camus is careful to avoid any flight into the
transcendent. Yet, is he not accepting a concept not quite consistent with his central notion of an absurd universe? If measure
becomes a cosmic principle of harmony (not only an idea necessary to the mind), what then becomes of the theory of the absurd,
so basic to Camus's philosophy? In trying to answer this new
question, we should once more remember that Camus's approach
is not intellectual but lyrical.

It is hard to imagine that the law of balance, in a form akin
to Aristotle's golden mean, could have much appeal to a man
of Camus's temperament. However, it can be linked lyrically
with the two basic dichotomies he experienced in his life: the
divorce mentioned in Sisyphus between man's aspirations and
the absurd world, and that of the frustration and enchantment of
the world as expressed in *Noces*. Thus, Camus sees men's fundamental experiences as composed of two antithetical forces, and
in the *Myth of Sisyphus* he repeats several times that no valid
solution of the human problem can be reached unless we always
keep in mind the dichotomy of the absurd universe and man's
aspiration.

Camus's second ambivalent experience, that of a world both
frustrating and gratifying, can also be found in the Greek tragic
poets. They certainly did not maintain that the world was actually
in harmony with man's wishes. What they did believe, as shown

27. *Ibid.*, p. 296.

in *Oedipus at Colona,* was that happiness and misfortune were
equally meted out to men, and that men, by a sort of creative
fatalism combining acceptance and hope, could help maintain
this mysterious harmony. Since there are indications in Camus's
works (especially *Noces*) that man's relation to the universe is
not solely one of frustration and rebellion, the Rebel, while maintaining the tragic tension between his aspirations and the mute
universe, can restore harmony by accepting the unavoidable part
of his existence, that is, fate, while applying to what is left to
his free choice the principles of dignity and measure (*ratio,
sophrosuné*).

Similarly, the rebellious slave, in reminding his master that
there is a limit that must not be transgressed, works for the
restoration of harmony, even at the price of his life, whereas a
resentful Spartacus would be at the antipode of measure. He
would yield to *hubris,* to overweening pride, which can breed only
more cruelty and more resentment. Finally, since man naturally
thinks according to the law of polarity, measure consists in keeping
both alternatives in sight, each one acting as a limit to the other
and thus working for harmony. In this respect, the policy of
suppressing the alternative in the name of totalitarian absolutes
is against the nature of man and things, and works for death.

In this way Camus welds together the main experiences in his
life and achieves a moral vision that is infinitely richer—and not
perceptibly more inconsistent—than that of the fellow-traveling
intellectuals reluctantly led to totalitarian revolution by existential
despair. Nevertheless, it cannot be considered as an altogether
satisfactory basis for ethics and politics in modern times.

5. Conclusion

Camus's proclaimed intention in writing *The Rebel* was to
express an ethics suitable for our time. It had to satisfy both the
mind and the heart and we know that Camus was attacked
both as philosophically unsound and emotionally obsolete. Philosophers reproached him for the uncertainty of his method, and it

should perhaps be admitted that Camus might have been a better philosopher had he never studied philosophy; in this respect, his desire to play up to the *Temps Modernes* team has confused both his methods and arguments. He tried his hand at dialectic, as we have observed, without much success. In fact, dialectic is practically absent from Camus's reasoning—either Hegelian dialectic spiraling up to a higher spiritual plane, or Marxist dialectical materialism, finding its solution in the historical process, or Kierkegaard's truncated dialectic; for, although Kierkegaard would have agreed with Camus that man oscillates between two incompatible poles, Kierkegaard saw a solution in a possible jump from the aesthetic to the ethical planes and from there to the realm of faith. This is precisely why Camus objects to him.[28] Camus wants to maintain at all costs the abyss between man's aspirations and blind fate.

Camus's approach to the problem of man's conflict with the order of things is in no way dialectical; it is clearly dualistic. Camus's novelty is that his is a horizontal dualism, ruling out any higher ontological status for human aspirations or achievements. Between the two poles of the conflict there is no movement, no oscillation as in Kierkegaard's sense, since Camus insists that both incompatible aspects of the human situation be kept in mind as a precondition of genuine revolt. After the duality of human experience has been discovered, Camus's dualism is perfectly static, the only movement in it being the effort to maintain the tension between the two poles of experience with the determination of a circus rider standing on two horses and holding them side by side. Once understood, the inner tension remains forever the same; only the application of the principle varies according to external contingencies.

Camus's method is not only imprecise; it lacks consistency. We are faced with two sets of values, not altogether compatible and resting on shaky foundations: Christian ethics of brotherhood, but without God, and Greek ethics of measure and harmony, but

28. *Myth of Sisyphus.*

with no Unmoved Mover and cosmic rationality. Humanity strives for unity in both the Christian and pagan sense of the world, but Camus's humanism has neither roots nor teleology. An eclectic, Camus borrows ideas from many philosophers, without carrying any theory to its end—a Kantian not believing in practical reason, a pietist without God, an Aristotelian without teleology, a bewildered existentialist who tries desperately to preserve a human essence hanging in a metaphysical void. Most striking is his imperfect blending of Christian and pagan elements; far from harmoniously completing each other, as in the classical tradition, they remain not exactly incompatible, but rather placed side by side without any link, for lack of a superior principle.

As for the subjective, lyrical value of Camus's political essay, it elicited much hate and irony in certain quarters, as will be seen later. Yet, its emotional appeal to the reading public was immense. The novelty of the approach was largely responsible for this success, and, to a large extent, what made it philosophically unsound increased its credibility. Here was an ethics offered to a bewildered generation, an ethics that did not toss them endlessly from Lenin to the Marquis de Sade, but offered them beauty, friendship, freedom, justice, commitment, and meaning; an ethics based on revolt, not on acquiescence; a hard ethics, without transcendental illusions, and yet imbued with all the tenderness and mystery of poetry, and proffering the hope of a humanitarian revival. A rest from history, no doubt. Yet, history was taken into account, and by linking historical to metaphysical experience, Camus was suggesting more than an ethics—a coherent view of man's place in the universe. Again this coherence might be more lyrical than logical for, in his characteristic discontinuous way of thinking, Camus fails to mention or examine the strong emotional link between his two sets of ethical values. By no stretch of imagination, as said before, can Christian notions of equality and brotherhood be deduced from Greek concepts of cosmic harmony and measure. Between the two sets of feelings there is a jump, a mutation. "This is of another order," as Pascal said, and Camus denied any ontological hierarchy of values. Instead, he perceives between the two systems an emotional association. Man stands in relation to Fate or the Gods as a slave to a cruel and whimsical master. He must revolt, but while revolting, he must know his limits. Metaphysical and social revolt are one, inasmuch as some men choose to behave like fate to other men, and transfer their humiliation and suffering to others. Prometheus and Spartacus are one, which is the reason for the homology, implied in the central chapters of *The Rebel,* between the metaphysical and the political revolts. But if Prometheus and Spartacus are one by their experience, they also have the same values and the same duties; they rebel not in order to conquer and oppress, but in order to free themselves, and others, from the master-slave system.[29] The political rebel, if he wins, must renounce oppression. The metaphysical rebel, who cannot win, can at least assert his dignity as a thinking reed. This means, in Camus's views, that he should refrain from convulsive satanism, and, instead of aping Fate by an indiscriminate use of whatever power he can grab, take the part of his fellow humans, defending his own and their dignity and happiness.

Whether the association Prometheus-Spartacus has any reality for the majority of mankind is highly doubtful, if one considers world history as little else than the chaotic story of power relations. But, Camus would argue, it is that little else that matters, and the minority of men who care for it.

---

29. The same message appears in Malraux's *Man's Fate* (especially in chapter 3, relating Kyo's dialogue with Koenig the torturer).

7
Perversion of Values:
1. The Philosophers

> Entre la folie de ceux qui ne veulent rien que ce qui est et la déraison de ceux qui veulent tout ce qui devrait être, ceux qui veulent vraiment quelque chose, et sont decidés a en payer le prix, seront les seuls à l'obtenir.
>
> —Camus, *Actuelles II*

Having discovered genuine values rooted in the existential experience of revolt, Camus proceeds to examine in this light the representative political doctrines of the past hundred and fifty years and detects in them a series of fundamental infringements upon the true spirit of rebellion. All aberrations studied by Camus have in common that they ignore the dual character of the experience of revolt and disregard one aspect of it: either the human aspiration to create meaning and unity in the world, or the limitation imposed on this wish by the human condition.

The second type of aberration is more frequent and is chrono-
logically earlier. It consists in seeking to realize absolute good on
earth, forgetting that man, as part of an absurd universe, is made,
as Kant observed, "of too crooked a wood for him ever to become exactly straight." In some cases, as with the perfectionists
of the Jacobin type, the absolute good is to be realized here and
now. In another, more modern distortion, the absolute good is
projected into the future and its realization entrusted to history.
Such is the case with Hegel and most of his disciples, especially
with those of the Marxist-Leninist school. In both instances, abstraction prevails, the concrete human being is forgotten, or rele-
gated to the second place. The irrational (Camus would say
absurd) element in the human condition is ignored; ethical and
political values divorced from reality are postulated as absolute.
Hence, life is transformed into abstract ideologies, an ideal breeding ground for "crimes of logic." This is one of the reasons why
"all modern revolutions have ended in a reinforcement of the
power of the State."[1]

The other and opposite type of aberration consists in ignoring
the fact that man is able and inclined to impose a certain amount
of order and humaneness on the absurd course of events, and in
arguing as if the whole of human affairs were ruled by blind
destiny. This exclusive acceptance of the irrational and contingent
element in life, best exemplified by Nietzsche's *amor fati,* leads
even more directly than the first set of doctrines to wholesale
massacres, perpetrated in the name of ideology.

These two types of betrayal of the initial experience of revolt,
that of the extreme optimists and that of the extreme pessimists,
each of whom sees only one half of the truth, Camus describes
by the somewhat misleading term of nihilism.

Following Nietzsche, he uses the term in its widest meaning to
describe all the phenomena accompanying the breakdown of
humanitarian values.[2] Camus speaks of nihilism in connection

1. Camus, *The Rebel,* p. 177.
2. Camus confirms this understanding of the term "nihilism" in
Actuelles II, p. 100, "Réponse à Jeanson":

with Jacobin virtue, naturalism, romanticism, biologism, and finally with historicism, expediency, and psychotechnological power.

We shall review these various kinds of "nihilism" in separate sections, starting with the perfectionism of the Jacobins and the historicism of Hegel and Marx.

1. The Philosophy of the French Revolution

Camus opens his review of political crime with the study of the abstract-theoretical revolutionary mind. Under this heading he would put all system-builders, the fanatics of justice, the believers in absolute rationality and righteousness in man and in the body politic—in short, all the formalists whom Nietzsche had in mind when he called Kant, unjustly regarded as their spiritual father, "the Mongol of Koenigsberg." Their common sin is abstraction. The way in which Camus uses this word requires clarification. By abstraction he does not mean the mental operation usually designated by this name, which is necessary to all rational thought. What he means is a psychological attitude that consists in seeing only the desirable principles of conduct and ignoring the concrete human individual who is called upon to fit in this Procrustean bed. Some psychologists have tried to detect the causes of this widespread attitude. Nietzsche and Scheler, whom Camus often quotes with approval, see in it a form of contempt, not devoid of resentment. Gabriel Marcel speaks in this connection of a "transposition of imperialism into the world of the spirit."[3] Camus would agree with Nietzsche and Scheler that this kind of flight from reality is not essentially an operation of the intellect, but a subterfuge of resentful passions, a neurotic deviation from

"le nihilisme pour moi coincide avec les valeurs désincarnées et formelles. La critique de la révolution bourgeoise et formelle de 1789 est parallèle dans mon livre à celle de la révolution cynique du XXème siècle et il y est démontré que, dans les deux cas . . . le nihilisme et la terreur sont justifiés."

3. Gabriel Marcel, *Les Hommes contre L'Humain* (Paris: La Colombe, 1959), p. 116.

the fullness of reality. It desiccates life, distorts all problems, corrupts the spirit, and turns passion into obsession.

When applied to political thought, this kind of abstract thinking usually gives preeminence to one category or class of persons, singled out from the rest of the living and endowed with absolute value. Abstraction in this sense pervaded the radical wing of the French Revolution. Camus probably considered that the Revolution, prompted by genuine rebellion, should have followed the spirit of the Girondists. It became distorted when the Jacobins let themselves be caught in the cogs of lifeless reason and abstract virtue.

This development Camus traces back to the philosophy of Rousseau's *The Social Contract*. No doubt Camus would readily agree with Anatole France that Rousseau "believed he was deriving his principles from Nature but did in fact deduce them from the ethics of Calvin." In *The Social Contract* Camus detects the Spartan, Stoic, and Jansenist roots of the Jacobin Revolution. He shows in *The Rebel* how the abstract unity of "The People," proclaimed absolute and infallible, is but another incarnation of the old punitive God of religious tradition: transcendent, all-powerful, and vengeful.

> The will of the people is, in fact, coercive; its power has no limits. . . . The will of the people is primarily the expression of universal reason, which is categorical. The new God is born.[4]

Nothing could be a more precise expression of this spirit of perfectionism than the concluding chapters of *The Social Contract,* in which Rousseau not only forbids opposition to the civil faith, but goes so far as to punish neutrality. There, the concept

---

4. Camus, *The Rebel*, p. 116. In his analysis of *The Social Contract* Camus simplifies Rousseau's thought, leaving out the distinction between the "general will" and the will of the majority. Since, however, Rousseau recognizes frankly the first notion as utopian, only the second one was taken into account and Camus's analysis is correct in practice if not in theory.

of "holy humanity" together with a merciless religion of virtue was born. The divinity of "The People" has found its gospel.

No more than other political utopians did Rousseau strive for balance of power; he further sought total political unity.[5] He had in mind a preconceived ideal of absolute reason and virtue, outside of which he saw no salvation. This was the Calvinist heritage in him. He conceived of no relative approach to human affairs. Nevertheless, Rousseau was far from desiring the Terror as a permanent institution.[6] In his idealistic mind he believed that, after the elimination of kings and bishops, enlightened nations would enthusiastically follow the path of nature and reason. It was to be the fate of his Jacobin disciples to find that in practice human affairs follow a different course.

"But once abstraction has taken root, it casts its pallid rays in all directions."[7] Rousseau's Jacobin disciples set out to build a concrete Spartan republic, in which everything would be regulated by "virtue." But what is virtue?

What, in fact, is virtue? For the bourgeois philosopher of

5. Hannah Arendt, *The Origins of Totalitarianism* (New York: Harcourt, Brace and Company, 1951).

6. A remarkable contribution to the analysis of the problem of freedom, as formulated by Rousseau and others, is contained in a paper by Raymond Aron, read at a conference held under the auspices of St. Antony's College, Oxford, 1957. In the series on *Changes in Soviet Society,* Aron delivered a lecture entitled *La société Soviétique et l'avenir de la liberté,* in which he says:

En une analyse simplifiée, on distinguera trois sens de la liberté, trois sortes de *libertés*: ce que Montesquieu appelait la sûreté, ce que les intellectuels de Hongrie réclamaient, c'est-à-dire le droit de dire la vérité sur tous les sujets, enfin la liberté de Rousseau, c'est-à-dire la participation à la souveraineté, les elections libres et la compétition des partis étant au XXe siècle l'expression de cette liberté-participation.

Rousseau has one failing in common with innumerable writers on political problems: he is totally unaware of this threefold aspect of freedom.

7. Ferdinand Peroutka, *Democratic Manifesto* (New York: Voyages Press, 1959).

the period it is conformity with nature and, in politics, conformity with the law, which expresses the general will.[8]

Such vague statements invite any arbitrary interpretation. Thus, to the Jacobins, Nature becomes an abstract principle: nature equals virtue, and the law equals nature. It is not long before "virtuous" becomes synonymous with "lawful"; and the primitive confusion of the holy and the lawful that it had taken centuries to separate, is formally reestablished. Thus, the laicization of political life, one of the main aspirations and achievements of eighteenth-century humanism, was revoked by the atheistic patriotic believers in the virtue of the French Revolution.

Camus then proceeds to show how terror was bound to follow from these abstractions.

That is why the Republic not only is an assembly, as Saint-Just forcibly says, but it is also virtue itself. Every form of moral corruption is at the same time political corruption, and vice versa. A principle of infinite repression, derived from this very doctrine, is then established.[9]

In theory there existed an abstract unity embodied in the general will and deriving from natural virtue. But in practice there were factions marring this theoretical unity.

Factions divide the sovereign; therefore they are blasphemous and criminal. They, and they alone, must be combated.[10]

Unavoidably, the Republic established in the name of virtue began to kill in the name of virtue. Its values were abstract, and so was the enemy. The enemy of the Republic was not just an obnoxious fellow but the enemy of holy unity. The concrete guillotine became the only support of abstract unity.

---

8. Camus, *The Rebel*, p. 123.
9. *Ibid.*, p. 123.
10. *Ibid.*, p. 124.

At the heart of this logical delirium, at the logical conclusion of this morality of virtue, the scaffold represents freedom.[11]

This is the meaning of Saint-Just's desperate cry: "Either virtue or the Terror!" And such was the outcome of the first attempt to establish a society based on an absolute principle, by men oblivious of the element of absurdity in the human condition. Abstraction, in Camus's sense, is inseparable from *hubris,* as are all moral attitudes that involve frustration and resentment, whatever moral and intellectual justification might be found for them.

2. Camus's Indictment of Historicism

> L'histoire est sans yeux et
> il faut donc rejeter sa
> justice pour lui substituer,
> autant qu'il se peut, celle
> que l'esprit conçoit.
> —Camus, *L'Eté*

Hegel, according to Camus, diagnosed correctly the causes of the Jacobin terror. He discovered them in the cult of abstract moral virtue that prevailed during the second part of the Revolution, when, as Camus describes it, "the rule of abstract law is identical with the rule of oppression."[12]

---

11. *Ibid.,* p. 126. Camus's indictment of the Terror is impressive, backed as it is by the psychological analysis of the ideological, abstract mind. Time and again, one is reminded of Anatole France's analysis of fanaticism in *The Gods are Thirsty.* It can be regretted that Camus did not show the same fairness as the old master of skepticism, inasmuch as he failed to mention the concrete historical situation in which the Terror developed: external war, civil war in the Vendée, shortage of food, and general obsidional fever; the result is that Camus's argument seems to proceed *in vitro.* However, incomplete though it is, it remains valuable in exploding a historical myth that is still very much alive among the French Left, perhaps due to the French special fondness for abstraction.
12. *The Rebel,* p. 133.

Hegel therefore sought means to preserve the living body of national and cultural tradition, the concrete spirit of the *Gemeinschaft,* in contrast to the abstract entity of the *Gesellschaft* of the Jacobins. The former entity he calls the concrete universal, as opposed to the abstract universal of the blueprint society. Hegel's concrete universal is undoubtedly less artificial than the abstractions of Saint-Just, but, as Camus remarks, it is also much more ambiguous. The transcendental principles of Justice and Reason, embodied in the French Revolution, were brought by Hegel and subsequent historicists into the flow of events through which the "concrete universal" is being shaped. The abstract principles, which the Jacobins intended to realize by one stroke of the pen in nations and cultures, were entrusted by Hegel to the dynamics of history, through which they were slowly to emerge. This was a momentous transformation. Camus writes:

> Up to this point, reason had soared above the phenomena which were related to it. Now reason is, henceforth, incorporated in the stream of historical events, which it explains while deriving its substance from them. . . . These values have ceased to be guides in order to become goals.[13]

Hegelian reasoning, as Camus understood it, thus dispensed with all fixed standards; it postulated the ultimate emergence of an Absolute, when the Idea would realize itself at the end of the

---

13. *Ibid.,* pp. 133–134. Here, Camus seems to oversimplify. What Hegel meant was probably that these values became manifest as historical goals and were regarded as progress. Camus reverses Hegel's argument and seems to interpret him as saying that the manifest goals of history were values ("values had ceased to be guides in order to become goals") or at least as making these goals so obscure ("action . . . must be performed in darkness while awaiting final illumination") that they lay open to any distortion. Thus, some Hegelians will use "Hegel's panlogism" as "a justification for a condition of fact" and other Hegelians to justify "every ideological encroachment upon reality." This is not the place to discuss to what extent, if at all, Hegel had relativised values; but Camus was certainly right in pointing out the bad faith of post- or pseudo-Hegelians who used historicism to justify whatever they pleased and turned their master's "reason" into "an inflexible passion."

historical process. In this philosophy human nature is not yet realized, but man can and should strive to bring about its final realization. It is against this conception of history and all forms of historicism derived from it that the bulk of Camus's argumentation in *The Rebel* is directed. Camus sees in Hegel one of the great villains of philosophy, the arch-enemy of true rebellion. It was he who, according to Camus, instituted the worship of totality in the social and historical process, he who relativized all norms, and endowed the process of history itself with absolute validity. Finally, it was he who introduced into the mind of modern man the idea that present societies are evil and sinful, absolutely corrupt, but ripe for eschatological salvation.

Many critics of *The Rebel* consider that Camus's simplification of Hegel's thought verges on crudity; and it must be admitted that his criticism of historicism does not show a profound knowledge of the problem. There are many hues of historicism. The British scholar Isaiah Berlin enumerates the teleological, metaphysical, mechanistic, religious, aesthetic, and scientific types of historicism; he further distinguishes between pessimistic and optimistic types of the doctrine. In spite of the many differences among the various schools, Berlin finds the following common denominator:

> that the world has a direction and is governed by laws, and that the direction and the laws can in some degree be discovered by employing the proper techniques of investigation; and, moreover, that the working of these laws can only be grasped by those who realize that the lives, characters, and acts of individuals, both mental and physical, are governed by the larger "wholes" to which they belong, and that it is the independent evolution of these "wholes" that constitutes the so-called "forces" in terms of whose direction truly "scientific" or "philosophic" history must be formulated.[14]

Few serious historians today would defend rigid historical determinism. Fewer still would present a teleological conception

---

14. Isaiah Berlin, *Historical Inevitability* (London-New York: Oxford University Press, 1954), p. 17.

of history, asserting the existence of purposes in the historical process, the predictability of these purposes, and the objective value of theories concerning such metahistorical aims. This, however, does not exclude relative beliefs as to a possible meaning of history. But Camus's attitude is one of sweeping denial. He not only denies that the historical process could be foreseen; he denies it any meaning whatsoever.

From several passages of *The Rebel* it could be gathered that Camus accepts the Greek conception of a cyclical or undulatory process in history. Occasionally he seems to borrow Nietzsche's conception of the "eternal recurrence of the same"; or he might be accepting the ideas, as expounded in Theodor Lessing's *Geschichte als Sinngebung des Sinnlosen,* of the absolute meaninglessness of the historical process, when he asserts that "l'histoire est sans yeux" (history is blind). In this absolute refusal of historicism, Camus does not distinguish between historicism as such, culminating, for instance, in the great work of Wilhelm Dilthey, in which history becomes an important clue to the understanding of man's thought and institutions, and any metahistorical prophecy that might choose to call itself historicist.

However, Camus's valuable contribution comes when, leaving aside all theorizing on the value of "historicism" as such, he concentrates on the abuse of the theory by various types of doctrinaire who claim to be privy to the most secret aims of history and, on that authority, attribute absolute validity to their utopian expectations, their desires, or their aversions. No doubt Hegel's new approach has encouraged all kinds of spurious interpretations of the purposes of history. For Hegel, according to Camus, has discarded all fixed standards of thought and conduct, such as human rights, or the principles of the Enlightenment; and although he has put his faith in the "goals" of the Spirit working through history, he is somewhat ambiguous as to the means of achieving them.

As for the means of attaining these goals, specifically life and history, no pre-existent value can point the way. On the contrary, a large part of Hegelian demonstration is devoted to proving that moral conscience, by being so banal as to obey justice and truth, as though these values existed independently of the world, jeopardizes, precisely for this reason, the advent of these values. The rule of action has thus become action itself—which must be performed in darkness while awaiting the final illumination. Reason, annexed by this form of romanticism, is nothing more than an inflexible passion.[15]

Camus would readily agree with Schopenhauer's pronouncement that Hegel's philosophy has inaugurated "the age of dishonesty" in Western thought. The "historical mission" is an abstraction, and once it has taken hold of the minds of people, intellectual honesty recedes into the background.

Thus, Camus's indictment of historicism turns out, in fact, to be an indictment of messianism and fanatic utopia, which masquerade under the cloak of historicism and, inevitably, end in terror. Camus rightly detects under historicism of the prophetic kind the age-honored tendency to explain historical events by the actions of Providence. He devotes a few pages in *The Rebel* to the historicism of the Judeo-Christian tradition, especially to Joseph de Maistre, and, incidentally, to Auguste Comte, but turns the whole impact of his argument against Hegel, Marx, and Lenin. In Marx he clearly differentiates between the diagnostician, whom he admires for having exposed the laws of nineteenth-century capitalism, and the prophet of a future society. His criticism of this prophetic element in socialism is, in the opinion of this writer, one of the most valid parts in *The Rebel*. It is also the part that evoked the sharpest criticism from the French Left, led by Sartre.

According to Camus's analysis it was Marx's prophetism, and not his criticism of the capitalist process, that made possible the development from Hegel to the theory and practice of the modern totalitarian state. The explanation of how a regime of Terror can develop from Hegel's prophetism is the heart of the argument in *The Rebel*. If history is "the march of God on earth," if the future

15. *The Rebel,* p. 134.

is an imagined God, then constant sacrifice of individuals can be justified in view of an end which is not only supremely good, but holy. We arrive at a conception akin to that of Jacobin "virtue":

> For the Jacobin, everyone is virtuous. The movement which starts with Hegel, and which is triumphant today, presumes, on the contrary, that no one is virtuous, but that everyone will be. At the beginning, everything, according to Saint-Just, is an idyl; according to Hegel, everything is a tragedy. But in the end that amounts to the same thing. Those who destroy the idyl must be destroyed or destruction must be embarked on in order to create the idyl. Violence, in both cases, is the victor. The repudiation of the Terror, undertaken by Hegel, only leads to extension of the Terror.[16]

Just as the Jacobins had divinized The People, in the same way the left-wing Hegelians, atheists though they were, were led to divinize history and the collective. And when history becomes a ground and the State an instrument for the manifestation of the holy, then the guillotine waits for its victims. In this respect the transition from Hegel to the Communist totalitarian state lies not in putting back the dialectic on its feet, but in the Marxist prophecy of justice, materialized through history.

Another dangerous aspect of Hegel's prophetism was that it is to be fulfilled through a collective. Neither man in his relation to the Absolute or to Reason, nor man in his relation to other human beings and their dignity, but rather society itself became endowed with absolute meaning as the exclusive bearer of dialectic progress, the total, true, and only reality through which the Absolute could manifest itself. Hegel had entrusted specifically the Prussian state with the mission of preparing the advent of the Absolute on earth. His disciples found other, equally commendable mediators: nations, races, classes, abstract humanity, "elites," or masses were endowed with a messianic mission and the destinies of men entrusted to the tender mercy of these inspired collectives. Similarly, any disposition in man can be endowed

16. *Ibid.,* p. 136.

with holy or regenerative functions. Such is the case with efficiency in our time. Here, again, the full effect of this attitude was to be seen only in the twentieth-century totalitarian states. When social interests are paramount, individual wishes become a mere hindrance; when history is absolute, man is but its instrument.

Among Hegel's ideas that were taken up and developed by Marx, there is one on which Camus concentrates his most violent criticism: it is the theory of the master-slave relations as outlined in Hegel's *Phenomenology of Mind*. According to Hegel the elemental desire of all men striving to be recognized by others brings about the struggle for life, and represents the basic content of the processes of history, which, according to him, will be fulfilled only when everybody will have been recognized by all other men. But while this struggle lasts, mankind is necessarily divided into masters and slaves. Such are the inexorable tensions of the world process. And Hegel takes pleasure in quoting Schiller's dictum: "Die Weltgeschichte ist das Weltgericht." History, then, is the story of labor and revolt, and not much else. It is a "slaughter-house."[17]

Camus's criticism of this theory is central to his thesis of true revolt. First, he shows that the master-slave theory linked with historicism has furnished modern man with the idea of welding metaphysical revolt to a secular revolutionary movement. All value judgments, including dignity and solidarity, have been abandoned, the entire existence of man and nations temporalized, an ugly subservience to the needs of one's nation or class initiated; all this leads to utter political cynicism in a world caught between the brute forces of masters and slaves—without recourse, without respite, and "without principles and innocence." This was, in Camus's opinion, the first philosophy of power, according to which all creation must necessarily be preceded by violence and

17. The echo of this theory can be found in most recent political literature, for example, Maurice Merleau-Ponty, *Humanisme et Terreur, Essai sur le problème communiste* (Paris: Gallimard, Essais XXVII, 1947). Here, Camus seems to mix up Hegel's theory of the master-slave relations with that of Marx, and disregards Hegel's dialectical resolution of the conflict.

destruction. This was the new nihilism which, due to the deification of violence, later takes its inexorable course toward "crimes of logic":

> Cynicism, the deification of history and of matter, individual terror and State crime, these are the inordinate consequences that will now spring, armed to the teeth, from the equivocal conception of a world that entrusts to history alone the task of producing both values and truth.[18]

And two pages further, Camus expresses the same idea even more forcefully:

> The sky is empty, the earth delivered into the hands of power without principles. Those who have chosen to kill and those who have chosen to enslave will successively occupy the front of the stage, in the name of a form of rebellion which has been diverted from the path of truth.[19]

The totalitarian regimes of the present age are far from saving man from reification by capitalism. Following the logic of abstraction, they are transforming him into a function of the abstract apparatus of the state, completely disrupting the organic entity of the community. Man becomes an atomized abstraction, to be replaced at will, and in conformity with the "needs of society." Cold planning reigns supreme. The destruction of all communities outside state control is followed by an alienation from the self. The totalitarian state completes the alienation of man and brings chaos and servility into his soul. In the name of a pseudo-revolutionary ideology, the betrayal of true rebellion is consummated.

"Liberated" from reason and God at the same time, the protesting human being finds himself left with a single value, the relativity of the historical process itself, which then is endowed with all the qualities of a deity. Man "will kneel before history," Camus says. That is how the nihilistic aberration of historicism is launched on its ill-fated voyage.

18. *The Rebel,* p. 146.
19. *Ibid.,* p. 148.

3. The Betrayal of Revolt by Titanic Romanticism

The other and opposite type of betrayal of genuine revolt, which Camus studies under the heading of "metaphysical revolt," consists in denying any validity (or existence) to man's aspirations to unity and justice. It is a protest of modern man against the whole of his condition and the entire order of the cosmos. This form of rebellion is nihilistic in Camus's sense, since it excludes one-half of human experience;[20] it is also nihilistic, in the accepted sense of the word, inasmuch as it denies the existence of any worthy purpose in the universe; it is tantamount to a denial of God and of any rational meaning, or to a full-fledged rebellion against Him.

As the perfectionist rationalists of the French Revolution forgot the irrational element in man and as many of the historicists forgot man's autonomy, so do some metaphysical rebels ignore the existence of values, because they do not see any traces of them outside the human conscience. They are, so to speak, more nihilistic than is strictly necessary; and, from this distortion of reality, a new set of "crimes de logique" originates. In his study of this third aberration, Camus draws many examples from the intellectual history of the past hundred and fifty years. Defiance against the general order of the universe is demonstrated by reference to such diverse examples as the Marquis de Sade, Dostoievski, and the "poètes maudits," especially Baudelaire, and Lautréamont. Max Stirner and the surrealist movement are also used to illustrate the cult of the absurd. But most relevant to this study is Camus's analysis of Dostoievski's Ivan Karamazov and of Nietzsche's "prophetic nihilism."

The majority of metaphysical rebels, notably Baudelaire and Lautréamont, insult God, which means that they still recognize Him. But Ivan Karamazov refuses God because He is unjust. God is judged and condemned. And, since a God who permits the suffering of innocent children is beyond imagination, then

---

20. *Ibid.,* p. 147.

God is dead; and with God's death, not only does man celebrate his final liberation, but he can proclaim his own divinity.

> But what does becoming God mean? It means, in fact, recognizing that everything is permitted and refusing to recognize any other law but one's own. . . . We can see that to become God is to accept crime.[21]

In Nietzsche the philosophy of "all or nothing" finds its first systematic expression. It is the quintessence of *hubris*. The problem of Ivan Karamazov was still to achieve unity by absolute justice, since he refused the God of Christianity on grounds of injustice. Ivan's followers tried to establish justice in its totality, that is to say, by any means. Thus, with the divinity of man, the Grand Inquisitor moved into action and attempted, according to an already known pattern, to unite mankind through the reign of terror and death. Revolt, as pictured by Dostoievski, was still incomplete, since Ivan attacked God in the name of values. Moreover, Ivan shrank from the consequence of his own ideas, and Dostoievski himself returned to the fold of the Russian Orthodox Church.

The metaphysical revolt of nihilism was completed under the "hammer blows" of Nietzsche's philosophy. For the traditional humanist, the world was basically rational, it had a structure or a goal or both. But Nietzsche's philosophy starts with the premise that there is neither unity, finality, or meaning anywhere. With Nietzsche, modern nihilism becomes fully conscious of itself for the first time.

This revolution starts with Nietzsche's criticism of generally accepted values. Camus explains at the beginning of *The Rebel* how Nietzsche, followed by Scheler, detected the autointoxication of Western civilization by resentment. The analysis of resentment as an underlying force of the majority of modern values is probably the greatest intellectual achievement of the tragic German philosopher. With uncanny insight Nietzsche demonstrated how

21. *Ibid.*, pp. 58–59.

much of our so-called values and moral aspirations, whether Christian, bourgeois-humanist, or socialist, is colored by impotent envy: "The evil secretion, in a sealed vessel, of prolonged impotence."[22]

Nietzsche, and Scheler after him, analyzed the originally passive aspect of resentment that, once released, leads to senseless destruction. Camus observes, rightly, that it was Nietzsche and not Marx who first foresaw the apocalyptic events of the twentieth century, and that it was Nietzsche who really unmasked the hypocritical values of the bourgeois world.

But when Nietzsche, having transferred Descartes's method of *tabula rasa* from the intellectual to the psychological plane, had exploded all European creeds, movements, religious beliefs, and ideologies, he found himself suspended in thin air, faced with utter loneliness and meaninglessness. It was then that he decided to go beyond the ruins he himself had caused. Man was at last without a God, and became God himself. And, as Camus shows, Nietzsche is fully aware that the moment man tries to become God he is "responsible for everything alive, for everything that, born of suffering, is condemned to suffer from life." Camus continues:

> It is he [man], and he alone, who must discover law and order. Then the time of exile begins . . . the most heartbreaking question, that of the heart which asks itself: Where can I feel at home?[23]

Faced with the absurd universe, Nietzsche asked himself whether man can live and create values without any metaphysical sanction for them. His answer was in the affirmative, since "man is a most courageous animal, who can survive even the death of his gods."

Camus unreservedly admires Nietzsche's assertion that the

---

22. *Ibid.,* p. 17.
23. *Ibid.,* p. 70.

emancipated nihilist must accept new obligations, but he introduces one important qualification:

> Absolute domination by the law does not represent liberty, but no more does absolute anarchy. . . . Without law there is no freedom.[24]

For in spite of all his admiration for Nietzsche, Camus does not exculpate him from the charge of having betrayed genuine revolt. After having discovered that in the absence of any lawgiver it is man himself who must lay down the law, Nietzsche did not attempt to make laws against chaos, that is, to take the part of man, the only creature who can oppose a senseless world and introduce a minimum of meaning into it. Instead, Nietzsche threw humanism overboard altogether, and accepted the reign of the absurd, thus betraying once more the Promethean adventure. When all values are destroyed, man is reduced to his bare vitalistic existence, or, as Heidegger writes in his profound study on Nietzsche, to pure voluntarism, to his "will to will."[25] In such a world there is only power and the will to power; all is pure becoming; only Heraclitus's change is eternal. Nietzsche's contribution was only to replace a passive acceptance of fate by an active and enthusiastic identification with it. Nevertheless, driven to this extreme, Nietzsche's rebellion ends with a complete subordination to the senseless flux of the cosmos. Man should be faithful to the world, but since there are no laws or values in a contingent universe, Nietzsche ends in absolute assent, in *amor fati*. This is nihilism in its purest form:

> This magnificent consent, born of abundance and fullness of spirit, is the unreserved affirmation of human imperfection and suffering, of evil and murder,.

---

24. *Ibid.,* p. 71.
25. Martin Heidegger, *Holzwege,* section "Gott ist tot" (Frankfurt: V. Klostermann, 1950). "Das Sein des Seienden ist Wille zur Macht."

Thus, Nietzsche is seen as ending in the glorification of blind fate:

> The joy of self-realization is the joy of annihilation. But only the individual is annihilated. The movement of rebellion, by which man demanded his own existence, disappears in the individual's absolute submission to the inevitable.

Nietzsche was the first fully to experience, on the reflective level, the void of nihilism—an experience that was to become the fate of modern man and modern society. But there were still inconsistencies in Nietzsche, for in his "cosmic complex," he still dreamt of tyrants that would be artists, and of "Caesars with the heart of Christ." But in spite of all his hatred of cruelty and mediocrity, his philosophy lent support to the glorification of evil. "The human spirit," says Camus, "bowed proudly before the inevitable." And this precisely constitutes the betrayal of the Promethean revolt. Those who followed Nietzsche did not feel so many scruples as the lonely thinker did. They distorted his philosophy into an ideology of blind violence: "The doctrine of the superman led to the methodical creation of submen."[26]

Such were the results of the betrayal of true rebellion. By identifying himself with blind fate, and by glorifying the will to power, Nietzsche has opened, along with other philosophers of the nineteenth century, a dangerous path.

4. Conclusion: The Logic of Insanity

In his analysis of the various perversions of values, Camus carefully avoids any sentimental or instinctive approach. He does not invoke the natural goodness of man or the beauty of brotherhood. Nor does he ever argue from the point of view of social usefulness. He attacks logical crime on strictly logical grounds,

26. Camus, *The Rebel*, pp. 72–76.

which means that he accepts his opponent's platform. It may be surprising at first that such pronouncements as those of the Marquis de Sade seem to him worthy of discussion. Many simply consider them to belong to criminal psychopathology. Has not Camus wasted much ink in refuting blatant nonsense, in demonstrating the obvious?

The fact is, however, that in our time unreason has imposed its standards in such a compelling way, and with such appalling results, while humaneness stands impotent and discredited, that one feels, as Camus says (to repeat his introductory remarks), "now, it is innocence which is called upon to justify itself." One could add that sanity also is called upon to justify itself, since insanity claims a monopoly on logic and consistency.

In taking up this "strange challenge," Camus therefore answers a need of our time. Moreover, he does it in a way that sheds new light on the problem. He accepts his opponent's platform because he recognizes that even madness has its logic. But the logic of insanity, or, to use a more classical term, "la logique des passions,"[27] has its own specific laws, the main one being that it correctly deduces consequences from spurious assumptions, the insanity of which the madman does not perceive. These assumptions usually proceed from emotional motives, well hidden in the logical madman's unconscious, so that his opponent feels, with increasing irritation and anxiety, that he is running around in circles, a victim of some gross but elusive fallacy.

This seems to have happened to Camus himself, in relation to the logic of destructive nihilism, to such an extent that he wrote *Caligula* as a kind of auto-exorcism. For, if Caligula was logical, then Camus's own attitude was not, since, although believing in absurdity, he refused to legitimize logical crime. He would then be caught in the dilemma of the absurd, in the very terms in which it was offered by the logical criminals.

The first type of solution Camus found for such a dilemma—as expressed in *Letters to a German Friend*—he called, rather

27. For example, Théodule Ribot, *Logique des Sentiments.*

loosely, "faithfulness." In *The Plague* the humanitarian characters are also prompted by this "faithfulness," for which they could give no rational account but which nevertheless drove them to action. Here, Camus came nearer than he ever did to the belief in an inner moral sense in man. In *The Rebel* his analysis becomes more precise, since revolt is presented as an existential mode and solidarity as its logical outcome. Here, "faithfulness" has a precise object: one should be faithful to the totality of the experience of revolt, ambivalent though it is.

However, there is more in *The Rebel* than an attempt at logical justification of humanitarian feelings. Besides this professed aim of the book, Camus follows, somewhat hesitantly, another line of thought. By psychological analysis, he unravels his opponent's argument until he digs out the spurious premises, charged with hidden passion, by which Caligula's insane logic was set spinning.

Camus observes that if the desire for unity has been frustrated and nihilism ensues, nihilism ends in a desire to destroy. This happened to Ivan Karamazov, to the Marquis de Sade, to Lautréamont, to Ernst Juenger, to the surrrealists; and if it does not happen consistently to Nietzsche himself, at least the presuppositions for it are present in his works and his self-styled disciples developed them to the full.

It is this "all or nothing" which constitutes the spurious premise. Since the human predicament is such, precisely, that man cannot have all his desires or ideals fulfilled, it is a foregone conclusion that those who demand all are, in fact, calling for nothing; and we have seen with Caligula how they bring this "nothing" about by systematic destruction of everything meaningful. When looking for the hidden emotional motive behind this spurious demand for "all or nothing," Camus correctly identifies it with pride, the enraged pride of man humiliated by fate, who wants to re-assert himself by a cosmic revenge—"Entruestungspessimismus," as Scheler calls it, in connection with the psychological roots of Schopenhauer's philosophy.

In order to make this point clearer, let us remember that in long-forgotten, quieter times, the problem of nihilism had received an entirely different solution. Few writers have been more despairing of the metaphysical and historical goals of man than the elderly Ernest Renan or Anatole France. Yet they did not find it imperative or "logical" to follow an "all or nothing" theory of violence. Instead, they preached humaneness, tolerance, and reason, and showed great fondness for all the fragile creations of the human spirit, so brutally denied by the cosmos. Their attitude was similar to that of Cherea and Caesonia, in *Caligula,* of Rieux and Tarrou in *The Plague,* and indeed, of Camus himself—a simple, sane, perfectly "logical" solution. It consists in assuming that the human condition can be improved to some extent. Something is better than nothing: this is the logic of the pleasure principle. All or nothing is the logic of pride, of neurotic honor. Camus's attitude is, in many ways, a vindication of happiness against the extravagant claims of neurotic pride. He even goes so far as to assign heroism the second place in human endeavors: "après, jamais avant l'exigence généreuse du bonheur."[28] This attitude entirely lacks the daemonic splendor of the all-or-nothing school, whose somber violence appeals more to our restless age. The logic of pride in relation to man's fate has so completely prevailed over the logic of happiness that it has almost become a cultural pattern in our day, both among the intellectuals and the youths; in some countries, such as Hitler's Germany, it prevailed among the masses as well. There was an urgent need to unravel this problem, and Camus has done this. He has exploded the myth of satanism and deprived the destructive nihilist of his monopoly of logic, thus striking at the psychological roots of one important aspect of modern insanity.

In Camus's opinion, true to the spirit of Aeschylus, Prometheus may choose to insult the gods, but he must not forget that man, the fragile being, is neither god nor beast. Man is a relative creature, and he must never forsake this relativity. Prometheus

---

28. Camus, *La Peste* (Paris: Gallimard, 1947), p. 157. It should be noted, however, that only "generous" happiness is valuable, which excludes gross materialism or empty contentment.

must never aspire to an absolute in history. Promethean revolt has to remain faithful to the limited nature of human experience. The only revolution that "is adjusted to the measure of man is to be found in the acceptance of relative aims and ambitions, which means faithfulness to the human predicament."[29]

This message of relative freedom, as contrasted with the total freedom that man, according to Sartre, is trying to capture by becoming *causa sui*—i.e., God—is expressed in a passage of great insight by the German philosopher Nicolai Hartmann:

> A being that had unlimited freedom would also be burdened with unlimited responsibility. But the boundaries are drawn very narrowly for man: he sometimes collapses under the limited responsibilities which he actually has to bear in everyday life. Man can bear only a limited measure of freedom. And even this measure he possesses only approximately. . . . For he can in seriousness only will those things he can see the means to carry out. To "will" is not a vague wishing or longing. It is initiative and decision in the face of recognized possibilities. Moral freedom is solely the freedom of initiative. The freedom of decision, the power of the mind is the highest gift which man possesses, the true miracle of his being, the most metaphysical and divine part in him. But it is a two-edged gift. Because of it man is an unsettled being, threatened at every step by the fall into the abyss, and existing all his life in crisis. Other beings, those without reason and personality, are from the first to the last step bound, led, and protected by the laws of their species; their actions are blind, but unerringly true to their being, and in this sense infallible. They are incapable of evil, just as they are incapable of good. Only man reflects, has the freedom of the pro and con with regard to laws of value which he regards as his own. He is his own protector, but a weak one. That is his inner instability. The great gift of freedom makes a demand upon him, calling him to heights to which he must raise himself. The mind first has to make itself into what it is. In no aspect of man's being is this more obvious than in his moral freedom. Moral freedom is precisely that inner form, that enigmatic ability man has to create—or not to create—himself as he is. The free being is

---

29. Camus, *Remarques sur la Révolte,* pp. 18–19.

the being threatened by itself. Only man is threatened from the inside. He carries self-realization and self-destruction within him.[30]

Similarly, Camus observes that Europe can be reborn on condition that man accepts the spirit of relative freedom. "A limit under the sun shall curb them all. Each tells the other that he is not God; and this is the end of romanticism."[31]

Meanwhile, "romanticism" had moved from philosophy into politics. For nihilism, like resentment, easily assumes a proselytic character. The desperate desire for unity is then transformed into a convulsive attempt to control the world and build the City of the New Man. But all this now has to be achieved by conquest, for in the atmosphere of nihilism only the naked will to power prevails. Thus, Camus ends his search for the causes of modern insanity with an analysis of the motivations of the nihilistic empire-builders.

---

30. Nicolai Hartmann, *Das Problem des geistigen Seins,* zweite Auflage (Berlin: Walter de Gruyter and Co., 1949), pp. 165–67. Translated by Ingrid Lotze.

31. Camus, *The Rebel,* p. 306.

8

Perversion of Values:
2. The Empire Builders

> It is the mission of the twentieth
> century to elucidate the irrational.
> —Merleau-Ponty

1. Meaning Values and Interest Values

Modern totalitarian philosophies and the ideologies of mass movements derived from them should be studied, Camus insists, not
as scientific or philosophic doctrines, but as hallucinations of
uprooted and desperate people searching for a meaningful existence. Under the influence of his former teacher, Jean Grenier,
and following the analyses of Michel Collinet and Jules Monnerot
(whose books are mentioned in *The Rebel*), Camus shows how
Nazism, Fascism, and Communism create a new warlike psychology
in the ruling elites and the masses, opposed to the cunning, mer-
cantile interest values of the bourgeois age. These doctrines
profoundly transform all concepts of ethics and politics and bring
to the fore a new class of professional revolutionaries bound by
absolute obedience to the leader of the party, whom they endow
with *mana*.

159

If we adopt Max Weber's distinction between meaning values and interest values, then the totalitarian movements, with their violent and dynamic features, are not carried by economic or political interests in the first line, but belong to the psychology of religion. The secularization of political life, which started with Machiavelli, is thus reversed, and politics becomes once more a religion, a means of salvation. The modern revolutionary is convinced of the absoluteness of his mission. He tries to eradicate all present evils by a total upheaval, to transform man and society at their roots. Accordingly, the hearts and minds of the alienated masses are filled with pseudo-religious hope. They expect grace. They wait for absolute security and total fulfillment at some future stage of history. In such a frame of mind, compromise becomes hardly possible: any adversary is regarded as a diabolic enemy, to be liquidated.

Leaning once more on Nietzsche's diagnosis, Camus sees in all these movements and their violent ideologies phenomena of nihilism, likely to disrupt all civilized life. In *The Rebel* he distinguishes between the "irrational terror" of Nazism and Fascism and the "rational terror" of totalitarian Communism. Both these movements, Camus repeatedly emphasizes, are the final outcome of Hegel's philosophy of history, transformed on the one hand by the Dionysiac philosophies of life, and on the other by Marx's, Lenin's, and Stalin's distinct contributions. In short, metaphysical and historical revolts have joined hands, and, supported as they were by the new technological possibilities of mass production and propaganda, they have created new, specific, politico-sociological phenomena.

2. The Irrational Terror of Fascism and National Socialism

In the case of Mussolini, we need not look long to find the origins of Italian Fascism in a combination of historicism and Nietzscheism. Mussolini himself was a crude Hegelian of a sort, seeing in the State the culmination of all human efforts. He welded together the more primitive parts of Hegel's philosophy of the state with some of Nietzsche's extreme pronouncements on the Will to Power, thus justifying the all-embracing structure of the Fascist State by Hegel and Fascist terror by Nietzsche. Finally, by adding some Caesarian bombast concerning the sacred mission of Rome, he emerged as the first theoretician of the totalitarian state in our time.

Nothing beyond the State, above the State, against the State. Everything to the State, for the State, in the State.[1]

These were the first resounding phrases of European totality. But the longed-for unity did not quite come about in Italy. The power of the Church, and of the Italian bourgeoisie, still stood in the way. Moreover, the industrial backwardness of the country retarded its development toward a perfect totalitarian state.

Camus finds an infinitely more fitting example of the "irrational terror" and "active nihilism" of mass movements in the German National Socialist revolution. This was nihilism in full action, and Camus would agree with the ideas expressed by Hermann Rauschnig in his *Revolution of Nihilism* and by Franz Neumann in his *Behemoth,* that this kind of dynamism was no more than a glorification of the most primitive instincts, a pre-logical and pre-civilized tribalism of *Blut and Boden.*

One reads in a Nazi newspaper:

Our divine mission was to lead everyone back to his origins, back to the common Mother . . . it was a truly divine mission. . . . National Socialism is the only faith which can lead our people to salvation.[2]

---

1. Camus, *The Rebel,* p. 182. A confirmation of Camus's view, can be found in Serge Hughes's *The Fall and Rise of Modern Italy* (N.Y.: Macmillan, 1967), together with an analysis of the socioeconomic and psychological situation in Italy, which is lacking in Camus's study.
2. *Ibid.*

However, it is not in Hitler's, Himmler's, or Goebbels's ideology of the gutter that Camus sees the most perfect expression of the irrational prong of modern nihilism. For even Hitler wanted to destroy in order to build his Third Reich for a thousand years. The purest expression of nihilism Camus finds in Ernst Juenger, the most inspired theoretician of the National Socialist movement and one of its few real intellectuals. It was the poet and philosopher Juenger who transformed Nietzsche's nihilism of creation into a systematic nihilism of destruction. Nietzsche dreamt of a noble, creative, and self-sacrificing elite who would rule for the sake of grandeur and splendor. From the ruins of the bourgeois world, from the pseudo-Christian, pseudo-humanitarian half-truths and the vulgar imperialism of money, a new renaissance was to be born. Ernst Juenger believed in none of these things. Instead, he frequently advocated an apotheosis of destruction and degradation, the total abandonment of all values, for, according to Camus's interpretation:

> The best answer to the betrayal of life by the spirit is the betrayal of the spirit by the spirit, and one of the great and cruel pleasures of our times is to participate in the work of destruction.[3]

Juenger was not satisfied with the official Nazi identification of all personal and national life with the lowest instincts. He had a vision of a "technological world empire" in which, as we shall see later, Nazi and Stalinist nihilism would join hands. The result combined Hegel's "worker-soldier state" and Juenger's own "concrete universal." This "universal" was removed from all pity, all beauty, and all intercourse with the intellect. Human beings were to be reduced to the level of delta minus of Huxley's *Brave New World*. Juenger's empire was simultaneously

> the factory and the barracks of the world, where Hegel's soldier-worker reigns as a slave.[4]

3. *Ibid.*, p. 178.
4. Ernst Juenger, *Der Arbeiter; Herrschaft und Gestalt* (Hamburg: Hanseatische Verlagsanstalt, 1932).

Man's entire existence was to be organized in terms of power and military efficiency. In direct reference to Montesquieu, Camus comments that in such a state all intermediary bodies are abolished, all balance of power destroyed, with all power emanating only from the top. In the finished state such a society would be fully atomized and man transformed into a helpless object—the perfect travesty of Hegel's suggested solution of the master-slave relation.

This is the organized rule of the modern Caligulas, which Camus characterizes in the following way:

> Irrational terror transforms men into objects, "planetary bacilli," according to Hitler's formula. It presupposes the destruction, not only of the individual, but of the universal possibilities of the individual, of reflection, solidarity, and the urge to absolute love.[5]

Since Camus seems to be unaware of the dangers of the power-instinct as a fundamental human drive, he tends to regard all these evils exclusively as the outcome of nihilistic resentment in Scheler's meaning. The power to kill, to humiliate, and to degrade saves the soul of the "irrational nihilist" from utter emptiness. Nothingness escapes into the worship of power, into cruelty, success, and domination. Under the terror machine of the "irrational" totalitarian state lie buried the freedom of man and his true rebellion, which defy history's blind mechanism.

3. The Rational Terror of the Soviet State

A previous chapter dealt with Camus's study of the utopian elements in Marxism. But at the turn of the century Marxism was enriched by a new doctrine, the teachings of Lenin, which later found their expression in the organized power of the Soviet state and its ideology of international Communism. Leninism, for Camus, is not just a continuation or amplification of Marx, but a radical departure from the original Marxian *Weltanschauung*.

---

5. *The Rebel,* p. 183.

Leaning on Collinet, Camus points out that Marx and Engels could never quite decide on the modes of seizure of power by the proletariat, nor on the ways of maintaining it in a future proletarian state. Moreover, Marx never entirely lost his faith in the creative capacity of the working class and its autonomous revolutionary mission.

It was left to Lenin to "modernize" Marxism in several important ways. His attitude toward the seizure and maintenance of power was not at all ambivalent like that of his teachers. Almost from the beginning of his activity in the Russian working-class movement, his primary concern was with the problems and strategy of power. It was he who regarded the creation of a professional elite of revolutionaries as the prerequisite for a successful seizure and maintenance of power. Lenin also destroyed Marx's belief in the inevitability of the Revolution, and concentrated all his efforts on teaching revolutionary zeal and activist ruthlessness:

> The authoritarian socialists deemed that history was going too slowly and that it was necessary, in order to hurry it on, to entrust the mission of the proletariat to a handful of doctrinaires.[6]

In this manner, Camus maintains, Lenin confiscated, for the benefit of a select group of technicians and strategists of power, the living message of freedom contained in the original idea of socialism.

Camus's study of Leninism contains some original ideas on how Lenin merged modern voluntarism with the utopian elements of Marxian historicism. It is almost certain that neither Lenin nor Stalin had ever read a line of Nietzsche's *The Will to Power* or were familiar with any of his ideas.[7] But for Camus it is significant

---

6. *Ibid.,* p. 217.
7. It is known that Lenin had read Max Stirner's *Der Einzige und sein Eigentum* and was probably also familiar with some of the ideas of Georges Sorel and Gaetano Mosca.

that Lenin had developed a strategy of power for the revolutionary elites in almost exact conformity with some of Nietzsche's basic ideas. The philosophies of power have become expressions of the *Zeitgeist* of our century. And, above all, what is most useful to the modern revolutionary is that power, or Neitzsche's "will to will," need not be defined. It is its own self-perpetuating goal.

Under Lenin's guidance the humanistic element of socialism was lost. The rebellion against the conditions of capitalism ended in an ideological intoxication with organization and efficiency. That is how the idea of a just social order, which was to follow the expropriation of the means of production, became perverted into an ideology of rational terror:

> Frenzy in terms of history is called power. The will to power came to take the place of the will to justice, pretending at first to be identified with it and then relegating it to a place somewhere at the end of history, waiting until such time as nothing remains on earth to dominate.[8]

It is therefore wrong, Camus points out, to speak of Lenin as a Jacobin. Jacobin perfectionism was a belief in principles, in reason, and in formal virtue. But Lenin was primarily interested in efficient seizure and maintenance of power. He battled against the reformists as well as against individual terror in the name of efficiency rather than of moral principles. For Lenin the revolution was a military affair.

In this connection Camus makes some interesting observations concerning Lenin's attitude toward the state. His *State and Revolution* is often used to demonstrate that Lenin remained faithful to the original anarchistic program envisaged for the second stage of socialism. There are indeed many passages in *State and Revolution* that deal with the withering away of the state apparatus as described in Marx's *Program of Gotha*. But Lenin shifted from Marx's original ideas in one important way. According to Lenin, the proletarian state should be used not only to crush the ex-

---

8. *The Rebel*, 225–26.

ploiting classes, but also to "direct the great masses of the population . . . in the management of the socialist economy." Thus, the provisional state of Marx and Engels is entrusted with a new mission, "which risks prolonging its life indefinitely."[9] Such a conception of the state was not that of Karl Marx, but of Lassalle.

No doubt, Lenin was a passionate lover of justice, but it was a kind of justice that had to be enforced by military means, not by spontaneous and organic action of the proletariat. Any rebellion that might disrupt strict discipline was to be crushed (as shown by Lenin's own action against the sailors of Kronstadt). And the longer Lenin ruled, the more doubtful he became of the advent of the second stage of socialism, when the state would wither away. In evidence, Camus quotes the following sentence from Lenin, without giving any reference:

> For the sake of greater clarity, it has never been vouchsafed to any socialist to guarantee the advent of the higher phase of Communism.[10]

Camus comments that at this point the hope of freedom held out by socialism definitely died; first Lenin announced that the end of the provisional and necessary dictatorship—no longer of the masses but of the professional revolutionaries—could no longer be foreseen, and later it was said that no one has ever promised the advent of such a higher stage of Communism.

This marked the birth of "Caesarian socialism," the final betrayal of the original ideas of socialism, which meant not only a fair deal for everybody but also dignity, solidarity, and freedom for everybody. For the sake of justice in a distant future, injustice was being authorized for an indefinite period, and thanks to this policy, the masses were to be kept in permanent servility. Freedom had been thrown overboard, the god had failed. Everything had to be sacrificed in order to conquer the Empire.

In a passage of great beauty, Camus describes the sequence of

9. *Ibid.,* p. 230.
10. *Ibid.,* p. 231.

mystifications by which humanitarian socialism, the dream of millions, was giving way to its totalitarian caricature:

> Therefore as long as there exists on earth, and no longer in a specific society, one single oppressed person and one proprietor, so long the State will continue to exist. It also will be obliged to increase in strength during this period so as to vanquish one by one the injustices, the governments responsible for injustice, the obstinately bourgeois nations, and the people who are blind to their own interests. And when, on an earth that has finally been subdued and purged of enemies, the final iniquity shall have been drowned in the blood of the just and the unjust, then the State, which has reached the limit of all power, a monstrous idol covering the entire earth, will be discreetly absorbed into the silent city of Justice.[11]

Such then, was the fate of the universalistic creed of socialism, when it became a cloak for the power ideologies of Lenin, Stalin, and the Soviet state. Until the final goal is reached, all wrongs, crimes, and falsehoods are justified:

> all freedom must be crushed in order to conquer the empire, and one day the empire will be the equivalent of freedom. And so the way to unity passes through totality.[12]

---

11. *Ibid.*, pp. 232–33.
12. *Ibid.*, p. 233.

9
Camus and Anarchism

Camus's attitude with respect to anarchism is particularly relevant in view of today's political trends. Dissenters have sporadically hailed Camus, together with Herbert Marcuse, as one of their forerunners. There is no use indulging in the idle game of guessing how Camus *would* have stood in relation to the New Left and what goes by the name of anarchism today. But it is important to assess his views on certain political attitudes that were dear to his heart and not yet popular at the time of his death.

The word anarchism means so many different things that a strict inventory is imperative. It covers practically every dissenting attitude, from bomb throwing to the kind of mild assault against authority in which the French have been indulging for many centuries. Mild or savage, the assault can express the indignation of individual consciousness at the sight of injustice or can spring from mere petulance. It can be aimed at "society" in general and the powers that be, or restricted to specific classes or groups. Finally, it can be a well-defined political theory—in many ways akin to Anglo-Saxon nonconformism—in which individual self-control would replace external coercion; or it can be a dream of chiliastic upheaval, a fascination with chaos.

Between the whimsical lawlessness of the immature, and the serious, though in many ways utopian, aspirations to a society based on self-discipline and voluntary cooperation, there is nothing in common except a word, this loosely applied, prestigious, and mystifying word *anarchy*. Needless to say that Camus had no sympathy for plain lawlessness (beyond the French hereditary compulsion to tease authority). In the chapter of *The Rebel* called "The Poets' Rebellion," which deals with Lautreamont, Rimbaud and the surrealists, Camus takes care to dissociate their literary talent, which he admires, from their social rebellion, which he calls "irrational" and "adolescent." After pointing out the contradiction between the violence of some doctrinaires and their professed love for humanity ("the rebel's eternal alibi"),[1] he observes that some of the most vituperative rebels of our century submitted to the absolute order of the Communist Party. In Camus's eyes, this is a clear case of perversion of true revolt by the "all or nothing" attitude, with its characteristic ambivalence: absolute innocence or absolute evil (as illustrated in Maldoror's mating with the female shark), or, on the political level, total chaos of individualism run wild, with its apologies of crime and madness, or total abdication to totalitarian order.

Although Camus can legitimately be reproached for oversimplifying the case of the poetico-political *avant-garde,* what interests us here, in connection with the development of his own thought, is his impatience with what he regards as the spiritual abdication characteristic of the nihilist: the appeal of suicidal passions let loose, and the submission to suicidal discipline.

As for the other type of anarchy, based on self-discipline— ethical anarchism, we might call it—it seems to be the mainstay of Camus's political philosophy. Ignorance of a long French tradition of anarchism, as well as confusion of thought on this point, may well be responsible for the widespread misunderstanding of Camus's concept of revolt and what seems to be his ambivalent attitude to anarchism. Indeed, Camus himself seems singularly ignorant of the French anarchists. It is unlikely that he ever studied the difficult works of the French constructive

1. *The Rebel,* pp. 81 ff.

anarchists, from Proudhon to Péguy, although, as we shall see later, he agreed with them on many points. He hardly mentions them and seems to have absorbed their ideas or, better, the atmosphere in which they lived, through his acquaintance with prewar revolutionary syndicalism. Serious doubts may be raised as to solidity of his knowledge when he lumps together in one sentence Saint-Simon, Fourier, and Proudhon.[2] But he is much better informed about the Russian anarchists and discriminates between their several schools.

1. Guilt and Innocence of Man

Whatever the school to which they belong, all anarchists have in common the anti-Christian conviction of man's innate innocence, by which they mean that he is inclined by nature to love his fellowmen. In this respect it should be remembered that all revolutionaries initially shared in this conviction, even if they later appeared to forget it. Camus himself never totally abandoned this belief, even after *The Fall*. However, in view of the conspicuous absence of brotherhood in human affairs, especially among those who undertake to enforce it by political means, some explanation was required for this contradiction between facts and theory.

The emergence of this problem in European civilization is comparatively recent, since the conviction of man's utter wickedness—or folly—prevailed even after the Renaissance. However, by the end of the eighteenth century, excessive Christian misanthropy was outbalanced by a no less excessive optimism as to human kindness, and it became imperative to find scapegoats in order to explain man's beastly behavior. "Society" was the first scapegoat;[3] but since it was not clear how the association of good

2. *Ibid.,* p. 187.

3. Although this attitude is usually credited to Rousseau, his own opinions on the matter were far less absolute than is generally believed; he maintained that man was favorably disposed to his fellowman when his interests were not involved; as for society, he regarded it not as intrinsically bad but as corrupted by property and the desire for luxury and other "vices" of hyper-civilized societies.

individuals could produce a beastly collective, it was assumed that only one part of society was bad, namely, the rich and those born in authority, while the poor and humble retained their primeval innocence. Camus seems instinctively to have shared in this persuasion, although he quickly rejected this simplistic social Manichaeism. Instead, he tended to ground all evil in metaphysical evil. Dimly in *Caligula,* more clearly in *The Rebel,* he indicated that man confronted with the absurd universe, an innocent sentenced to death, had the choice between two ways: either take the part of his fellow sufferers—the path of "genuine revolt," or try to ape Fate by using whatever power he could seize in order to crush the weak. To explain why this latter choice so often prevailed is the main object of *The Rebel,* the very conception of which seems to indicate how deeply undermined Camus's hopes were at that time, although his belief in the essential goodness of *most* men does not seem to have been really shattered until *The Fall* and *The Renegade.* The unresolved conflict in his mind is particularly visible in two chapters: *Guilt and Innocence of Man,* in which he denounces excessive expectations concerning human virtue as a perversion of genuine revolt, and *The Fastidious Murderers,* in which he tries to draw a line between justified and criminal violence.

2. The Social Manicheans

How Jacobin terror was to follow an ideology of virtue and power is not difficult to guess. But Communist terror has certain features of its own that enable it to destroy, better than any other, not only the bodies of men but their souls as well. In an attempt to illustrate this point, Camus concludes his chapter on the rational terror by a subtle study of the question of guilt and innocence of the people under totalitarian regimes.[4] In the section on the Jacobin terror we saw how the creed underwent a strange transformation. Initially, the Jacobins were believers in the goodness of human nature, which their doctrine was supposed to

---

4. *Totality and Trials, The Rebel,* p. 233.

express in politics. Faced with the rise of factions, they attributed it not to any fault in their doctrine, but to the wickedness of a few perverse individuals whom they had regretfully to sacrifice to the common good. However, there came a moment when the number of dissidents became large enough to point to some discrepancy between human reality and Jacobin theory. The Jacobins did not hesitate long. The purity of the doctrine had to be kept intact at all cost; therefore it was the people who had to be castigated, and the reign of terror ensued. While the guillotine did its work, however, the dogma of the basic innocence of the people was maintained, and the whole hideous business of repression was blamed on "the enemies of the people."

A similar phenomenon reappeared, on a much larger scale, in what Camus calls Caesarian socialism. There, the realization of the ultimate goodness of human nature had been promised for a future date. But as this realization receded into an ever more distant future, and as ever-recurring obstacles barred the way to it, Communist nihilism gave birth to a theory, first cautiously pronounced, then generally accepted: that of objective guilt. This was a logical solution to the dilemma before which Jacobin logic had shrunk; since it could not be admitted that the premises of the revolution and the Soviet state might be wrong, it must be man who was at fault—man, but not his nature. For in socialist theory man has no nature; he is the product of social and economic conditions. He must therefore have been corrupted by his capitalistic past and will remain "objectively guilty" until he has been readjusted to the new system. Whether corrupted by a desire for property, or turned counter-revolutionary by lack of party discipline or by lack of faith in the socialist future, or poisoned by "subjectivism" and therefore blind to the demands of the historical situation, he has to be reeducated and readjusted, and no one can tell how long this process will last. Meanwhile, maladjusted deviationists have to be liquidated in the interests of the revolution. Moreover, their liquidation is just, since they are "objectively guilty," that is to say, they are obstacles to the realization of the Ultimate End.

Together with this notion of the "objective guilt" of the people, the phrase *engineers of the soul,* coined by Lenin, made its appearance in early Communist literature. Engineers of the soul were supposed to adjust man to history by means of education and propaganda, fully in keeping with the Communist doctrine of man's determination by his surroundings. But what those engineers primarily did, in fact, was to dwell on the permanent and ineradicable "objective guilt" of the people so as to make everybody feel guilty somehow, somewhere, against an oscillating party line, and the loyalties and duties it commanded.

Gradually, this feeling of an "objective guilt" was instilled in the minds and hearts of the majority of citizens living under Communist regimes, and produced subjective phenomena peculiar to those regimes. The part of Koestler's Rubashov was reenacted over and over again at every party congress, at each meeting of writers and artists behind the Iron Curtain, and even at insignificant meetings of party cells in the smallest villages. Every citizen is made to feel guilty, but like Kafka's hero in *The Trial,* the nature of his guilt is hidden from him. This "objective guilt," also stressed in Orwell's *1984,* is a most primitive but oppressive feeling, infused into modern minds by the political climate of totalitarian countries. The citizen feels guilty because he is disapproved of and punished.[5] Feeling guilty, he tries eagerly to regain his lost innocence by ever-increasing subservience and conformity, but in vain. He can never catch up. The rational terror culminates in the universe of trial. The regime relentlessly preaches the innocence of history and the guilt or ill will of the people. History, like the God of yore, has become the judge who pronounces the original sin of man.

Such are the results of the rational terror. At the beginning of the insurrection of man against arbitrary power and exploitation, rebellion started from the premise of an erring but innocent human being. The rational terror ends with the proclamation of man's "general culpability" before the demands of history and the party:

---

5. See, for example, Fauconnet's study on responsibility.

the faithful are regularly bidden to attend strange feasts where, according to scrupulous rites, victims overwhelmed with contrition are offered as sacrifice to the god of history.

Neutrality is also a crime.

Under the regime of the Empire, the man who is neutral is considered hostile objectively to the regime.[6]

Thus, the betrayed revolution produced the degrading phenomenon of general servitude and conformity. Under the constant impact of the terror and guilt propaganda, everybody was reduced, first to outward conformity, later to inner submission. The elite and the masses, in the grip of utter helplessness, found their salvation in acceptance: "The real passion of the twentieth century is servitude."[7]

In modern psychoanalytical parlance, this attitude is called masochistic withdrawal. The majority of men in a totalitarian society reacts to public affairs by passivity and fatalism. The most sensitive become listless, desperate, and conformist. The robust part of totalitarian society, on the other hand, turns fatalism upside down, and gives it a sadistic impetus, creating a climate not dissimilar to that prevalent in Islam during its most virulent periods. The energetic part of totalitarian society is gripped by a wild dynamism, a primitive élan, fully at the service of the ruling elite. Both these attitudes, the passive and the active, are characteristic of the modern totalitarian societies.

This is the most perfect transformation of living men into objects of state power. The sadistic torturer of the irrational terror fought his individual victim by trying to break his freedom. But Caesarian socialism, by proclaiming the infinite malleability of man, has created, says Camus, a new "physics of the soul" that makes the degradation complete:

6. Camus, *The Rebel*, pp. 243, 244.
7. *Ibid.*, p. 234.

Guided by a determinist hypothesis that calculates the weak points and the degree of elasticity of the soul, these new techniques have once again thrust aside one of man's limits and have attempted to demonstrate that no individual psychology is original and that the common measure of all human character is matter.[8]

This is the final result of nihilism, "the cancer of Europe." The chapter in *The Rebel* that deals with rational terror ends with a parable of tragic beauty, by which Camus expresses the cruel betrayal of socialist and humanitarian hopes by an ideology of power:

Here ends Prometheus' surprising itinerary. Proclaiming his hatred of the gods and his love of mankind, he turns away from Zeus with scorn and approaches mortal men in order to lead them in an assault against the heavens. But men are weak and cowardly: they must be organized. They love pleasure and immediate happiness; they must be taught to refuse, in order to grow up, immediate rewards. Thus Prometheus, in his turn, becomes a master who first teaches and then commands. Men doubt that they can safely attack the city of light and are even uncertain whether this city exists. They must be saved from themselves. The hero then tells them that he, and he alone, knows the city. Those who doubt his word will be thrown into the desert, chained to a rock, offered to the vultures. The others will henceforth march in darkness, behind the pensive and solitary master. Prometheus alone has become god and reigns over the solitude of men. But from Zeus he has gained only solitude and cruelty; he is no longer Prometheus, he is Caesar. The real, the eternal Prometheus has now assumed the aspect of one of his victims. The same cry, springing from the depth of the past, rings forever through the Scythian desert.[9]

3. The Problem of Violence

Characteristically, the next problem Camus takes up is that of violence or, to be more precise, of the right to resort to vio-

---

8. *Ibid.,* p. 239.
9. *Ibid.,* pp. 244–45.

lence in the face of oppression. After *The Plague,* Camus was criticized for eschewing the problem by using, as his central symbol, a disease, that is to say, a nonhuman form of oppression, which enforced solidarity and excluded violence against human beings. In *State of Siege,* in which the Plague is personified, Camus came to a more precise grasping of the problem; however, in such an extreme situation, the right to violence was taken for granted. Feeling, presumably, that he had not analyzed the question to its existential roots, Camus came back to it in *The Rebel* ("Individual Terrorism") and in his play *The Just Assassins,* performed in 1949, one year before the publication of *The Rebel* but apparently written at the same time.[1] In both his essay and his play, Camus attempts to differentiate between just and unjust violence.

The chapter devoted to anarchism in *The Rebel* ("Individual Terrorism") deals exclusively with Russian anarchists. Although the theory of the individual against society had been shaped by French and mostly German philosophers (culminating in Stirner and Nietzsche), it was in Russia that it was first carried from books to life by a handful of intellectuals amidst a silent populace.

In the absence of any clear positive theory among the Russian anarchists, Camus distinguishes three layers among them: the Decembrists, the school of Bakunin and Netchajev, and finally the initiators of individual terrorism—mostly the social revolutionary group in Russia—who touched off a wave of bomb assaults in Europe, and especially in France, in the eighteen nineties.

Of the Decembrists Camus speaks very briefly, noting that they did not see themselves as revolutionaries but as martyrs, aiming not at efficiency but at exemplary protest—an attitude that, Camus says, persisted throughout the terrorist movements.

Pisarev, Bakunin, Netchajev, and their disciples are studied more extensively. What Camus dislikes about them is their propensity to ideologies. The three main leaders of the movement were first Hegelians, then turned Hegel's method against his

---

1. In addition, he produced a stage version of Dostoievski's *The Possessed,* which deals, in part, with Netchajev's disciples.

system and claimed the individual's right to absolute freedom, to a "fullness of life,"[2] which they failed to specify. In their refusal of history, and society as its embodiment, these anarchists claimed to exercise "the power of the negative," thus rushing headlong into what Camus condemns as nihilism: rebellion for rebellion's sake, irrespective of values.

Camus then proceeds to study the three main theoreticians of nihilism, Pisarev, Bakunin, and Netchajev, with frequent references to Dostoievski's *The Possessed,* pointing out that all of them, while demanding "storm and life" and "a world without laws,"[3] ended in the glorification of dictatorship: having accepted the fatal "all or nothing," they became the "cruel high priests of a desperate revolution," "an order of murderers" or "the contemptuous aristocrats of the revolution," whose heirs exercise power in today's Soviet Union. But, Camus asks, is a lawless world identical with a free world? There is little doubt as to his answer. By turning revolt into a fetish, the rebels lost sight of their initial experiences, and revolution "explicitly separated from love and friendship" went the way of dictatorship.[4]

As to the last group, which he calls "les meurtriers délicats" ("fastidious murderers"), Camus had in mind here the terrorist groups called "Will of the People" or "Russian Social Revolutionaries," who were responsible for the murder of Tsar Alexander II and Grand Duke Sergei. Camus is ambivalent about them, but shows enough sympathetic interest in their case to depart for the first time from his own concept of true revolt. Theirs had been a real and personal problem for Camus during the Resistance, when he knew that for every assault against the occupying authorities, innocent hostages would be shot. It would be of no use to argue that Camus never caused such deaths by murdering a German official with his own hands, for he surely considered that anyone who participated in the Resistance or regarded it

---

2. *The Rebel,* p. 152.
3. Dostoievski's phrase *The Possessed* became the subtitle of a section in *The Rebel* ("Three of the Possessed"), p. 153.
4. *The Rebel,* pp. 160, 163, 158, 161.

as legitimate shared in the responsibility. The blood of innocent hostages was on their hands. The choice was between submission and the death of others. Risking one's own life was the only extenuating circumstance. Camus experienced this problem in full when, in starting to write for *Combat,* he chose freedom at the price of murder. Hence his interest in the "fastidious murderers" or, as he calls them in the play, the "Just Assassins."

Camus perceives the nihilistic trend in this kind of revolt, which, in Russia, ended in Chigalev's ruthless doctrine: "Nihilism, intimately involved with a frustrated religious movement, thus culminates in terrorism." However, Camus is impressed by the scruples and nobility of this unusual group of terrorists (Kaliayev refraining from throwing his bomb at the Grand Duke's carriage because two children were sitting in it), as well as by their courage and solidarity—their chivalrous spirit, as he calls it—and their hope that, by their sacrifice, they would save the indifferent people from both tyranny and inertia. Since then, Camus says, men have become accustomed to sacrificing themselves for "an ideal of which they knew nothing, except that it was necessary to die so that it might exist." Having experienced "the Rebel's destiny, in its most contradictory form," they "demonstrated for the last time in our history that real rebellion is creator of values."[5]

Here, a basic ambiguity appears in Camus's thought. Are values created by revolt, or merely discovered in the act of revolt, as preexistent to it and vested in human nature? The second hypothesis is that of Camus in the theoretical chapters of *The Rebel.* Here, on the other hand, when speaking of those values of which one knows nothing except that it is necessary to die in order that they may exist, Camus leans dangerously toward one form of what he himself regards as nihilism, namely, turning formal virtue into an absolute. Here, this formal virtue is self-sacrifice. Not everything for which men are willing to die is holy, and giving away one's life does not exculpate one from murder. Only one consideration can exculpate them, and that is the enor-

---

5. *Ibid.,* pp. 165, 166, 169, 172.

mity of the oppression, which leaves them no choice. Having indulged for a time the romantic fate of murderers who are as careful with other people's lives as they are reckless with their own, he finally asserts that their ultimate justification is that they are fighting oppression of such a nature that the means available to them are extremely limited. In this respect—mostly in view of the general apathy of the population—their situation is similar to that of the Spanish republicans or the French resistance groups, among which Camus learned the tragic dialectic of freedom, murder, and sacrifice. In other words, the paradox offered by this group of rebels has confused Camus's usual lucidity by tempting him with the kind of extreme ambiguity that fascinated him: absolute respect for the life of others, absolute disregard for one's own; absolute respect for innocent life (the Grand Duke's children), absolute right to take the life of the guilty. Lucidity prevails, however, in fact, if not in words; both Camus and his heroes escape the coils of ethical formalism. For the rebel's obstinate clinging to extreme poles of the ambiguous experience of revolt has one very concrete meaning. Whoever is able to live out this contradiction is *not* made of one piece, is *not* a dogmatic man, a man of ideologies. He is human. While living for an idea, he bears in mind the human consequences of his acts. He might temporarily place principles above life, but he remembers that men's happiness is the supreme principle and that its denial is an "unnecessary and unjustifiable" exception. This is why the person who can keep both extremes in mind—performing the murder and detesting it—even if he errs tragically in his conduct, keeps his human integrity, "the spirit of compassion," in contrast to the modern nihilists, whom Camus defines as follows:

Mediocre minds, confronted with this terrible problem, can take refuge by ignoring one of the terms of the dilemma. They are content, in the name of formal principles, to find all direct violence inexcusable and then to sanction that diffuse form of violence which takes place on the scale of world history. Or they will console themselves, in the name of history, with the thought that violence is necessary, and will add murder to murder, to the point of making history nothing but a continuous violation of everything in man which protests against injustice. This defines the two aspects of contemporary nihilism, the bourgeois and the revolutionary.[6]

What Camus finds most tragic about Russian anarchists, at any rate those of the first and third groups, is that, although they succeeded, by their very sacrifice, in incarnating "a new value or virtue which did not cease even today to challenge tyranny and help true liberation,"[7] the historical outcome was not in keeping with their expectations. *The Rebel*'s chapter ends with Chigalev paving the way for Lenin; *The Just Assassins* ends with similar doubts and premonitions.

Camus's ambiguous attitude toward anarchy reflects his own contradictory thoughts about the legitimacy of violence. Thus, Camus was a passionate supporter of the Spanish republicans, and only tuberculosis prevented him from fighting on their side. On the other hand, he opposed the war against Hitler, on the ground that the Versailles Treaty had been an injustice, and that all efforts at conciliation had not been brought to bear. He had to see France actually occupied and crushed before he joined, wholeheartedly, in the Resistance, with feelings presumably akin to those of *The Just Assassins*. He does not seem to suspect that a minimum of preventive violence in 1936 would have saved millions of lives three years later.

This contradiction may be due to Camus's mistrust of large organized groups resting on *de facto* power. "I do not like institutionalized violence," Camus said to an interviewer. "Neither states nor parties (including revolutionary parties) are innocent, for the simple reason that they wield power, or have wielded it and misused it at one point." Camus is primarily a pacifist and, if necessary, a partisan; least of all he is a soldier or a militant; but as an enraged quietist, he views with indulgence—though within strict limits—the acts of small self-appointed groups of

---

6. *Ibid.,* p. 169.
7. *Ibid.,* p. 183.

individual terrorists, bound together by their common horror of humiliation and injustice. The underdog is always right, and he alone has the right to violence, always within limits. This oversimplification accounts for much of Camus's political illogicalities. Although he watches closely for the moment when the underdog becomes the overdog and loses his rights together with his innocence, this moment is not always easy to determine. This could be the clue to Camus's changing attitude toward the Algerian revolutionaries: he showed understanding for the terrorist FLN as long as they were fighting a desperate battle against a strong colonial power; he blamed them when they turned terror into a system and coerced their fellow Algerians into practicing of indiscriminate violence. This is in keeping with the Rebel's doctrine, but who can say whether Camus would have been so perceptive had he not been born a French Algerian.

Failure to identify the overdog can be detected in Camus's romantic bias for the revolution and his equally romantic dislike of "capitalist countries." Here, many examples come to mind of the intricacies arising from Camus's unrealistic conviction that the underdog is always right, especially in his attitude toward international Communism. He was among the first to perceive that communist power was increasing and he did not share the complacency of most of his fellow intellectuals toward the sins of the Communist bloc. He nevertheless reproved resistance by "capitalist countries," so strong was his pro-revolutionary bias, encouraged by postwar slogans ("un anticommuniste est un chien: l'anticommunisme est le commencement du fascisme"), that for a long time he could not go further than to regard both camps as equally guilty.[8] In spite of his loathing of Soviet methods, and even after he had lost all hope for a change, as shown in *The Rebel,* he maintained the fiction of equal responsibilities of both camps, until the crushing of the Hungarian revolution led him definitely to side with the West. Had he lived through the stormy sixties, it is impossible to predict whether Camus would have

8. See Pierre Nora "Pour une autre explication de *L'Etranger,*" in *France Observateur* (Paris, January 5, 1961), p. 12.

sided with Third World countries and their New Left defenders at home. This sort of "fiat justicia, pereat mundus"—justice being understood as no coercion—is the greatest paradox in Camus's ethics. His ethics rests on preservation of life, entirely disregarding the fact that if "institutionalized violence" had been applied in time, endless massacres could have been avoided. Had not Camus reached an impasse in his political thought when the international situation began to change after the publication of *The Rebel?*

10
The Outcry

After the publication of *The Rebel,* Camus found himself under the crossfire of many opponents led by the existentialists group round *Les Temps Modernes;* Jeanson, soon followed by Sartre, criticized Camus in the magazine, while later Simone de Beauvoir in *Les Mandarins* gave a satirical portrait of him as a vacillating intellectual, mainly interested in big words and young girls. Their reproaches can be summed up as follows: on the philosophical plane, hollowness and confusion; on the political plane, ignorance of economic facts, a disregard for concrete political exigencies, and an untimely insistence on "academic principles." In short, Camus was reproached for incompetence and utopia, aggravated by bourgeois smugness; the main reproach, however, was his "betrayal" of the Marxist creed.

Camus's answers printed in *Les Temps Modernes* and reprinted in *Actuelles* go a long way toward clarifying not only his own attitude toward the main political issues of our day, but also these issues themselves, distorted by too much passionate discussion. Camus's approach to these questions is characteristic. His chief method is dissociation. Time and again, as he defends *The Rebel* against criticism, he distinguishes between the intellectual and the emotional content of his opponents' arguments, weighing the one, unraveling the other. In so doing, he explodes many political fallacies that had gained ground since the Soviet revolution, especially certain fictitious antinomies in which the absolutist mind is prone to enclose itself. "Either—or," says the absolutist. Either justice or freedom, either sterile individualism or party discipline, either bread for everyone or high principles. Camus refuses all these "either-ors" as oversimplifications of the abstract mind, and his effort to rediscover the original human motives under layers of theoretical accretions may well be one of the most important attempts at clarification in present-day European political thinking. Even an interval of two decades has not made it irrelevant.

The most dangerous of these false antinomies created by the abstract mind is, in Camus's eyes, that of justice and freedom put forth by the Jacobins and perfected by the Leninists. It runs as follows: Freedom remains our cherished aim. But, man being what he is (or the historical situation being what it is), freedom has to be sacrificed, "temporarily," for the sake of justice. Camus does not limit himself to showing that this temporary sacrifice tends to become a final holocaust; he challenges the validity of the antinomy itself, a perfect product of the abstract mind.

Why separate freedom and justice, as if they were incompatible? The true rebel demands that his political, economic, and human rights be respected, in other words, that his ruler's whims and power be curtailed. But he also claims a right to fight for his due according to his own lights, and to understand it in his own way. It is freedom that provides the possibility of protesting. Freedom is what guarantees human communication. "The dialogue," as Camus calls it, is in his view the prerequisite for all civilized existence. Inspired by the same ideal, Marx and the utopian socialists had protested against the "reification" of man by capitalism (*Verdinglichung*). But, now, the "rational terror" denies this most important prerogative of the human spirit: man's capacity to decide for himself where his own good lies. It disturbs all human relations by propaganda which is the monologue of the ruling elite. This abandonment of the idea of freedom by the revolutionary party is, according to Camus, the gravest tragedy of the twentieth century. A great hope has disappeared from the world, and with all meaning lost, utter loneliness spreads in the hearts of millions of our contemporaries.

True, whatever the Communist Party removes from freedom it claims to sacrifice on the altar of justice. But to choose freedom does not mean to abandon justice. In fact, the opposite is true. To abandon freedom is to reject justice.

> Si quelqu'un vous retire votre pain, il supprime en même temps votre liberté. Mais si quelqu'un vous ravit votre liberté, soyez tranquille, votre pain est menacé, car il ne dépend plus de vous et de votre lutte, mais du bon plaisir d'un maître. La misère croît a mesure que la liberté recule dans le monde, et inversement.[1]

There exists a subtle interrelationship in every society between the demand for justice and the demand for freedom. And it is not permissible, in the context of socialism, to subordinate freedom to justice as a means to an end. The false antinomy of freedom and justice entirely distorts the original idea of socialism. Camus quotes Ernestan's sentence: "If socialism is an eternal evolution, its means are its ends."[2] In fact, Camus denies the very existence of an "end" in the complexity of the historical process. Here, he tries to unearth a central fallacy in Marxist thought. Its dialectic, the author of *The Rebel* maintains, is "only nihilism—pure movement that aims at denying everything which is not itself."[3] This is why this kind of dialectic can so easily be misused for purposes of mystification.

Caesarian socialism has upset the true dialectical relationship between freedom and justice by proclaiming history the only value and by invoking "an imperialism of justice," an absolute end, justifying any means:

The revolution of the twentieth century has arbitrarily separated,

---

1. *Actuelles II,* pp. 167–68.
2. *The Rebel,* p. 224.
3. *Ibid.*

for over-ambitious ends of conquest, two inseparable ideas.
Absolute freedom mocks at justice. Absolute justice denies
freedom. To be fruitful, the two ideas must find their limits in
each other. . . . there is a justice, though a very different kind
of justice, in restoring freedom, which is the only imperishable
value of history.[4]

Absolute freedom means titanic romanticism, as analyzed in
the section on Nietzsche. It would give power to the strongest, it
would be the rule of absolute injustice, whereas absolute justice
attempted by the Jacobins, and once more by Leninism, would
mean the abolition of all contradictions, arrest and impede the
dialectical process of life itself, and establish a *rigor mortis*. Both
are manifestations of impotence, divorced from the real issues of
life. Here Camus follows Jean Grenier's comment in his *Entretiens
sur le bon usage de la liberté,* that absolute freedom would be the
destruction of all values, while, conversely, the demand for absolute
justice would mean the destruction of all freedom. Some Renaissance and Protestant philosophers used a similar argument against
their Catholic opponents. If there is absolute truth, the argument
ran, freedom has no reason to exist. The same applies to the
absolute truths of Marx-Leninism. The belief in an absolute
truth is precisely what Camus calls "abstraction": it tends to
isolate and freeze up important areas of the living sources of
the spirit.

The second false antinomy that Camus distinguishes is that of
individual conscience and party discipline. In certain respects
it coincides with the broader antinomy of freedom and justice,
since the question arises whether ethical judgments should prevail
at the risk of jeopardizing the party's chances of establishing
justice (by first achieving success). This old debate about truth
and *raison d'Etat* was to be revived, at the time of the *Temps
Modernes* controversy, by David Rousset, who had aroused public
opinion by making available data about Soviet concentration
camps. This is also the question debated by Henri in *Les Man-*

4. *Ibid.,* p. 291.

darins. The general tone of these polemics is not edifying. At one point the attacks against Camus in *Temps Modernes* become charged with so much personal animosity that one cannot help thinking that Camus's analysis had touched a more sensitive spot in his opponent than regard for Marx or Hegel. Perhaps the essence of the misunderstanding between Sartre and Camus should not be sought in their political attitudes, but in the recesses of their respective personalities as explored by themselves in *The Words* and *The Right and the Wrong Side of Things.* The critic Thibaudet, speaking of some writers' reactions to the Dreyfus Affair, coined the phrase "left-wing childhoods"; he was trying to establish some natural predispositions to docility or revolt. However, such natural dispositions do not necessarily coincide with economic conditions. Whether proletarian or bourgeois, some childhood experiences lead to later revolt because the child feels threatened or frustrated in its very being. Even when postponed until adolescence, as in the case of Sartre, such revolts are usually implacable and total, as if carried away by their very irrationality.

On the other hand, it frequently happens in the poorest families, that children enjoy security and self respect. Such was the case with many left-wing writers prior to Camus: with Charles Péguy, Jean Guéhenno, and Louis Guilloux, for whose book Camus wrote a preface. This also was the case of Camus himself. He was brought up, like his predecessors, in artisan surroundings. Security and self-respect in work are the first demands such men are likely to make upon society. From revolutions they demand the creation of a just and stable order; for them a revolution is not savage revenge against bourgeois meaninglessness and all established order. Such people are the typical anti-utopians, predisposed to reform, not to the destruction of all that is.

Camus and pro-Communist groups had been close friends in the resistance. They had shared the same hopes and indignation at the sight of humiliation and crime, the same admiration for the part played by the Communists in the struggle. Then, many had been caught in the dilemma of *Les Mains Sales,* when postwar power politics replaced wartime heroism. Camus solved the problem in an uncompromising way, by refusing to sacrifice moral principles, even temporarily, to necessities. At this point one could argue that Camus was not betraying the working class but denouncing Moscow for doing so, as Sartre himself was to do a few years later, after the Hungarian revolution. The truth is, however, that Camus felt no loyalty to the working class as class—that is to say, as a power group. He felt loyal to the workers as human beings whose dignity was trampled on. In so doing he follows the principles of classical humanism and also his own theory of rebellion, according to which a doctrine that singles out one part of mankind as the bearer of a holy mission becomes an "abstraction" and, by the encouragement it gives to the collective power instinct, a justification of "crimes of logic."

In *Actuelles III,* Camus applies the same criterion to the case of the Arab rebellion in Algiers. And he takes great pains to clarify his attitude on this point: he backs the Arabs as men whose human rights have been ignored, but he refuses to follow them and is even ready to fight them when they behave as a chauvinistic power group.

Thus Camus has found a way of circumventing the well-worn dilemma of ends and means. The real question in his eyes is what the end actually is. Camus knows only too well that, as Lenin said, "when forests are being felled, splinters will fly." And he is ready to accept this necessity. What he finds revolting, however, is the indifference shown to the splinters by the devotees of efficiency. Their crime is precisely to regard the victims of "the historical process" as mere "splinters"—or even as "objectively guilty" of obstruction. This is no crime of passion. It is not even, as Sartre believes, a crime of negligence committed by people who are busy building up an empire. It is the perfect crime of logic; for the logic of genuine rebellion says that a human being is not the raw material of the historical process, but the aim of this process. And the so-called "negligence" presupposes exactly the opposite belief: it reveals a tendency to the "reification" of man, which constitutes the typical crime of logic.

Camus's own practical solution to this problem, as he works

it out in *Actuelles,* is austere to the point of formalism. One has a right to kill in defense of human dignity, he says, but only on condition that one is willing to stake one's own life. One might be tempted to regard such scruples as exaggerated in a fight directed, for instance, against Nazi torturers. But what Camus wants above all is that, whatever the circumstances, murder should keep "son caractère d'infraction honteuse." And he feels that the security of human life has to be reasserted more firmly than ever in times of revolution. For, the moment a revolutionary becomes *reconciled* to the idea of murdering for the Cause, he loses the genuine sense of rebellion, which aims at creation and preservation, not at destruction. Thus, for the true rebel, there may be a tragic opposition between ends and means, but there could not be any antinomy of the kind construed by the abstract mind.

The second reproach leveled against Camus, that of ignoring the concrete economic aspects of political questions, cannot be disposed of as creating a false antinomy or resting on abstraction. It is an argument *ad hominem.* It is, of course, grossly unfair to accuse him of indifference to working-class misery because he does not deal with economic problems in *The Rebel.* But it can be regretted that an analysis of political aberrations in our time does not mention this important element. Thus, Camus ignores the specific economic (and political) aspects of Czarist Russia when trying to elucidate Lenin's conception of the Revolution. Another shortcoming of Camus's thinking in this field is his complete disregard of the problem of social organization. A writer who undertakes to analyze the ills of his time cannot concern himself exclusively with abstract therapy. If he does so, he does not fully reflect the problems of his time.

We must not forget, however, that Camus did not undertake to give an exhaustive analysis of the causes of our predicament. He is not an economist but a psychologist, and any writer is free to choose whatever aspect of a question he likes, provided that he does not try to validate his conclusions by denying the importance of other aspects. In the present case, Camus does not deny the importance of material want in the development of mass

nihilism; he rather takes it for granted. His own experience of
misery made him fully conversant with the subject and he had
shown no signs of bourgeois smugness since fortune smiled on
him. He just left out the economic aspects of the problems because he felt more competent to deal with the others.

The same applies to the solution Camus advocates. He does
not oppose the economic system of socialism. He surely agrees
with much of the Marxist analysis of the capitalist system. Nor
does he tackle the idle question of whether one should first alter
the economic situation, or change the heart of man. Of course,
material considerations should come first, since there is no spiritual
ideal for hungry stomachs. But material improvement comes first
in the order of necessity, not in the order of value. That is why
the antinomy of the Yogi and the Commissar is a pseudo-prob-
lem, invented again by the devotees of efficiency to conceal their
lack of interest in human values. Once more, the abstract mind
creates spurious antinomies where there is only a question of
priorities.

Camus does not limit himself to exploding the fallacies of the
absolutist mind and restoring the free play of the dialectical
process. According to his familiar method, he distinguishes the
emotional from the logical elements in his opponent's philosophy.
What lies behind this denial of freedom for the sake of justice, of
individual conscience for group loyalty, of spiritual for material
considerations? According to Camus it is despair and loneliness,
compensated by a wish to create the absolute unity of which
man is deprived by the absurd universe. This yearning for totality
can be found at the bottom of all nihilistic creeds, whether on
the level of the instincts, as in National Socialism, or on the
level of total justice, as in Lenin's fanaticism of the State. Justice
so conceived is nothing more than a grandiose and misguided
desire to achieve meaning in an absurd universe. Meaningful
unity, in Camus's sense, can be achieved only through a solidarity
born of the fight for human dignity, whereas totalitarian yearnings
are only perverted and misguided attempts by nihilists to transcend
the solitude to which man is condemned since the loss of his

religious and metaphysical creeds. Totality is a vain attempt to recapture the lost unity. By the Jacobin revolution as well as by the Hegelian-Marxist-Leninist revolution, man had freed himself from the rule of a whimsical Providence. But instead of searching for the difficult unity born of solidarity with others, modern man has handed over his freedom to the power of Caesar for the sake of his fallacious promises. The struggle today is between Caesarism and genuine rebellion. Rebellion does not offer any fixed or formal value like Jacobin "virtue" or Communist "justice." It offers only an incentive to those who have preserved the integrity of the rebel's initial experience.

11

The Rebel in Politics:
The Psychologist and the Moralist

1. A New Approach: Psychoanalysis of the Revolutionary Spirit

The most original part of Camus's political message is his special treatment of the psychology of politics, or rather his psychoanalysis of revolutionary movements. Camus takes great care to distinguish between the inner revolutionary message and subsequent accretions. Here, many questions can be asked. Do there exist collective neuroses, which by the mechanism of rationalization give rise to mass ideologies? And, if so, what is neurotic and what is nonneurotic in politics? Moreover, the concept of neurosis can be understood only with reference to an assumed state of normalcy. What, then, can be considered normal, or sane, in ethics and politics, by a man who does not believe in revelation, either divine or scientific?

What is neurotic and nonneurotic in ethics and politics? Here, Camus is fully original. He does not argue that normalcy consists in having this or that so-called natural feeling or thought (everything that exists is natural). Nor does he consider normal what has always been done, or what is done by "everybody," by the majority. In fact, he cares little for normal and nonnormal. His definition of neurosis and sanity in politics is precisely that of individual psychopathology, although he does not take the trouble to define this point clearly. To be neurotic is to live under some inner compulsion, usually unconscious, at least as to its origins. To be neurotic is to be deprived of one's free will by some compulsion not consciously felt as such. Not knowing and not wanting to know that he is enslaved, the neurotic builds rationalizations. Camus's method consists in analyzing these rationalizations by mercilessly isolating from every political philosophy its unconscious, compulsive elements. These neurotic components are already known: resentment, the sense of guilt, humiliation, alienation, loneliness, despair. Similarly, there are neurotic remedies, such as glorification of the power instinct or the insane resentment at humanitarian solutions. Underneath political theories, Camus unearths a wish to punish, or a wish to demonstrate to man his utter abjectness, by rubbing his nose in it, as Caligula does. It should be noted that in his analysis Camus does not condemn these feelings as such: he does not say that resentment or a sense of guilt are wrong *per se;* they can be perfectly legitimate. He regards them as dangerous when they assume a compulsive character which points to some unconscious conflict.

Political neuroses, like individual ones, have a specific odor: their power component makes them frantic, absolute, given to *hubris;* the elements of resentment and guilt in them make them cruel; the unconscious character of all these trends gives rise to a need for rationalization and justification that leads to *crime de logique;* finally, all neuroses entail a loss of contact with reality; all political neurotics are paranoids of one kind of another, and the neurotic "realists" are the most paranoid of all, because the kind of scientific rationalism they have chosen makes them deny even scientific facts.

If neurosis is defined by inner compulsion, lack of lucidity, and lack of realism, then the sane attitude in politics is one that involves lucidity, the use of one's inner freedom, and acceptance of unpleasant realities. Once more, we encounter the two prongs of man's genuine revolt: proud assertion of his Promethean gifts, and modest acceptance of his limits.

Camus's main demand on political theoreticians is that they be not neurotic. Apart from that, one can assume that he is an eclectic. He may have his own preferences, but he would not feel entitled to impose them on others, not only from an innate tolerance and respect for another man's freedom, not only from fear of systems, but because he believes that plurality of opinions in a society is salutary. It is the neurotic who, by his wish for unity, tries to stop the dialectical process of life. This is probably the last word of Camus's political philosophy: eclecticism, within the limits of sanity. The practical value of this attitude now has to be considered.

2. An Old Approach: The Moralist in Practical Politics

After following Camus's analysis of political aberrations in our time, we come to the question his somewhat elusive thought invariably suggests to friends and foes alike: What does he concretely advocate? He does, of course, favor a moral attitude that corresponds broadly to that of humanistic, non-Marxist, socialism. Socialism means for him a society "qui serait en même temps heureuse et digne, qui voudrait que les hommes soient libres dans une condition enfin juste."[1]

But how does he expect to bring it about? How does his criterion of genuine revolt apply to the political situation of today; how does it help against tyranny and injustice? Many critics feel that Camus's answers on these points are vague, and they regret that one of the noblest writers of our time does not offer a more precise message.

In his *Problems of Ethics,*[2] Moritz Schlick distinguishes between the moralist and the philosopher of ethics. The aim of the philosopher of ethics is knowledge and nothing else. The moralist,

---

1. *Actuelles II,* p. 153.
2. Moritz Schlick, *Problems of Ethics* (New York: Prentice Hall, Inc., 1939), pp. 1–2.

on the other hand, wants to edify, preach, attack, and defend values. In *The Rebel,* in which Camus attempts to do both these things, his contribution to the epistemology of political philosophy remains full of ambiguities; as a moralist, however, he deserves in many ways to be called the witness and conscience of our time. He is not primarily interested in practical issues of politics. Although for many years he worked as a political journalist and left no major problem of our time untouched, his interest centers on principles more than on practical results. He is not a theoretician of politics either, for in all problems, be they those of war and peace, relations with Moscow or Washington, or the Algerian war, one feels that although his principles are inflexible, his solutions are *ad hoc*. They do not proceed from any political theory, let alone a party program. Of course one could hardly expect a man of Camus's disposition to produce a system or even a systematic program. *Actuelles* is essentially a series of concrete examples of how men of good will could, by rule of thumb, "reintroduce morality into politics."

To that effect, he thinks a "new social contract" is necessary, the first law of which must be the safeguarding of free speech. We have to fight fear and silence everywhere, and destroy the walls between men. There is no humanity without "a dialogue." The second clause of this new social contract should be the abolition of the death penalty, by which society treats man as "a parcel" (un paquet). Life is fragile, tenuous, and relative. Therefore we have no right to kill, not even to execute criminals. All conscious life is tragic and sacred.

As far as social organization is concerned, Camus relies mainly on the idea of revolutionary trade unions. Political problems should, in his opinion, be solved inside the factory or profession, where people know each other and have concrete problems calling for concrete solutions, without interference of abstract ideological issues. The driving force should be an individualism transformed into solidarity.

> This individualism . . . is perpetual struggle. As for knowing

if such an attitude can find political expression in the contemporary world, it is easy to evoke . . . what is traditionally called revolutionary trade unionism. . . . Trade unionism started from the concrete basis. . . . Trade unionism, like the Commune, is the negation, to the benefit of reality, of bureaucratic and abstract centralism. . . . The revolution of the twentieth century, on the contrary, claims to base itself on economics, but is primarily political and ideological. . . . It begins in the absolute and attempts to mold reality. . . . Rebellion relies on reality to assist it in its perpetual struggle for truth. . . . Rebellion . . . takes the part of true realism. . . . Politics, to satisfy the demands of rebellion, must submit to the eternal verities.[3]

It is regrettable that Camus's ideas on trade unionism and his emphasis on "natural" communities remain confined within the Continental tradition. In his groping for "natural communities," Camus follows Tolstoï and Kropotkin; and, we may assume, Proudhon, as well as the tradition of French *Syndicalisme révolutionnaire,* still alive before the war. It is characteristic of the insularity of French political theory since the First World War that the author of *The Rebel* probably never heard of Guild socialism as propounded by G. D. H. Cole, or of the pluralistic socialism propagated in his earlier writings by Harold Laski in England. Neither in *The Rebel* nor in the many discussions following the publication of the book did Camus or any of his supporters or detractors even mention the concept of Guild socialism. Had Camus been familiar with this trend of thought within Fabian socialism on the other side of the Channel, this could have given a more practical turn to his advocacy of a *koinonia* for an industrial society.[4] This lack of concreteness of his theories increases the impression that Camus's "revolutionary trade unionism" is inadequate, feeble, and sentimental—a relic

---

3. Camus, *The Rebel,* pp. 297–98.
4. In contrast to Camus's utopian approach, R. Aron in his *Leçons sur la Société industrielle* and his numerous other works shows a thorough acquaintance with Anglo-Saxon political thinking.

from the nineteenth century quite unfit to solve the intricate problems of a mass society.

Interference by the state should, then, be reduced to a minimum. In this Camus approaches sentimental anarchism of the Tolstoian, or Kropotkin types, with all their pitfalls and infantilisms, clothed in a new philosophical language and somewhat adjusted to the experience of our decades. Hence all the quips about the "Red Cross state" so frequently applied to Camus's works. Camus almost entirely disregards the problems of social organization, of the whole intricate structure of power needed by any social group that wishes to hold together and perform social and economic functions.

The question arises whether Camus does not misunderstand the power instinct altogether. He distinguishes correctly between revolt and resentment, and understands the effects of humiliation and resentment on the historical process. But he does not differentiate between revolt and the pure power drive. This is the weakest spot in his analysis. He recognizes crimes of passion; all others he regards as crimes of logic, the results of abstraction and nihilism. But he forgets about crimes of power, which blend compulsive greed and the coolness of logic. The specific character of power, its incurability, escapes him. More serious still, he does not realize that group power works as a crude and blind mechanism and that, even though "reason" can sometimes be forced into the mind of a power-ridden individual, power-ridden groups will not be deterred by abstract fear, but only—if at all —by threat of immediate retaliation. Indeed, Camus does not seem to be quite aware of the fact that power is not just a historical or transitory phenomenon in the evolution of social groups, but an essential category, an indispensable evil without which any society—let alone the complex industrial society of the industrial age—would simply stop functioning.[5]

---

5. This subject has been treated extensively by Bertrand Russell in *Power; a New Social Analysis* (London: George Allen and Unwin Ltd., 1938), partly to offset the doctrinal optimism concerning the withering away of the State in a future socialist society. Camus feels

This lack of understanding of the power instinct may be the reason Sartre and others so mercilessly criticize Camus for his lack of realism. Moreover, a writer who wants to "understand his time" cannot be spared the reproach of not having dealt with the question of how freedom, justice, and tolerance can be safeguarded and extended in the modern industrial and social systems.

3. The Moralist and the Sociologist

In this fight, which was to be Camus's last, it would be interesting to compare Camus to a social thinker with a positive bent of mind and attached to humanitarian Western values—Raymond Aron, the well-known French sociologist and one of the last liberal theoreticians of the West.

Aron does not require any introduction to American students of sociology and political thought. The bulk of his vast body of thought is now available in English, and even his adversaries do not question his enormous erudition and his intellectual acumen. Camus, the political moralist, was probably quite unfamiliar with Aron's prolific and incisive writings. Yet, some important similarities between the lyrical poet and the positive sociologist have been pointed out by Roy Pierce.[6] The points of contact or full agreement touch upon Camus's main ideas: the refusal of political Utopia and chiliasm, the refusal of hollow and pretentious abstractions, the stress on relativism of all political thought and action, and finally loyalty to Western values and faith in Western political institutions.

All utopian thinking seems to both thinkers childish and dangerous, breeding false hopes and eventually violence. (And no additional volumes by Sartre on the Dialectical Reason can talk away the fact that Marxism as interpreted by the "Left Bank

---

equally skeptical as regards the communist state, but implies that such withering away could take place in an anarchistic society based on "natural groups."

6. Roy Pierce, *Contemporary French Political Thought* (New York: Oxford University Press, 1966).

ideologues" is anything but utopian as soon as it leaves the solid ground of analysis and begins to promise a "second stage of socialism" or the "jumping out of historical necessity into the realm of freedom.") In this respect, Camus and Aron are almost identical. As far as the dislike of "abstraction" is concerned, Aron's sociology provides a much-needed theoretical support for Camus's thought. As already seen, Camus defines "abstraction" in *The Rebel* as the propensity to isolate one aspect of human "nature" and turn it into a fetish. Aron does not deal with human nature but with the nature, or essence, of a given society. One of his most original contributions to sociological thought and thereby to the sociology of political thought is certainly his notion of "social wholes."[7] The concept emphasizes the structural unity of *all* the components of a specific social and political system. According to Aron, there is an essence inscribed, or imprinted, in each social and political regime, which constitutes its inherent structure. The usefulness of this concept may be gauged when applying it to concrete political opinions and actions. Aron's criticism in this respect ranges from eye-opening truisms, (e.g., "one cannot desire the advantages of capitalism and destroy the capitalists," and "one cannot reject technology and expect the eradication of poverty,") to his radical challenge of current illusions: "one cannot desire dictatorial political controls and expect liberty."[8] And Aron contends even more devastatingly: "the Left Bank intellectual Marxists are partisans of a regime never yet seen, which would be both as strictly organized as that of the East and as liberal as the institutions of the West,"[9] or: "the

---

7. Aron's concept of "social wholes" is broader than Max Weber's ideal types of society. Its origins can be found in Tocqueville and mostly in Montesquieu's search for the "principle" of a government, that is: what makes it what it is, such as "virtue" for a republic or "honor" in a monarchy. For Aron—and Camus—the "principle" of democracy is liberty.

8. Raymond Aron, *Opium des intellectuels* (Paris: Calmann-Levy, 1955), p. 169; and *La lutte des classes* (Paris: Gallimard, 1969), p. 173.

9. Cours de Sorbonne, Paris, 1963, p. 160. Also *Les Etapes de la pensée sociologique,* (Paris: Gallimard, 1967), p. 250.

Marxists are trying to establish an ideal society with fragments borrowed from the most diverse regimes but no doctrine is "more dangerously utopian," and moreover, "political and social wholes have their own structure; they cannot be dissociated into elements and rebuilt or reshuffled at will." In other words, according to Taine's well-known formula, one cannot build a constitution as one builds a house, according to the simplest and most practical layout. In this respect, "Left Bank intellectuals" tend to act like a farmer who would pull apart a cow and a horse in order to construct a more satisfactory animal. This is not Utopia, although it can proceed from it, but a lack of perception of the self-contained, resistant character of social structures.

In his *Opium of the Intellectuals,* Aron analyzes such abstractions as the "revolution," the "proletariat," and "hierarchy," and tries to demythologize many of the political concepts of the Left and Right, showing that they are meaningless, pure fictions in the sense of Feuerbach. But their lack of concrete meaning does not prevent them from becoming powerful disruptive forces, leading to terror, violence, and destruction. And Aron shows conclusively, as did Camus in his deliberation on the rational terror of the Soviet Union, that the simple transfer of means of production to the State will not change an iota as far as the dignity of the daily life of the workers or citizens at large is concerned.

Camus did not perceive this structural intractability of institutions. When he criticizes "abstraction"—the tendency to single out one principle (such as "justice" or "freedom") and endow it with supreme value—he sees in it a failure to perceive the imperfection of human nature. His vague theory of "measure" or "balance" can probably best be substantiated by the sociologist's insight into the structure of "social wholes": not Nature but the nature of human communities supplies the criterion of what is possible.

The rejection of both Utopia and abstraction leads to relativism. Society can never be tailored to man's needs. "Relativism is the authentic experience of politics," Aron writes,[10] and Camus advo-

---

10. *Opium of the Intellectuals,* p. 169.

cates "an active consent to the relative."[11] As far as the role of values in politics is concerned, the similarity between the two writers is all the more striking since they started from opposite poles. Aron started from Max Weber's concept of "valueless science." He nevertheless realized that, as a citizen and as a man, he was committed to the defense of values. The dividing line was clear: value judgments must be excluded from the analysis of society, but such analysis is meaningless if it does not lead to the improvement of society by the enforcement of values. Science is value-blind, the citizen is not; but both fields must be kept divided, lest abstraction and Utopia rule. Aron's unequivocal warning in *Opium of the Intellectuals* is that the reality principle is inescapable.

Camus came from exactly the opposite direction. Values were paramount to him. He had little use for reality; like almost everyone else, he was a political utopian in his youth and painfully learned the lesson of facts. His ethical demands were never forgotten, but he gradually came to regard them as guides, rather than absolute, workable goals. This painful evolution, initiated with *The Plague,* gradually led Camus to insist on conservation of what is irreplaceable in Western institutions, as well as in the values they embody. What values? Here, again, the agreement between Aron and Camus is complete: Freedom, of course, is the main value, but freedom is vague enough to include Caligula's freedom. Camus's concept of relative freedom is defined by its limits. "Restraint"—as a cosmic principle—is his answer both to Caligula and to the perfectionists of virtue. Translated into political terms, this means freedom of criticism, the willingness to let the opponent live and speak. This is what liberals mean by democracy. But, here again, when it comes to finding the correct relation between value and the institutions in which it can be embodied, Camus fails to focus his thought on relevant issues, while the sociologist has been trained to do just this.

"The essence of Western culture," writes Aron, "the principle of its triumphs, the source of its radiance, is liberty. Not universal

---

11. *The Rebel,* p. 290.

suffrage, a late and debatable institution of the political order, not the parliamentary jousting, a procedure, among others, of government by opinion; but the liberty of research and of criticism, progressively conquered, of which the historical conditions have been the duality of temporal power and spiritual power, the limitation of state authority, the autonomy of the universities."[12]

Institutions are defined functionally, not formally; what is needed is a device, whatever it is, whereby "the limitation of state authority" can be achieved. This limitation, not universal suffrage, is the essence of Western democracy, whose active principle is liberty. Such a radical analysis is alien to Camus. When faced with a problem of ends and means, he compensates for his lack of practical political sense by lyrical emphasis on the end—hence the vagueness and even seeming utopianism with which he has often been reproached.[13] But then, poets are here to inspire, not to advise.

---

12. *Opium of the Intellectuals,* p. 269.
13. When he gets down to brass tacks, as in his plan for an Algerian constitution (see above, chapter 13, 1), his impracticality becomes glaring.

PART V
The Last Decade: Camus Ostracized

12
Innocence Reconsidered

After Camus had so clearly taken sides on ethics and politics, the literary works of his last decade showed a sharp decline: three thin volumes, one of enigmatic beauty—*The Fall,* the other two[1] made up of short stories dating from different periods and of unequal artistic value. All these works reflect in allegorical form Camus's ethical and sometimes political preoccupations. In contrast to his previous periods of intellectual effervescence, Camus's last decade was a time of reflection and reappraisal, during which all the contradictions in his thought came to the fore, as well as the hopeless conflict between his ideal and the new historical situation that was taking shape. Many of Camus's later works have their roots in *The Rebel,* but develop in unexpected directions under the impact of new experiences.

1. The True Antinomies of Concrete Thought

Marx and Lenin regarded ethics as a superstructure of the mode of production. In their eyes, Camus would have been an idealist, because of his effort to ground ethics outside institutions and history: a proper Marxist should recognize only "objective guilt"—a crime against revolution to be punished, irrespective

---

1. *Summer* and *Exile and the Kingdom.*

of intentions. Adherence to this Marxist concept of ethics did not prevent communists and fellow-travellers from endlessly activating shame and subjective guilt in their opponents. Sartre does little else in his polemics with Camus about *The Rebel.* But Camus remained as immune to the Marxist sense of sin as to the Christian one. Just as he could enjoy bodily pleasures without any qualms of conscience, so he remained unimpressed when accused of being a bourgeois intellectual. Alien to any puritanic sense of guilt, he seemed equally insensitive to the kind of social guilt that thrived in French *avant-garde* circles of the period. This does not mean that he was indifferent to the fate of the destitute. On the contrary, his whole work is animated by a passion for justice which won him the unwanted epithet of "Camus le Juste"[2]—a moralist, almost a preacher. But while defending the oppressed and the poor, he remained free of guilt as to his own privileged situation. He had known from his youth what it meant to be poor ("I did not learn revolt in Marx . . ."), and he had not abandoned the underprivileged in his new and relative prosperity. But he did not feel obliged to limit his activities to the "service" of the proletariat. As an artist, he was convinced his function was to create beauty and joy for himself and for others. In contrast to cultural snobs, his humanistic inspiration excluded no one; he wrote his novels and plays in very much the spirit of the *Théatre de l'Equipe* in Algiers.

Until his death, joy and happiness remained his paramount value. Camus was perhaps the only defender of the ethics of joy against immoderate commitments. Revolution for him was a means of making happiness possible, insofar as it depended on social conditions. However, an important qualification is introduced in *The Plague* in this respect: when Rambert eventually finds a way to escape the quarantine town on the grounds that "he does not belong there," he gives up his plan voluntarily at the last moment, although no one blames him or lectures him, because he feels that "there is some shame in being happy alone."

2. *See* Georges Hourdin, *Camus le Juste* (Paris: Les Editions du Cerf, 1960).

Camus's approval of this attitude, in contrast to his open hostility to the ethics of atonement preached by Father Paneloux, makes the lesson clear. Sacrifice for its own sake or as a means of appeasing one's conscience by self-punishment is abhorrent to Camus (Christianity remained to him the symbol of this medieval aberration); but there are many instances when personal happiness has to be sacrificed for the sake of dignity or solidarity. Thus a line has been drawn between what Camus regards as meaningful creative sacrifice and neurotic self-immolation, as practiced by some "bourgeois intellectuals" on the altar of the proletarian revolution.

Along with these reflections on guilt, striking changes took place in Camus's belief in the essential innocence of man. For all his hedonistic philosophy, Camus was probably as guilt-ridden as any of his contemporaries, but it took a long time before his reflection consciously became centered on this point. The central idea of Camus's early works—the origin of his metaphysical revolt—is that man is an innocent unjustly sentenced to death by fate. This is axiomatic with him. Meursault the Stranger is not only innocent but exemplary enough to be compared to Christ ("the only Christ we deserve"). Sisyphus is innocent, of course. Even Caligula is innocent, since "men die and are not happy." Yet, there was something forced in such assertions—a false tone. It is not Father Paneloux but Meursault who incidentally remarks: "on se sent toujours un peu fautif." It is not without significance that both Caligula and Meursault practically ended in suicide—a passive suicide—by refusing to defend themselves, actually by helping their murderers. At the same time, both Caligula and Meursault—the latter only at the very end of his life—stand as judges over the society that condemns them, thus offering, as in a filigree, the initial pattern of the penitent-judge who delivers the ironical monologue in *The Fall*.

Not until *The Plague* is the theme of guilt fully developed. It appears not only in Tarrou but in the entire conception of the book which so puzzled Camus's critics; why choose an illness, an act of God, as the symbol of such an obviously man-made evil as war? Why, if not in order to reject the comfort of discovering a scapegoat and allocate responsibility to where it properly belongs, inside of each of us? Men rarely have the luck to be involved in a historical situation in which good and evil are so clear-cut as during the Second World War, a situation in which the horror of killing was so well compensated by the certainty of acting for the sake of humanity. Yet, Camus—who still remembered Versailles in 1939—rejected this comfort by insisting that the Plague was in all of us, less in Grant than in Cottard, to be sure, but present in all. Is there better proof of a sense of guilt in him, not personal but historical guilt, collective guilt "unto the seventh generation"?

In *The Plague,* Rieux still says that he finds more things to admire than to despise in man. Yet, *The Plague* marks the end of the hopeful humanistic period, which started with the *Letters to a German Friend.* In *The Rebel,* the dream of innocence is replaced by a search for "reasonable guilt"[3] (une culpabilité raisonnable). *The Fall* indicates that even this wish has to be given up.

2. The Fall

This "haughty confession," as Maurice Blanchot calls it,[4] might have been prompted by Camus's personal problems which fall outside the scope of this study; but it is not irrelevant to mention here that the two versions of *Jonas*—mostly the unpublished one, as well as some parts of *The Fall*—suggest that Camus had his share of the well-known artist's egocentricity and disregard for others. Although in other works he called it his "natural indifference" and almost tended to regard it as a virtue,[5] it seems to have weighed on his conscience and contributed to the radical self-examination in *The Fall.* The decisive factor, however, might

---

3. *The Rebel,* p. 11.
4. *N.R.F.,* June 1951.
5. See the introduction to *The Right and Wrong Side of Things.*

have been the bitter controversy with Sartre, clear echoes of which are perceptible in the book.

This masterpiece of ambiguous irony reproduces, at least outwardly, this famous clash between two personalities and two solutions to the same insoluble problem. Although it would be ridiculous to identify Camus with Clamence, the first part of *The Fall* does suggest a caricature of Camus as seen by his enemies; "Camus le Juste" has become a well-to-do barrister who thrives on the defense of widows and orphans. His partiality for noble causes has won him money, glory, and self-esteem. This perfect pharisee even uses his spare time to help blind men across the street. Camus has obligingly drawn parts of Clamence from Simone de Beauvoir's Henry of *The Mandarins* and Sartre's various "bourgeois," "belles âmes," or "salauds." Conversely, in the second part, Clamence is partly a caricature of what Camus ought to be to win his enemies' approval. Clamence has given up his profitable philanthropy and lives as a bum in a shady bar in Amsterdam. He has not reached for Sartre's "engagement," but has assumed his complex posture of "penitent-judge" while practicing revolt in the manner of Jean Genet, for he has also become a thief. Characteristically, the stolen object is Van Eyck's picture of The Three Judges. Clamence hopes to be found out and to crown his career as penitent-judge with the palm of martyrdom.

Between these two parts, something has happened. First, the warning laugh—this peculiar hallucination. Then, the real tragedy of Clamence's failure to help the drowning woman. Why did he not help her? It was not even necessary to dive into the icy black river. He could have pressed the alarm signal. But he remained frozen. Literally speaking, he lost himself, as well as his sense of external reality, just as Meursault did when he shot the Arab. Was it not a sign that he lived in a fictitious world, and experienced the fatal impotence of nightmares when faced with the real world in which people despair and die, and real bullets come out of real revolvers?

A subtle counterpoint of irony and serious psychological in-

sight gives *The Fall* its enigmatic character. Undoubtedly, Camus
makes fun of his critics when he obligingly draws his own caricature for them. But what if that crude mask was meant both to
hide and expose the other mask behind which, perhaps, another
Camus—or perhaps Man—was hiding from himself? Also, Meursault was a mask and, obviously, Caligula. Where is truth?

The Fall is a deep and desolate reflection on the inevitable
loss of innocence and the belated understanding of the concept
of the Fall, be it Clamence's fall from grace, his ultimate sinking
into the underworld of the Zuider Zee, or the unknown woman's
fall into despair and her plunge into the river. Psychological and
physical symbolism are mixed here. The innocence so often
asserted in earlier works perhaps never existed, except in extreme
youth when the reflective mind is silenced by passion. But youth
fades away and its innocent sensuousness passes into the self-
complacency of the aging pleasure-seeker. This fall from grace
the reflective mind is quick to register. Camus knew it. But he
experienced another kind of innocence, the new and tragic innocence born of revolt, resistance, and revolution—the brotherhood of the fighters for justice. Unfortunately, this also petered
out into pettiness, tyranny, and general indifference during the
postwar years. The reflective mind also registered this fact and
shed doubts on past idealism. Does not all idealism become
rhetoric in the mirror of the reflective mind? Clamence has only
a reflective mind left to him; he is indeed exceedingly intelligent
and well-read, but he has no soul, not even his "beautiful soul"
of yore, as he unrolls his endless, futile monologue, or dialogue
with a mute listener—perhaps himself, knowing that on the
following day he will start all over again. He offers not the
caricature, but the tragedy of bad faith. Indeed, Camus has lost
his innocence. Time has carried away the innocence of *Nuptials,*
and history has eroded the regained innocence of the fighter for
justice. *The Fall* marks a turning point in Camus's development
by its emphasis on man's guilt. If we regard *Nuptials* as the expression of genuine innocence, *The Stranger* as a forcible clinging
to the feeling, and *The Plague* as an admission of unavoidable

guilt, then *The Fall* can be considered a radical, though inconclusive, reappraisal of the very foundation of Camus's ethics. Is the first J. B. Clamence defending noble causes in pompous, harmonious sentences, a malevolent caricature or a true aspect of "Camus le Juste"? Is Clamence an archetype of all idealists?

The Fall, however pessimistic, does not bring Camus's belief in man's innocence to its lowest ebb. An obscure short story, fittingly entitled "Un esprit confus," explores the depth of man's addiction to evil. Everything is deliberately confused in this text, the only one Camus wrote in the *avant-garde* style of the inner monologue, without punctuation. The ambiguity begins with the title: *The Renegade or a Confused Mind.* It is impossible to decide whether the *or* in French is correlative or disjunctive. In the first case, the tragic-romantic notion of betrayal is neutralized by the Cartesian irony of the subtitle: betrayal is the result of the *hubris* that the hero, in his mental confusion failed to perceive. In the second case, a question of almost metaphysical dimension is raised: is evil—as embodied in *The Renegade*—a betrayal of man's mission, or the result of intellectual deficiency?

As far as a plot can be discovered in this nightmarish vision, it concerns a missionary prompted by charity or pride, or both, to evangelize a particularly savage tribe in the desert. "The town"—a frightening caricature of Camus's beautiful Sahara— is cut out of salt mines, with houses built of salt and the burning bitterness of salt in every mouth and every soul. The sun, always an ambivalent symbol in Camus, is no longer a symbol of justice, lucidity, and measure as it was in *Thought at the Meridian,* but casts the burning spell of folly, as on the beach where Meursault becomes a murderer "à cause du soleil." In this inhuman landscape, the missionary is seized, outraged, tortured, and finally enslaved. But the fascination of the inhuman city and its inhuman inhabitants is such that he himself becomes an incarnation of evil, willful evil, and the voluntary slave of the town's evil fetish. He betrays his religion and, in the last scene, he is shown hiding behind a rock with a gun in order to shoot the new missionary who has been sent to replace him.

What can be the meaning of this haunting story? Caligula's last return, a plunge into the furious world of all addicts of violence, whose "all or nothing" attitude was analyzed in *The Rebel*? Once more, the hideous temptation of absolute evil has been expressed. Evil is shown at the depth of man—at the depth of nature also, if one remembers the animal grunts that punctuate the evil man's monologue.

Surely it does not express a temptation, a wish to understand, as in the days of Caligula. It sounds like a deep cry of disgust at the sight of this ever-renascent, never-relenting wickedness, which might be—who knows—the true essence of man and nature.

13
Racial Brotherhood

1. The Guest

Although Camus had spared no effort to help the Arabs out of
their poverty and to fight the colonial system, charges of racism
were wildly flung at him when he refused to condone F.L.N.
terrorism. Camus, the "racist," the "colon," "the pied noir," soon
became a scapegoat and a symbol, and his previous works were
screened for traces of racism. Such traces were suddenly detected
in *The Stranger*. Did not Meursault murder an Arab, designated
by no other name than "The Arab"? Did he not do it out of
racial solidarity with his friend the pimp, having helped him
in his shady love affair with an Arab girl, equally anonymous and
called by an almost derogatory word, "une mauresque"? With
more haste than logic, Camus's critics pointed out a) that in
order to show Meursault as a victim of society Camus had to
make him murder a man of no importance, a mere Arab; and
b) that capital punishment for an almost accidental manslaughter
showed the deep-seated guilt complex of a racist society.[1] This
is, of course, a muddled argument, confusing fact and judgment,
identifying the author and his hero and making Camus responsible

---

1. See: Pierre Nora, *Les Français d'Algérie* (Paris: Gallimard,
1961); Paul Amash, *Romance Notes* 9 (1967), no. 1, p. 6; Renée
Quinn, *Revue d'histoire littéraire de la France* (March 1968): p. 251.

for the state of affairs he merely described. Yet, *The Stranger* stresses, perhaps unwittingly, the surprising fact of the almost total lack of fraternization between Arabs and Europeans, even in poor districts where they lived side by side. The fact that Meursault records without comment what he sees around him seems to indicate that both for him and his creator this state of affairs was natural. These charges contain an element of truth and require elucidation.

Although many personal relations existed between intellectuals of both races, and intermarriages were frequent, there was practically no fraternization among the non intellectual groups of the two races, least of all among the proletariat. It is doubtful whether international brotherhood at the level of the proletariat ever existed, except in the imagination of political idealists. Primitive men of all nations and races think and feel through their groups. This was the situation in which Camus grew up, and the most superficial observer of prewar Algeria would have noticed a similar though less marked estrangement between various European groups: French, Spanish, Italian, Maltese, and even between native Algerian French and those from the Metropolis.

The word racism is far too strong and inadequate to describe this state of affairs. For one thing, the rejection was mutual, and it is no exaggeration to say that it was more difficult for a Frenchman to penetrate Arab society than for an Arab to assimiliate and make a career, whether as a tram conductor or as a lawyer, within the French system. Moreover, racism is a pseudo-scientific concept, a theory of blood determinism invented by Gobineau and others, later taken up self-righteously by American Southerners, then used savagely by the Nazis. Simple people do not think so far. They are conscious of cultural differences or, to put it in plain language, of different ways of life; they prefer their own and feel more at ease with their own group.

Meursault reflects the view of his surroundings uncritically. It can be assumed that Camus endorses it, since he covers the whole of Meursault's conduct generally with the cloak of innocence. It is even conceivable that he took it for granted, even when fighting colonialism and showing his sympathy for the Kabylian peasants. Such contradictions are not unusual. He took it for granted, because this was the way people were, and in his French exile Camus was nostalgic and totally uncritical of his old country.[2] Thought came later; not before *Exile and the Kingdom* did he reflect on the possibility of racial brotherhood. The difference between Camus and his critics on this point is that most of his critics start from the abstract idea that brotherhood is *natural,* that it would exist if it were not prevented by vested interests, capitalism, racism, and so on. None of this Manichaeism is found in Camus. He knows that interracial brotherhood does not exist spontaneously among simple people whose identity is rooted not in themselves but in their group. Racial brotherhood is not a fact of nature; it would be truer to say that cultural differences are a second nature. Camus's concern in *Exile and the Kingdom* is to detect the seeds of brotherhood behind cultural barriers.

The first short story in *Exile and the Kingdom* is enigmatically called "The Adulterous Woman." It shows how a French-Algerian woman, reaching the end of her youth, discovers the country and the people she had seen all her life without ever noticing them. She too takes things for granted. The cultural barriers were facts she never examined. She found nothing special about the Arabs. They were there, that was all. The occasion of her discovery was a journey to South Algeria that she reluctantly undertook to accompany her husband, a commercial traveler. They were a reasonably happy couple, which meant that they had become familiar to the point of forgetting each other's existence. They were tolerably well off, with a comfortable apartment furnished in a half-Moorish style. They had no wish for adventure of any

---

2. An example in point is *Le Minotaure* (in *l'Été*), which humorously describes the childish joy of the people of Oran at a boxing match, and their fierce competition with the people of Algiers.

kind, and the Saharan journey through a midwinter sandstorm
was utterly distasteful to them. The husband was mildly conscious
of his racial superiority, although he did not really succeed in
impressing any Arab. "They think they can get away with anything now," he grumbled when slighted. For him, the journey
was a trite business duty. For his wife, this journey, so unpleas-
antly begun, ended in a brief awakening. The adulteress did not
treat herself to a Berber lover. She was overcome by a feeling
of strangeness: the nomadic shepherds, their aloofness, their mystery, became perceptible to her for the first time. Then she discovered the desert with its endless horizon of rocks and moving
sands and, finally, the stars. She sneaked out of the matrimonial
bed at night, and ran to the top of the tower to look at the wide
skies. An adulteress indeed, unfaithful to the reasonable, secure
life of her clan, suddenly swept away from her pragmatic Western
background. She experienced for the first and last time in her
life the divine flight of inspiration in the unknown country of her
birth.

Another extremely ambiguous case of racial contact is offered
in the short story called *The Guest*. A French-Algerian schoolmaster lives in an isolated village beyond the Atlas, at the time
when the Algerian rebellion is about to gather momentum. The
French police chief of the locality brings him a manacled Arab
who has murdered his kinsman. The schoolmaster is requested
to keep the prisoner for the night and take him to the district
prison the next morning. The Frenchman's attitude reveals
Camus's distaste for official justice, as well as his search for
brotherhood.

The schoolmaster, a lonely man living in almost monastic
poverty, is akin to Dr. Rieux in his unassuming, spontaneous
sense of human freedom, and to the Stranger in his union with
nature and his indifference to events. He is deeply attuned to
the country and its landscapes, which are never romantically
described but ever present, just casually mentioned as if habit

had welded to the very substance of the man what it removed from his consciousness. He just perceives "the purple mass . . . where the gap has opened onto the desert." This was his country of birth; anywhere else he would have felt an exile. There is a touch of oriental fatalism combined with Western lucidity in Camus's comment, that the country was a cruel one, "even without men—who did not help matters either." The schoolmaster's relation to the inhabitants of this cruel country is similar to his attachment to the land—sober, but unbreakable; without illusion and beyond question. He squarely refuses to give up the prisoner. Instead, he takes him to the crossroad and shows him the way to the Berber tribes that would shelter and adopt him. For unexplained reasons, the prisoner chooses the other road and walks on his own to the French town where trial awaits him. When the schoolmaster comes back home, puzzled and heavy-hearted, he reads a sentence scribbled on the blackboard: "You handed over our brother, you will pay for this."

There is nothing attractive about the prisoner, with his thick lips and narrow forehead. The schoolmaster even feels angry, not only with him as a murderer, but with all men for "their damned wickedness, their tireless hatreds, their lust for blood." Camus does not clearly divide mankind into the innocent and the guilty (the germ of the plague is in all of us; this makes him loath to play the part of judge). The schoolmaster not only refuses to give up his prisoner to the authorities, but also unties his hands, shares a meal with him, and spends a somewhat uneasy night, hoping in vain that his unwanted guest will escape.

The pathos of the story rests not in any humanitarian sentimentality, but, on the contrary, in the incomprehension of the two men whose life experience is similar in so many ways. For Camus, all the tragedy of the Algerian war lies in this contrast: the solidarity that links him to the prisoner is their common participation in this inhuman country and the monastic poverty it imposes. In this respect the description of the shared meal has evangelical undertones in a modern setting, as the schoolmaster—or missionary, or biblical character—bakes the flour in oil and, while it slowly cooks on the kerosene stove, brings cheese, eggs, dates, and canned milk.

This simple rite of hospitality links the twentieth-century characters to the immemorial past or eternal present of the human condition, hardly sheltered by civilization. It is the desert which makes life real and pure. The schoolmaster's attitude is that of neither a French-Algerian nor an abstract humanitarian, but a hermit who has learned to regard all men as a common species and knows he has nothing to fear from them so long as they share in this essential humanity. The country reminds them that they are all compatriots in the metaphysical sense.

Yet, in other respects, the gap between them is absolute, as if their incompatible cultures—their mysterious pre-human conditioning—had buried the seeds of understanding too deep for them ever to germinate. It is not only that the Arab looks rebellious and frightened, and that the Frenchman, after some hesitation, slips a revolver furtively under his pillow; mutual fear is less important than each man's inability to understand the other's motives. Why did the Arab murder? Did he regret the deed? The murderer looks uncomprehendingly. Here, oddly enough, Camus seems to expect from him what the Court—to Camus's indignation —expected from Meursault: regret. Has Camus changed, or does he see nothing in common between regret admitted by one man to another and the declaration of regret institutionalized as a social demand?

He seems to have kept his faith in an improbable, yet real state of nature, a state that does not exist but can occasionally be conjured up into a fleeting potentiality. This fleeting moment of essential harmlessness and freedom is all that matters. Camus knows with his rational mind that it cannot be the basis of social order; still, he is willing to sacrifice security for this spark of brotherhood—"I shall not hand him over"; "I can't see a man with his hands tied up." Camus does not deny the irrationality of his attitude, nor does he blame those who defend law and order. Like a conscientious objector, his only concern is to keep the fleeting flame alive. He is not a militant anarchist; he just follows a sort of instinct, preaches to no one, and claims no privilege but the right to withdraw, at his own risk, from the system of social repression.

Camus is fully aware of the unrealistic character of this impulse. The fleeting moment cannot be extended into any lasting understanding. We are soon back to the paradox of two civilizations living side by side but unable to understand each other. Why does the Arab not escape? Why does the fool give himself up, unless some obscure symbolism is suggested in the Arab's ambiguous question: "Are you coming with us?" This could be simply an invitation to accompany his friend and guest when the officer takes him to the police court or, to do what so many Parisian intellectuals did, desert the French and join the Arab cause. This Camus declines, not out of conventional faithfulness to his French fatherland, still less for a community of interests with the French settlers, but simply out of faithfulness to himself. In contrast to the abstract humanitarian, he knows that the common horror of colonial oppression cannot unite the French and Arabs in a common struggle. He feels a solidarity with the Arabs as men, not as Arabs. He likes and respects them; still, he is not one of them. No amount of distaste for the colonial system or the war can make him deny that solidarity with his own culture has become part of himself. Characteristically, his hero is a schoolmaster, and the map of France hangs on the blackboard. The spreading of French culture in overseas territories was regarded by Sartre and his friends as an imperialistic enterprise. Camus, in all simplicity, regarded it as sharing a common heritage. French culture, in his view, was humanistic before being French.

Camus's dream of an amicable solution to the Algerian problem is explicitly stated in this story, as well as his awareness of the impossibility of his dream. It is easy to ridicule it as unrealistic, to sneer at "separate but equal" or "cooperation and mutual respect." But Camus's attitude is more complex. It combines a Quaker's dream of nonviolence and the anarchism of a partisan: "If I am attacked, I shall defend myself." He is fully aware of the contradiction and impracticality of his attitude. The cogs of war and rival nationalisms were already in motion to grind friends and foes alike. Institutions are stronger than men; but anything institutionalized is bad and spreads death: "You gave up our brother, you will pay." He will die indeed,[3] not for having betrayed anyone, but, as Pascal says, for having been born on the other side of the river. He will pay for crimes he neither committed nor abetted and he will suffer the crimes of the opposite clan. The karma of nationalism, the karma of group action, invariably overcomes the fleeting moment of brotherhood. Camus knows this, yet he refuses to give up.

Exile and the Kingdom, however, ends on a more optimistic note in the last short story: *The Stone that Grows.* Here, the action is set in a small village in Brazil, where a French engineer comes to build a bridge. The initial scenes suggest a kind of brotherhood through work, in which nature itself participates. When the engineer crosses the immense river on his arrival, "the long liquid muscles" act as flying buttresses to carry the raft that black oarsmen guide skillfully. Yet, the raft is but a speck of wood on the river—the water spreads on all sides while its powerful current carries the raft slowly "through the dark forest towards the sea and the night."

Upon his arrival, the "massive and warmhearted" Frenchman is seized, like a new Gulliver, by swarms of local officials, and the first bout of irony in the story lies in the contrast between this puny world of obsequious busybodies and the luscious spontaneity of nature and the common people. The official world—mayor, judges, notables, and church dignitaries—are depicted with good-natured humor, their self-importance neutralized by the tropical exuberance of the forest; there is even something touching in their efforts, as a naïve rite of hospitality, to honor Monsieur l'Ingénieur as he deserves.

---

3. A schoolmaster was murdered under similar circumstances at the beginning of the war.

The engineer's first attempts to get acquainted with the population are not too successful. He asks to visit a hut, where he is accepted with a hostile look. Poor people are ashamed of their misery in front of him. He is offered a glass of local alcohol, as courtesy demands. The whole village gathers to take a good look at him and disappears in "impenetrable thickets." Here, again, as in *The Guest,* Camus describes with great subtlety a kind of racial barrier unknown to the theoreticians of race equality. The barriers erected by the poor and the illiterate against the outsider are the result of their shyness and pride. But something more subtle makes them impenetrable. It is not the stranger's wealth or education that makes them shy: They accept such things in their own elite, provided they do not feel abandoned by it. But the fact of his being alien to their cultural pattern is insuperable. Can these cultural, sociological barriers be overcome? This is the question asked.

The natives are easygoing and talkative, but the gap between them and the stranger is deepened, rather than eased, by the popular festivities that take place at the moment of the engineer's arrival. For the Western man has lost a certain capacity for primitive joy, the childish delight of the village folk in their songs and dances. He feels painfully isolated from the Dionysiac ecstasy of the clan. His age and awkward bulk make physical participation impossible, and he is equally alien to the elders of the tribe, because centuries of Western rationalism prevent him from vicariously enjoying the feast as the native old folks do. True, this very rationality enables him to help them by building the bridge. But no amount of philanthropy can overcome the gap. The Western man knows it. Confronted with the simple exuberance of the dancers, he experiences something like a fall from grace. His self-consciousness weighs on him. Does he hopelessly belong to the world of fussy officials? Not even the friendly prattle of his driver and a native helper nicknamed "The Cock" can dispel his gloom.

Camus's story, as said above, has an optimistic ending. It suggests another kind of participation in which the Western man,

while remaining himself, can use his specific qualities to restore
the lost brotherhood. It so happens that The Cock has vowed to
the Holy Virgin to carry an enormous stone on his head to the
church on the morrow of the festival. It is a miraculous stone,
one that grows as crowds of faithful touch it. The Cock wants
to keep his vow, as honor and religion demand, and he begs
his friend, the Frenchman, to keep him from wasting his strength
at the evening dance. But, alas, the sound of flutes and tam-tams
is irresistible and The Cock joins in the dance, at first gingerly,
and then with all the savage energy of his youth. On the next
day, while carrying the stone, he inevitably falters and falls to
the ground, his vow unfulfilled, his honor shattered. Here, the
reasonable Frenchman intervenes. He carries the stone for The
Cock—not to the church, though, for Camus's objection to a
religion that denies man's innocence remains adamant, but to
The Cock's hut, where he deposits it on the hearth. He is re-
warded for having saved his friend's honor by an invitation to sit
in the circle round the hearth.

This complex allegory suggests the faltering Christ whom
Simon the Cyrenian helped carry His cross, except that here the
figure of Christ is purely human; the fulfillment of the vow is
something The Cock owes to himself as much as to the Virgin—
indeed, the Virgin might well be but a projection of what he
owes to himself. On the other hand, the action of the Western
man is strangely reminiscent of the White Man's Burden, except
that in the context of the story his act suggests no self-righteous
philanthropy, but an exchange, in which everybody gives what is
best in his culture—the primitive his unspoiled energy and joy,
his carelessness, the Western man his science, patience, and self-
control. The latter helps; the former rejuvenates and inspires by
the gift of innocence.

On reading the three stories, one finds it difficult not to be
reminded of romantic socialism, with its subtle allotment of parts
between the intellectual and the people. Some call it paternalism
—"il était féodal," says Simone de Beauvoir, in her *Memoirs*.
Let us simply call it exchange and solidarity. Each gives what he

has and remains what˙he is. Nature and civilization can be complementary.

2. The Algerian War

Camus was an Algerian, bred on Arab land, and at the same time a Frenchman. His loyalties were divided. From the beginning of his adult life, he kept protesting against the misery of the exploited Arab population. The fate of the Arabs was his main reason for joining the Communist Party in 1934, and for leaving it in 1937, when he realized that the Party was less interested in the concrete fate of the exploited Arabs than in the propaganda value of their exploitation.

Later he supported the Popular Front of Léon Blum, accepted with some hope Minister Viard's proposal that 80,000 Arabs should receive French citizenship and that some improvement be made in the social status of the others. But even this modest aim failed, not through the fault of Paris, but because of the stubborn resistance of the rich French settlers in Algeria. No sooner were the Nazis expelled from France than Camus resumed his plea for the Algerian Arabs. He was at that time an almost daily contributor to the formerly underground paper *Combat*. In a series of impassioned articles, he tried to familiarize the French public with the plight of his homeland. The usual misery and exploitation were compounded by two additional factors. When a near-famine situation broke out in Algiers toward the end of the Second World War, a large number of the Algerian Arabs found the American and British then occupying Algerian territory to be infinitely more humane than the French settlers and government. Moreover, tens of thousands of Arab workers received three to four times their usual wages from the Americans, for whom they built bridges, roads, and airfields. When the French administration returned, the *status quo ante* was quickly reestablished, with predictable consequences. Camus's warning of 1944–45 remained unheeded. And of necessity events proceeded to their tragic denouement.

It was not until 1956 that the war reached its peak. However, a series of some twenty articles by Camus appeared in *l'Express* as early as 1954–55.[4] In denying the fatality of the Algerian situation, Camus fought on two fronts. He continued to point out that the settlers' resistance made the situation insoluble; at the same time he opposed the view held by Sartre and his friends that the Algerian war was "nothing but" a pure colonial war against imperialism and a first stage in the inevitable march towards a socialist Third World.

By then, Camus was branded a bourgeois lackey by the French Communist Left and a traitor by the political Right. In the name of man's dignity and free choice, he protested vehemently and conclusively against the abuse by both sides of the theory of "historical fatality."

> People are too readily resigned to fatality. They are too ready to believe that, after all, nothing but bloodshed makes history progress and that the stronger always progresses at the expense of the weaker. Such fatality exists perhaps. But man's task is not to accept it or to bow to its laws. If he had accepted it in the earliest ages, we should still be living in prehistoric times. The task of men of culture and faith, in any case, is not to desert historical struggles nor to serve the cruel and inhuman elements in those struggles. It is rather to remain what they are, to help man against what is oppressing him, to favor freedom against the fatalities that close in upon it.
>
> That is the condition under which history really progresses, innovates—in a word, creates. In everything else it repeats itself, like a bleeding mouth that merely vomits forth a wild stammering.[5]

Then followed another and yet another appeal against terrorism, and against senseless violence on both sides. Camus's unique position in this war was that he attempted to see the rights and wrongs of both sides as objectively as possible. This attitude,

4. Many of them reprinted in *Actuelles III*. See chapter 1, 4.

5. *Resistance, Rebellion and Death* (New York: A. Knopf, 1961), pp. 141–42.

reminiscent of Romain Rolland's *Au dessus de la melée* (Above the Battlefield) in 1914–1918, predictably earned Camus many enemies and few supporters. He nevertheless persisted in his double condemnation of violence:

> When violence answers violence in a growing frenzy that makes the simple language of reason impossible, the role of intellectuals cannot be, as we read every day, to excuse from a distance one of the violences and condemn the other. This has the double result of enraging the violent group that is condemned and encouraging to greater violence the violent group that is exonerated. . . . Most often the Right ratified, in the name of French honor, what was most opposed to that honor. And most often the Left, in the name of justice, excused what was an insult to any real justice. In this way the Right abandoned the monopoly of the moral reflex to the Left, which yielded to it the monopoly of the patriotic reflex. The country suffered doubly. . . . It seems as if metropolitan France was unable to think of any policies other than those which consisted in saying to the French in Algeria: "Go ahead and die; that's what you deserve" or else "Kill them; that's what they deserve."[6]

Even as he criticized the *colons* intractability, he warned against a pan-Islamic solution, against Nasser's growing influence among the Arabs, and the Soviets' use of this explosive situation. This is the gist of the answer he published in *Encounter* to one of his detractors, P. L. Caracciolo.

Obstinately, Camus pleaded with both parties for the respect of civilian populations on both sides and the opening of a dialogue between all contending parties, including the large number of Algerian Jews, who were an almost forgotten issue by that time.

> And, to achieve that, each of us must preach pacification to his people. The inexcusable massacring of French civilians leads to equally stupid destruction of the Arabs and their possessions. It is as if two insane people, crazed with wrath, had decided to turn into a fatal embrace the forced marriage from which they cannot free themselves. Forced to live to-

6. *Ibid.,* pp. 116–17.

gether and incapable of uniting, they decide at least to die together. And because each of them by his excesses strengthens the motives and excesses of the other, the storm of death that has struck our country can only increase to the point of general destruction. In that ceaseless attempt to go one better, the fire is spreading, and tomorrow Algeria will be a land of ruins and dead which no force, no power in the world, will be capable of reviving in this century.[7]

In February 1956, when the horizon was already very dark, Camus again lectured in Algiers with an appeal for a civilian truce. After his appeal failed, Camus tried again: this time, he actually offered a concrete plan for a solution (printed as a post-script to *Actuelles III*). This long statement deserves not only to be summarized, but extensively quoted. Camus first sums up what is legitimate in the Arabs' complaints:

1) Colonialism and its abuses, which are man-made.

2) The perennial lie of constantly proposed but never realized assimilation, a lie that has compromised every evolution since the establishment of colonialism. The faked elections of 1948 in particular both illustrated the lie and utterly discouraged the Arab people. Until that date the Arabs all wanted to be French. After that date a large part of them no longer wanted to be.

3) The obvious injustice of the agrarian allocation and of the distribution of income (sub-proletariat)—injustices that are, moreover, being irreparably aggravated by a rapid increase in population.

4) The psychological suffering: the often scornful or off-hand manner of many French, and the development among the Arabs (through a series of stupid measures) of the complex of humiliation that is at the center of the present drama.[8]

What is illegitimate in Arab demands, according to Camus, is the wish to become an independent state. Here, in sharp con-trast to other French Left Wing intellectuals, Camus maintains that there is no such thing as an Algerian nation, and that their

---

7. *Ibid.*, pp. 128–29.
8. *Ibid.*, pp. 143–44.

demands spring "wholly from emotions" and "revolutionary romanticism." In Camus's opinion, Algerian nationalism was a pan-Islamic dream—the kind of group imperialism of which he disapproved, the only result of which would be the emergence of a nation unable to sustain itself economically, a prey to misery, and a stepping stone for Soviet expansion in the Mediterranean.

The French government's mistake was that it did not perceive these distinctions. The remedy was to state clearly:

1) That it is ready to grant complete justice to the Arabs of Algeria and to liberate them from the colonial system;

2) That it will give up none of the rights of the Algerian French;

3) That it is unwilling for such justice to mean a prelude to a sort of historical death for the French nation, and for the West the risk of an encircling that would lead to the Kadarization of Europe and the isolation of America.[9]

In passing from diagnosis to solutions, Camus quotes a plan for a federal association among the various sections of the Algerian population and Metropolitan France, put forward by Marc Lauriol, a professor of Law at the University of Algiers: there should be established two bodies in the French Parliament in Paris, a Metropolitan and a Moslem body, each dealing with its own affairs, with a gradual expansion of the common sphere of interest until the two nations in Algiers coalesce.

In 1958, these suggestions by Camus bordered on the ridiculous, not only because they had no chance of ever being accepted, but because, even supposing they had been accepted, the presence of several hundred Moslem deputies in the French Parliament would have offered such superb opportunities to disrupt the country by subversion that one is surprised that the Communist Party did not back the suggestion.

At the end of his article, Camus announced in a rather solemn fashion: "this is the last warning that a writer who for twenty years

---

9. *Ibid.,* pp. 147–48.

has been devoted to the service of Algeria feels he can voice before resuming his silence."[10]

Then, indeed, complete silence followed. Never again did he touch on the problem until his death in January, 1960. He fought a gallant but naïve battle for reason, compromise, sanity, and reverence for life in an absurd universe, in an absurd political situation.

Camus, the man of political dialogue, failed. We may ask once more: was he at heart a political anarchist, sharing in the naïve belief that society could do away with political power altogether if only the people could unite against their masters and governments?

14

Class Problems

"I did not learn rebellion in Marx, I learnt it in misery," wrote Camus when lectured by Sartre about working-class solidarity. The fact is that, in contrast to many French radical intellectuals of bourgeois background, Camus related to the proletariat without effort and had no feeling of hereditary sin concerning his origins. Accordingly, there is nothing compulsive in Camus's attitude with regard to social problems, and he is not obsessed with revolutionary romanticism. In fact—leaving out *State of Siege,* in which the Plague symbolizes the totalitarian system, not capitalism— Camus's writings are inspired only twice with a revolutionary mood: during the Spanish war, with *Revolt in Asturia,* and, for a brief period, after the liberation of Paris.[1] Otherwise, Camus was a radical reformist convinced that social justice could and should be enforced by democratic means. This, however, did not exclude conflict; indeed, it presupposed unrelenting pressure, and nothing could be further removed from Camus's outlook than a naïve belief in plain good will. A convinced trade-unionist, he believed that nothing could be gained without strikes and the threat of social disorder. What worried him was the increasing control of the French trade unions by the Communist Party, and

---

1. See *Actuelles I.*

the dehumanization of the class struggle in the age of large industry, materialism, and the masses.

In 1955, Camus came back to journalism after a long interval, and wrote in *L'Express* about "La condition ouvrière" (The Workers' Lot). In the same year, he published a short story conceived a few years earlier, about a strike in a small cooper shop in Algiers.[2] The comparison of the two texts is illuminating. The short story, *The Silent Men,* which describes the coopers' feelings, was called half jokingly by Camus "an exercise in socialist realism."[3] The coopers had always been silent, and in exploring their inner lives Camus goes back to the figures of his childhood: his silent mother and the uncomplicated men and women of Belcourt. The "Mediterranean man," as described in Camus's earlier short stories, had a brief youth, centered on bodily pleasures, then an endless middle-age, the boredom of which was relieved by work, the reading of sports papers, and an occasional drink of anisette. Such was his fate, for "there was no other form of happiness in this country" than physical life "and that happiness disappeared with youth."[4] The picture is familiar to every reader of Camus's books. Yet, as we know, the "Mediterranean man" does not become positively unhappy, for he has a sense of the beauty of the world and lives attuned to nature. Thus feels Yvars, watching the night fall on the terrace at the moment his neighbors "would suddenly lower their voices": "At least he felt in harmony at such moments; he had nothing to do but wait quietly, without quite knowing for what."[5] Such was his basic understanding of the world. His wife and child were so much a part of the substance of his existence that he was hardly conscious of their presences, yet they added warmth and security to his life. Yvars would call himself "happy," meaning that he was, on the whole, content.

For such a man, work in a small cooper's shop had nothing

2. *Exile and the Kingdom* (New York: A. Knopf, 1958).
3. See Camus, *Théâtre, Récits, Nouvelles, Pleiade,* p. 2045.
4. *Exile and the Kingdom,* p. 64.
5. *Ibid.,* p. 64.

in common with the industrial inferno Camus later discovered in Paris. The work required skill and care, and Yvars was proud of his proficiency. The love of work well done as an essential part of a worker's life is never mentioned in the story, but it is suggested as closely as possible as the reader follows Yvars's thoughts: "The good cooper, the one who fits his curved staves and tightens them in the fire with an iron hoop almost hermetically, without rafia or oakum. . . ."[6] The concrete terminology drives the point home. Camus's uncle had worked in such a small cooper's shop; such talk must have been familiar to him as a boy.

The kind of life described here is that of artisans. It is a hard life, but lived at a human level. The work itself, far from being a curse, could give meaning to one's life if only the pay were a little better, so that there would be no need to work overtime on Saturdays and even on Sundays to bring one's child up decently. The other men were old acquaintances; comradeship in work *almost* blotted out national and racial difficulties, although the Arab mentioned here is only a helper. As for the boss, "he was not a bad sort." He still remembered that his father had been an apprentice; he lived in a modest middle-class house almost enclosed in the shop, in which his whole life was encompassed. Hardly more sophisticated than his workers, he remained chummy, although he had become Monsieur Lasalle; moreover, his whole life, his very presence, was a reminder that every good worker could become a boss in due course. This had happened to Camus's own uncle and would have been the luck of his father, too, had he not been killed at Verdun.

This was a human world, or rather had been a human world, for it was dying out. Camus is acutely conscious of this: "What can coopers do when the cooper-age disappears?"[7] The pathos of this deceptively simple story is derived from the subtle interplay of human emotions and inhuman economic laws which drive men against each other and reject them out of humanity.

---

6. *Ibid.*, p. 66.
7. *Ibid.*, p. 65.

What can coopers do in the age of the large container factory? "One does not change trades at forty." This is not due to dumbness, but to something else: "You don't change trades when you have gone to the trouble of learning one. . . . Changing trades is nothing, but to give up what you know, your master craftsmanship, is not easy."[8] Your trade is part of your being. But all trades are disappearing, together with the cooper-age, and craftsmen become gradually hollowed out. One day, they will go and work in a container factory, submit to clock work and the assembly line, and forego their pride of craftsmanship. This is the tragedy of the men whose human dignity is threatened because their talents are no longer wanted and they themselves are destined to a kind of work in which the difference between good workers and bad workers is blurred; all are interchangeable, and none of them will ever be able to build a shop of his own.

What can cooper bosses do if the situation pits them against one another as competitors and against their employees for the sharing of diminished profits? Then the worst features in human nature come out. Until then, patriarchal conditions had prevailed. Camus does not idealize them, knowing the kind of conflicts and unavoidable resignation they entailed. But he clearly prefers them to the industrial world. In the cooper-age, the system was hierarchical, yet it did not exclude human equality, born of daily contacts and mutual esteem; and it was alleviated both by the hope of a better lot for oneself or one's children, and by the existence of trade unions, whose equalizing role was the main source of the workers' dignity. Small enterprise and trade unions made working conditions bearable. However, conditions were changing and Camus's prevalent mood was pessimistic at the time he wrote the story; his compulsion to go back to the world of his childhood at that time was probably due to his nostalgia for a dying world that was hard materially, but in which the absurdity of life was compensated by human values and natural beauty. To Camus, the new world seemed not only hard materially, but without

---

8. *Ibid.*, pp. 65–66.

beauty or values. This new world is not shown in the story, since the protagonists are not aware of its looming. They just feel that times are getting difficult, and they react by hardening their relations to one another: The boss refuses a raise, although he knows that the cost of living is going up. He acts selfishly, in order to preserve his profits. How else should it be? Can one expect the boss to be a saint? Moreover, he has to act as other bosses do, or face ruin. He is partly selfish and partly caught. The workers understand that. They need a raise. So, they resort to their old weapon: the strike. A half-hearted strike, half-heartedly backed by the union, which has other business to take care of than looking after a handful of outmoded artisans. The strike fails, of course, and the class conflict between boss and workers hardens into irreparable hostility which nobody really wanted.

Once again, as in *The Guest,* the tragedy is one of lost brotherhood and mutual incomprehension. The initial guilt rested with the boss. He not only refused the raise, but did it in an offensive way—probably to overcome his bad conscience and his suspicion that his own trade was becoming unwanted. His take-it-or-leave-it attitude infuriated the workers, who embarked on a punitive strike. Here was a subtle paradox: embittered class conflict prevailed where all were unconscious victims of a developing new order of things. The boss stood by his bosshood, the workers by their rights, although it was really a matter of coopers surviving the end of the cooper-age and, in fact, of independent work.

After the failure of the strike, the defeated workers devised another punishment for the boss: silence. Perhaps devised is the wrong word, for nothing was agreed among them and none of them decided it. It was less a decision than a natural outcome of an inextricable situation. On the day work resumed, Yvars's wife was worried: "What will you men say to him?"—"Nothing." Indeed, there was nothing to say. And a wave of silence fell upon the workshop. The boss had intended to show his masterhand once more by letting the men wait in front of closed doors in the morning, and then return to joviality; but his high spirits collapsed before the sullen silence of the men. In an interview

with the oldest worker, he said what he should have said before
the strike: that "when business picks up," he would give them
the raise without even being asked. His proposal failed to dispel
the gloom. Why? Were they so hurt by his earlier high-handed-
ness, or did they all know that business would never pick up, that
it was all "wind"? Sullenness set in, as in *The Guest*. Nobody
wanted it, but it happened. Perhaps they were taking out on
each other their anguish at being survivors of the cooper-age? All
that is obscure. Only, "anger and helplessness sometimes hurts
so much that you can't even cry out."[9] Here, as in *The Guest*,
it is insinuated that at one point men lose their grip on the situation and inhuman laws start grinding. In *The Guest*, the fleeting
moment when brotherhood and generosity could prevail was
hardly perceptible, and the blind determinism of race hatred was
unmistakably symbolized by the writing on the wall: "You handed
over our brother, you will pay for this." In *The Silent Men*, the
opposite occurs: the fleeting moment becomes a clear opportunity
to make peace—when the boss's child is taken dangerously ill
and all the men are genuinely anxious. However, the men remain
silent. Not that they want to, but they cannot help it. They were
silent by nature, shy in expressing their emotions; then they become deliberately silent. Now, they are numb. Although the boss
has again become a man to them, they still find nothing to say
to him: "When it occurred to Yvars that someone ought to call
him, the door had already closed."[10] Later on, when talking about
it to his wife, he concluded: "It is his own fault!" Here the words
on the wall are written almost imperceptibly. But they are written.

In this story of refusal, a minute symbolic incident is inserted.
It is as ambiguous as in *The Guest*. The workers' hostility to the
boss brought them nearer to each other. In this new atmosphere
of warmth, during the lunch break, Yvars suddenly noticed Saïd,
the Arab helper, lying in a pile of shavings. Perhaps he dimly
sensed that they had been behaving to Saïd as the boss to them.

---

9. *Ibid.*, pp. 68–78.
10. *Ibid.*, p. 84.

In the new mood of class brotherhood, he approached him, somewhat hesitantly, and asked him if he had already finished. Saïd said he had eaten his figs. Yvars stopped eating. The uneasy feeling that hadn't left him since the interview with Lassalle suddenly disappeared to make room for a pleasant warmth. He broke his bread in two as he got up and, faced with Saïd's refusal, said that everything would be better next week. "Then it'll be your turn to treat," he said. Saïd smiled. Now he bit into the piece of Yvars's sandwich, but in a gingerly way, like a man who isn't hungry.

The Silent Men inevitably brings to mind some pieces of prewar French social literature, such as Jean Guéhenno's *Journal d'un homme de quarante ans* and, Louis Guilloux's *La Maison du Peuple,* to which Camus wrote a preface[11] in 1953 for a new edition. Guilloux's short masterpiece is in many ways in keeping with Camus's own feeling of life among the poor, as expressed in *The Silent Men* and *The Right and the Wrong Side of Things.* This similarity is due to complex factors. First and foremost is the fact that both writers were born among the poor and could speak from firsthand experience. As Camus observes ironically in his preface to *La Maison du Peuple,* "Almost all the French writers who set themselves forth as speaking for the people today were born of rich or well-to-do families. . . . One can try to explain this paradox by asserting—like a wise friend of mine— that by speaking of what you don't know you eventually learn it." What Camus resents in those self-appointed spokesmen is what he regards as their false tone: either a glorification of "the proletariat" or "the masses," born of the bourgeois intellectual's own guilt feeling or revolutionary busybodiness (it is easy to guess whom Camus has in mind); or the high-handed sociological approach of the "experts in progress" who study the proletariat as "a tribe with peculiar customs." It is hard to say what is more insulting—the "disgusting sycophancy" of the former or the "candid contempt" of the latter. Those who have experienced

11. See Camus, *Essais* (Paris: Bibliothèque de la Pleiade, 1965), p. 1111.

poverty, Camus observes, tend to be impatient with those who speak about it without firsthand knowledge.

Besides their proletarian origins, Camus and the social writers he mentions have something else in common: they speak of a world that is no longer theirs, since they have become intellectuals and comparatively well off. Moreover, they speak of the world of their youth that was already anachronistic at the time they lived in it. Their warmheartedness is mingled with a double nostalgia— for their youth, and for the by-gone age of artisans, when work still had a soul.

Today's proletariat has little in common with old-time artisans. It looms on the horizon as an unknown factor in history and has indeed acquired the quality of "a tribe with strange customs"; *the masses* is a hideous phrase, suggesting some human raw material, explosive and undifferentiated, that aimlessly proliferates where there used to be men and women of the people. Although Camus does not care to admit it, the new proletariat is as strange to him as to "bourgeois intellectuals" or "experts in progress." Camus's notes and letters show that the discovery of large-scale industry was a kind of nightmare to him. The industrial inferno he discovered in Paris and Saint Etienne on his arrival in Metropolitan France found no place in Camus's artistic work. Perhaps the experience was too overwhelming. It just influenced—negatively—the nostalgic remembrance of *The Stranger* and *Exile and the Kingdom*.

Camus's opinions on problems of *modern* industrial work can be found in his journalistic articles. He repeatedly praised Simone Weil's *La condition ouvrière,* and introduced in *L'Express* a much less impressive inquiry by Beatrice Beck on the same subject. "Wages were notoriously insufficient," he said, and the large gap between rich and poor irked the poor.[12] To Camus, however, something seemed still more revolting than the material difficulties of the workers, and that was their spiritual isolation. Camus made

---

12. The minimum wage in 1955 represented a little over one third of what it was in the U.S. (in relative real value). Camus's article appeared on December 13, 1955.

this point in a short, extremely condensed article, "Les Déracinés" (The Uprooted Ones). The workers of the Renault Factory had won a wage increase without a strike. Camus the reformist welcomed this fact, rebuffing equally those who would rest satisfied with this insufficient alleviation of an unacceptable material situation, and those who regret such partial improvements as an opiate, which dulls revolutionary fervor. Camus preferred reform to violence, on condition that reformism was not turned into comfortable resignation to the misery of others.

From these remarks, Camus moves further. Considering the worker's condition as a whole, he deplores his spiritual isolation as much as his material poverty.

It is this inner exile, which separates millions of men from their own country.

> Camping at the gates of the cities, crammed in hideous-looking suburbs, chained by miserably small wages to a kind of toil which debases man by its very mechanical character, French workers, actually suffering from segregation, no longer feel that they belong to a nation which imposes duties on them without letting them partake of its joys. They produce what others enjoy. Can one wonder, then, if the nation henceforward identified with its traders, go-betweens and public entertainers is equally uprooted?

And Camus goes on with this grave warning: "Can there be a nation where there is no people?" Indeed, there are two nations. The exiled proletariat constitutes "a state within a state," for "it has chosen the fatherland of its dreams since it could not find in its own fatherland what was its rightful share."[13]

He concluded this substantial article by urging that the unions participate in the administration of the national income, but wished that these (Communist-dominated) unions would devote as much attention to the improvement of the workers' education as to the establishment of a political hierarchy.

---

13. "Les Déracinés," in *L'Express,* November 25, 1955. (Translated by the author.)

In expressing the worker's spiritual estrangement, Camus deliberately chose the word *uprooted,* which belongs to the terminology of Barrès, the nationalist, of Péguy, the Catholic, and of Simone Weil,[14] who almost converted to Catholicism. He deliberately avoided the word *alienated,* which belongs to the Marxist terminology. The two words point to the same fact of working-class isolation within modern society, but their connotations are far apart. For the Marxists, the workers' estrangement is due exclusively to economic inequality and capitalist rule. Therefore, it is automatically eliminated by the establishment of Communist rule. For Camus, the situation seems far more complex. Uprootedness to him does not exactly mean what it meant to Barrès or Péguy—estrangement from the past. This son of a young overseas colony seems to have little use for the past. His relation is with nature rather than with culture. (Indeed, his many eulogies of the philistine "Mediterranean man"[15] and the whole character of Meursault leave him open to suspicion of obscurantism.) Yet, his former teacher, Jean Grenier, once noted that, as a child of a practically illiterate family, Camus had an almost naïve respect for culture.[16] It can be felt time and again in *The Rebel* how much Camus's values owe to the humanistic tradition, both French and European. Even a quick glance at the program of his *"Théatre de l'Equipe"* and his later theatrical adaptations gives additional proof of this fact.[17] This article, then, raises an important question concerning proletarian education, which Camus never studied systematically, but which underlies most of his thought and work. If, as he notes, racial antagonism is based largely on cultural differences, could not the same be true of class differences, with the gap between the educated and the uneducated widened by the ugliness of industrial suburbs? The working class has no culture

---

14. See her book, *L'Enracinement.*

15. Especially in *Le minotaure ou la halte d'Oran* (in L'Eté), a description, full of humorous vigor, of amateur boxing in Oran.

16. Jean Grenier, *Albert Camus, Souvenirs* (Paris: Gallimard, 1968), p. 159.

17. Particularly Dostoievski's *The Devils.*

of its own, Camus warns in his *Express* article, and is separated from the nation's cultural mainstream.

Similarly, Camus implies in his *Express* article that their cultural vacuum leave modern workers uprooted (or alienated) from the rest of society. Here we may be standing on the brink of a dangerous chasm, for if it were true that there exists an unbridgeable gap between the oppressed proletariat and the "educated classes," it might follow from there—as Sartre repeatedly argues—that humanistic culture, the pride of the West, was simply a bourgeois superstructure, with no universal value, which must be displaced by a new working-class culture. Although Sartre and other fellow-traveling French intellectuals are nauseated by what goes under the name of "socialist realism," they reject humanistic values without being able to clarify what is "bourgeois" about them and what should replace them. Camus never lost himself in this maze. He does not seem to doubt the universal value of culture, as long as it refers to human (and not to class) experience. In his view, Dostoievski is no less accessible to an intelligent and sensitive worker than to any member of the "educated classes"—which is the reason why he so tirelessly adapted great works for the theater, as the best medium to attract work-weary audiences. Camus was not alone in pioneering this road, and it could not be said, after the creation of the *Théatre National populaire,* that such efforts did not receive intelligent official encouragement. Nevertheless, when Camus felt the shock of working-class philistinism, not only intellectual but moral, spiritual philistinism, his reflex was to speak of uprootedness and blame the educated ruling class. The question arises: to what extent was Camus's reaction justified? Other writers as perceptive as Camus and as far left as he was, such as the charming Raymond Queneau, give an altogether different picture of a perfectly adjusted proletariat, interested in cars, television, popular films, *tiercé,*[18] and bloudjines.[19] As for the so-called educated classes, supposedly

---

18. Horse betting.
19. French for blue jeans, according to Queneau's popular heroine, Zazie.

depriving the workers of cultural nourishment, they seem hard to locate. Who *are* the educated class in modern technocracy? Top executives have notoriously no time to waste on Dostoievski, and they spend their leisure very much as the workers do, only with larger cars, higher bettings, and so on. The same life patterns are found among traders and clerks (and there are indications that they exist in revolutionary countries as soon as they grow wealthy). Where, then, are the educated classes, the bearers of culture? Sartre ironically remarked in *What is literature?* that the writer's public was "introuvable." One is reminded of the woman who observed as she watched her son's regiment marching by: They are all out of step except our Johnny. What if the intellectuals themselves were out of step in a society that just needed a little more leisure, more income, and a better distribution of it, to reach a balmy state of perfectly homogeneous philistinism?

In Camus's humanistic universe, all differences—racial, cultural, social—could be remedied if only the flickering light of human communion was preserved. But what dialogue could possibly exist with those, be they workers or bourgeois, rich or poor, Communist or capitalist, who are committed to shallow living and mass entertainment? What communication can there be with those who do not communicate with themselves? Here the humanistic brotherhood ceases; and it may be fortunate for Camus that he did not live long enough fully to digest this fact.

15
Camus and the Communist World

"After that the case is closed," Camus wrote after the Hungarian Revolution; "What Spain was for us twenty years ago, Hungary will be today." Coming from a man who, after one generation, was still in the Résistance,[1] these words carried weight. They raised the dead and conjured up undying ghosts of honor and liberty.

Since *The Fall,* Camus was assailed with doubts. He thought sterility had overcome him and he would never write again. He was near despair, dissipating his life. But suddenly the old Camus awoke. His genius was not dead, but stifled and starved in the mediocrity of the time.

No perceptible evolution took place in Camus's ideas concerning Communist countries in the early fifties. After he had analyzed and condemned them in *The Rebel,* he kept silent. It is even conceivable that Stalin's death brought back some hope in him. But, after Budapest, "the case was closed." Nothing in *The Rebel* announced the total refusal, the urgency and passion that mark the 1957 texts on Hungary:

For it is indeed a counter-revolutionary state. What else can

1. He resigned his post at UNESCO in 1952 to protest Franco Spain's admission.

241

we call a regime that forces the father to inform on his son, the son to demand the supreme punishment for his father, the wife to bear witness against her husband—that has raised denunciation to the level of a virtue? Foreign tanks, police, twenty-year-old girls hanged, committees of workers decapitated and gagged, scaffolds, writers deported and imprisoned, the lying press, camps, censorship, judges arrested, criminals legislating, and the scaffold again—is this socialism, the great celebration of liberty and justice?

No, we have known, we still know this kind of thing; these are the bloody and monotonous rites of the totalitarian religion! Hungarian socialism is in prison or in exile today. In the palaces of the State, armed to the teeth, slink the petty tyrants of absolutism.[2]

There is thunder in this voice. Only a few pages are written about the subject, but they are of great beauty, a beauty that bursts through the mediocre frame of newspaper articles and interviews, that departs from Camus's usually subdued style—the tired style of *Letters to a German Friend* and of *The Plague*. This is the full-blooded, rugged beauty of the *Revolt in the Asturias,* the style of a man standing alone. It has the beauty of an oath: the locked jaws, the clenched fists of the Resistance fighter; the beauty of the Maquis. Once more, Camus was on the side of the rebels who said "No" and this time denounced the tyranny that pretended to speak in their names. A cloud was dispelled. Camus felt that tyranny was on the Left, conformity was on the Left, and lies, too. He had known it since *The Rebel*. But now it became part of himself. He perceived not the capitalists, but the new Eastern empire builders and their Western advocates as the menace. So far, Camus had shown up the fraud in *The Rebel,* and withdrawn. Hungary was an awakening. Prior to 1956, Camus was hesitant and confused when he advocated remedies, because he had to speak of the world of power and was not quite a man of this world. However, in denouncing tyranny, he recaptured his original élan. Such an impassioned appeal had not been heard

---

2. Camus, *Resistance, Rebellion and Death,* p. 158.

since André Malraux's great days in the 1930s. It reads in part as follows:

I am not one of those who long for the Hungarian people to take up arms again in an uprising doomed to be crushed under the eyes of an international society that will spare neither applause nor virtuous tears before returning to their slippers like football enthusiasts on Saturday evening after a big game. But I am not one to think there can be even a resigned or provisional compromise with a reign of terror that has as much right to be called socialist as the executioners of the Inquisition had to be called Christians. . . .

Contemptuous teachers, unaware that they were thereby insulting the working classes, had assured us that the masses could readily get along without liberty if only they were given bread. And the masses themselves suddenly replied that they didn't have bread but that, even if they did, they would still like something else. For it was not a learned professor but a Budapest blacksmith who wrote: "I want to be considered an adult eager to think and capable of thought. I want to be able to express my thoughts without having anything to fear and I want, also, to be listened to."

As for the intellectuals who had been told and shouted at that there was no truth other than the one that served the cause, this is the oath they took at the grave of their comrades assassinated by that cause: "Never again, not even under threat and torture, nor under a misunderstood love of the cause, will anything but the truth issue from our mouths." (Tibor Meray at the grave of Rajk.)

. . . there is no possible evolution in a totalitarian society. Terror does not evolve except toward a worse terror, the scaffold does not become any more liberal, the gallows are not tolerant. Nowhere in the world has there been a party or a man with absolute power who did not use it absolutely.

The first thing to define totalitarian society, whether of the Right or of the Left, is the single party, and the single party has no reason to destroy itself. This is why the only society capable of evolution and liberalization, the only one that deserves both our critical and our active support is the society that involves a plurality of parties as a part of its structure. It alone allows one to denounce, hence to correct, injustice and crime.

It alone today allows one to denounce torture, disgraceful torture, as contemptible in Algiers as in Budapest.[3]

And, continues his appeal,

> We must admit that today conformity is on the Left. To be sure, the Right is not brilliant. But the Left is in complete decadence, a prisoner of words, caught in its own vocabulary, capable merely of stereotyped replies, constantly at a loss when faced with the truth, from which it nevertheless claimed to derive its laws. The Left is schizophrenic and needs doctoring through pitiless self-criticism, exercise of the heart, close reasoning, and a little modesty. Until such an effort at re-examination is well under way, any rallying will be useless and even harmful. Meanwhile, the intellectual's role will be to say that the king is naked when he is, and not to go into raptures over his imaginary trappings.
>
> . . . The idea, still voiced among us, that a party, because it calls itself proletarian, can enjoy special privileges in regard to history is an idea of intellectuals tired of their advantages and of their freedom. History does not confer privileges: it lets them be snatched away.
>
> . . . Alienation is in any case too noble a word to describe the attitude of those who insist on seeing nothing but doves in the East and vultures in the West. Blindness, frenzy of the slave, or nihilistic admiration of force seems to me a more exact term.
>
> . . . Can it be that the Communists and progressive militants feel such love for the Russians they have never seen? No, but they feel such a loathing for a part of the French, the part that loathed them enough to be willing to serve the cause of Hitler. If France is to disappear, rest assured that she will die poisoned by these two hatreds.[4]

The sometimes facile hope that appeared in *Actuelles* is absent from these pages. These stress the tragic realization that the true heroes of our time are the defeated ones. There can be no victorious heroes at a time when all ideals become bastardized.

---

3. *Ibid.*, pp. 157–61.
4. *Ibid.*, pp. 171, 161–62, 167, 169.

Greatness consists in refusal. Heroes were those who have the courage to say "No!" Other ages had positive heroes—men whose misuse of power was redeemed by faith, or who wielded the sword with innocence. Our century has no faith, and offers no victory to the just.[5] At a time when power is wielded by bureaucrats and pseudo-theologians in tanks, helped by secret police, greatness is on the side of the conquered, of those who can do no more than say "No." Here Camus recaptured the spirit of tragedy. The hero is he who dies upright in a world that is not worth living in. These pages are marked with the true spirit of tragedy, of loneliness and death:

> In the battles of our time I have always been on the side of the obstinate, on the side of those who have never despaired of a certain honor. I have shared and I still share many of the contemporary frenzies. But I have never been able to get myself to spit, as so many others do, on the word "honor." Doubtless because I was and am aware of my human weaknesses and of my injustices, because I instinctively knew and still know that honor (like pity) is an unreasonable virtue that takes the place of justice and reason, which have become powerless. . . .
>
> At least we shall try to be faithful to Hungary as we have been to Spain. In Europe's present solitude, we have but one way of being so—which is never to betray, at home or abroad, that for which the Hungarian combatants died and never to justify even indirectly, at home or abroad, what killed them.[6]

Camus did not become "a reactionary," as they said of him. He never idealized the West: "The defects of the West are innumerable, its crimes and errors very real"; "We are fighting a lie in the name of a half truth."[7] He had at long last come to the conclusion that the West was a lesser evil for its half truth, and its quarter truth called liberty:

---

5. The first who recognized this predicament was Nietzsche. Hence his search for the tragic hero.

6. *Resistance, Rebellion and Death*, pp. 240, 167.

7. *Ibid.*, p. 247.

And liberty is the way, and the only way, of perfectibility. Without liberty heavy industry can be perfected, but not justice or truth. Our most recent history, from Berlin to Budapest, ought to convince us of this. In any case, it is the reason for my choice. I have said in this very place that none of the evils totalitarianism claims to remedy is worse than totalitarianism itself. I have not changed my mind. On the contrary, after twenty years of our harsh history, during which I have tried to accept every experience it offered, liberty ultimately seems to me, for societies and for individuals, for labor and for culture, the supreme good that governs all others.[8]

After this courageous stand, the fateful question *What next?* could not be avoided. The answer Camus gave is unfortunately so ambiguous as to blur the clarity of his previous political pronouncements.

What means did Camus suggest to defend liberty from Communist encroachments? When scrutinizing Camus's last writings for an answer to this unasked question, one finds strong words and confused thinking. Like a horse whose élan carried it up against a roadblock, Camus balks, chafes, and finally comes to a standstill. When the Hungarian uprising started, he had obviously hoped for world opinion to support the freedom fighters and outlaw the oppressor until oppression relented. Nothing of the kind happened, nor could Camus hope for long that it still could happen; hence the tone of melancholy contempt at the beginning quoted above, of the Kadar speech: ". . . an international society that will spare neither applause nor virtuous tears before returning to their slippers like football enthusiasts on Saturday evening after a big game." What then was to be done?

All hopes of "rolling back" or even mitigating Soviet tyranny failed when the repression in Hungary went unpunished. The only realistic alternative for the enemies of Communism was a realistic policy of containment. How was this to be achieved? By relying on the moral pressure of a "world opinion" whose lack of morality or opinions the Hungarian crisis had just ex-

---

8. *Ibid.*, p. 248.

posed? Or by the traditional device of meeting force by force, which meant NATO or a "balance of terror." Camus's attitude on this issue is, to say the least, ambiguous. In the above-quoted text about fighting a lie in the name of a half truth, he not only fails to specify by what means the lie should be fought, but, as his thought develops, the emphasis imperceptibly shifts from the determination to fight, suggested by the initial recalling of the days of the Resistance, to an empty eulogy of liberty.

Although the Hungarian crisis showed Camus that uprisings for freedom were "doomed to be crushed" by the indifference of those who wished to "return to their slippers," many lines in *The Wager of Our Generation,* six months later, indicate that the die-hard Utopian in him had already reconstructed the old castle of illusions. Having recalled the "solitary struggle" that preceded the writing of *The Rebel,* Camus slides into a pious optimism in strange contrast to the situation.

> A gigantic myth collapsed. A certain truth, which had long been disguised, burst upon the world. And if the present is still spattered with blood and the future still dark, at least we know that the era of ideologies is over, and the force of resistance, together with the value of freedom, gives us new reasons for living.[9]

Camus probably never saw any way out, except a change of heart; he persevered in the "difficult hope" that "in the end, the spirit proves stronger than the sword" (forgetting Voltaire's warning that God is on the side of big battalions); and when reality shattered the dream he took shelter in historical—perhaps historicist—quietism. If we succeed in avoiding global destruction, he says, begging the question, then unity will prevail—European unity, that would come about as a natural trend of history:

> If Europe is not destroyed by fire, it will come into being. And Russia will in time be added to it, with its individual differences. It will take more than Mr. Khrushchev to make me

9. *Ibid.,* p. 242.

forget what links us to Tolstoy, to Dostoievski and to their
people. But that future is threatened by war.[10]

Destruction or unity, this is the choice before us, or, as Camus
calls it, "our wager," "the Wager of Our Generation."

Strangely enough, Camus does not seem to be worried about
the utopian character of his "Wager." He very quietly states that
the choice is between the improbable change of heart he advocates
and the extinction of the planet by atom war. The possibility of
resorting to a wise use of balance of power (or balance of terror)
in order to create relative security in international relations does
not seem to occur to him. Not that he would reject this solution
as an ethically impure method (this kind of *fiat justicia pereat
mundus* would probably fall into the category of the moral perfectionism he condemns as nihilistic). Rather, Camus does not
believe in the possibility of achieving a balance of power in the
postwar situation. So strong was the impression the atom bomb
made on him that he assumed classical diplomacy to be totally
impracticable in the world of tomorrow. The situation called for
a totally new approach on both sides and the alternative in his
view was reform or perish.

Such an attitude is not without an element of bad faith of
the moralist who bears impatiently with the power game of history
and too readily persuades himself that, due to extraordinary circumstances, power politics is at an end and something new has
to be invented. This is, of course, a fallacy: there is always the
possibility of choosing a bolder, more subtle use of power politics.
Those who prefer peace to conquest must know that without
strength there is no peace.

---

10. *Ibid.,* p. 243.

Conclusion: Humanism in Our Time

1. Camus and Classical Humanism

Camus's view of life does not differ in substance from the views of the classical humanists of the Graeco-Roman and European traditions. One can easily find similarities to such writers as Erasmus, Montaigne, Voltaire, Anatole France, Alain and Bertrand Russell. One may even point to analogies with Seneca, whom Camus so often resembles in his effort to bring humaneness and sober reason to an age of incipient decadence. Camus follows those humanists in his principles: he believes that freedom is the highest value and tolerance the greatest virtue. He demands humaneness and decency in politics. He gives the highest place to respect for life and happiness and denounces the senselessness of ambition and conquest—Burckhardt's *Erwerbs und Machtsinn*. Like the humanists, he believes in the open society and warns against all forms of tribal magic, bound to end in the Inquisition or the police state.

In his mistrust of groups and political parties, with all the pragmatic compromise they impose, Camus often recalls another much-abused humanist, Julien Benda, who provoked a storm comparable to that in *Temps Modernes* when he reminded "clerics" in the late twenties that their function was not to follow Caesar, even for the good of mankind, but to redress him. However, Camus has none of Benda's prophetic intransigence. He is willing to adjust his demands to the concrete situation. Like Dr. Rieux in *La Peste,* who said: "Le salut de l'homme est un trop grand mot pour moi, c'est sa santé qui m'interesse,"[1] Camus is content with a limited application of his principles. The social reformer should not refuse the ant-like work of the sanitary worker, if that is all he is allowed to do. In this soberness Camus resembles Voltaire or even Montaigne, who did not expect much from man, and often aimed at no more than inserting a minimum of humaneness and tolerance into the refractory fabric of society.

Finally, he resembles many a classical humanist in his emotional makeup, uniting as he does metaphysical pessimism with a tender, affectionate disposition. He values friendship and friendliness, love, and compassion as the most precious achievements of man, and intellectual lucidity is for him the basis of a heroic life. His innate tendency is to preserve human values out of love and respect for the fragile thing that is man. Camus's philosophy might be summarized in these words of Bertrand Russell:

> Brief and powerless is man's life; on him and all his race the slow, sure doom falls pitiless and dark. Blind to good and evil, reckless of destruction, omnipotent matter rose on its relentless wave; for Man, condemned today to lose his dearest, tomorrow himself to pass through the gate of darkness, it remains only to cherish, ere yet the blow falls, the lofty thought that ennoble his little days; disdaining the coward's terrors of the slave of Fate, to worship at the shrine that his own hands have built; undismayed by the empire of chance, to preserve a mind free from the wanton tyranny that rules his outward life; proudly defiant of the irresistible forces that tolerate, for a moment, his knowledge and his condemnation, to sustain alone, a wary but unyielding Atlas, the world that his own ideals have fashioned despite the trembling march of unconscious power.[2]

1. *La Peste,* p. 261.
2. Bertrand Russell, "Free Man's Worship," in *Mysticism and other Essays* (London: George Allen and Unwin Ltd., 1917), pp. 56–57.

Similarly, Camus asserted that man is the only creature in the absurd universe that has meaning because he alone demands that there be meaning.[3]

Such striking analogies have not escaped Camus's contemporaries, who point to the lack of originality of his concrete precepts. Others may feel frustrated by his soberness. The Communist intellectuals call him a bourgeois. The *avant-garde* call him a petit-bourgeois.

If Camus had done nothing else than reassert the validity of humanism, that would still suffice to win him a place among the thinkers of an age that discards it, either openly, like the Nazis, or, like the Communists, by paying lip service to it while making it dependent on a system that denies it.

But Camus has done more than simply restate some threatened or forgotten values of the past. No two generations are exactly alike, and their problems are never the same. Even if we fully approve of the principles set forth by former humanists, our emotional experience differs from theirs; we arrive at their thoughts by different roads, informed by a different historical experience. Values have to be asserted anew by each successive generation. Camus has reasserted the age-honored values of humanism in the metaphysical, emotional, and historical setting of the twentieth century.

Some resignation was expected from a well-brought-up writer at the time of Renan, when nihilism was still limited to philosophic circles and had not yet acquired the obsessive character it assumes now that it has entered politics. This is why today tolerant skeptics of previous generations are generally ignored, even abused. They are regarded as tame, sentimental, mawkish, maudlin, and petit-bourgeois.

The emotional experience of Camus's generation is tragic and convulsive. It was Malraux who coined the phrase *tragic humanism,* by which he defines his own and much of his contemporaries' attitude. This applies exactly to Camus's endeavor. For

3. Camus, *Lettres à un ami allemand,* pp. 78–79. See also p. 67.

all its soberness and serenity, Camus's philosophy was born at a time when values had to be defended at the price of life in a world that denies them. Hence, the general heroic coloration of Camus's or Malraux's ethical thinking.

This difference between present and past humanism is revealed outwardly by a difference in tone. Irony was the traditional weapon of the humanist who had long fought fossil prejudice and shamefaced interests. Against the decadent *ancien régime,* as against the traditionalism of Paul Bourget, the irony of Voltaire or Anatole France was the correct weapon. But more than irony is needed against the Inquisition or the police state. Humanism was on the winning side then. Now that it is hunted down and imprisoned, it has given up irony. Nothing can be more revealing of the changed situation than this stylistic difference. Those were happy times in which irony sufficed.

Another difference between Camus and the classical humanists lies in their respective conceptions of man's aims in life. Both Camus and the humanists want "happiness." But the classical humanist usually understands by happiness tranquillity, achieved by curtailment of desire. His ideal is stoic-epicurean: a state of tameness and repose, which he calls "reason." Whether he achieves this state naturally or by self-discipline is irrelevant. Happiness— the only kind at which man can aim—is, in his opinion, the outcome of resignation, sometimes coupled with pride. In contrast to this, Camus is close to the existential attitudes of philosophy. For all his criticism of Nietzsche, he remains his disciple in matters of personal ethics. His aspirations are heroic and romantic. Self-fulfillment, not tameness, is his ideal, the only difference being that in his eyes this fulfillment should come from solidarity in the struggle for freedom, and not from egotistic conquest. And there are indications that in advocating this, Camus feels more faithful to the Nietzschean message than Nietzsche himself, since he encompasses the whole of human nature, part of which Nietzsche refused. To be fully understood, Camus's plea for the acceptance "of the whole of human nature" has to be seen in its historical context. At the time of Nietzsche traditional ethics consisted mainly in curbing and curtailing man's instincts. Accordingly, Nietzsche's plea for a total liberation of man was directed against hypocrisy, which is the reason it could so easily be understood as an apotheosis of raw instinct, that is to say, of barbarism. Such was still the climate when Freud published his *Civilization and Its Discontent*. But times had changed, and many of Camus's contemporaries were beginning to feel the discontent of barbarism. After so many crimes committed in the name of Holy Instinct, and after the tragic solution of the master-slave relation by totalitarian Communism, many writers were taking a second look at human nature. They were trying to discover whether the life force must necessarily aim at egotistic domination or at "reification" of one's fellowman, or to state it differently, they were searching for a more successful "unfolding" of the instincts and a more satisfactory balance between freedom and social discipline than those offered by Nietzsche and Lenin respectively. In other words, they wanted to avoid the onslaught of the Barbarian as pictured in Kafka's story, when "even their horses ate flesh."

What Camus believed to be the mission of the artist was to keep the barbarians away and, as time went on, the barbarians became linked with history, the effect of which, according to Camus, was merely to replace one set of barbarians with another, in an endless shifting of the master-slave relationship. "The role of the artist in society"—such is the title of the speech he read in Sweden when he was awarded the Nobel Prize for Literature in 1957—is usually regarded as Camus's spiritual testament. (He died in a car crash in 1960). The subject of the acceptance speech was not chosen lightly. It coincided with the reasons stated by the Academy for awarding him the Prize, "for his important literary work, which puts forth with penetrating seriousness problems presented to the conscience of man today."[4] In choosing as his theme "the role of the artist in society," Camus was dealing in fact with his lifelong commitment. His real subject was the

---

4. Statement by Dr. Anders Osterling, the Nobel Committee's Chairman, on the Swedish Radio, October 17, 1957.

confrontation of the artist—and the thinker—with history and, broader still, with that part of man which must be saved from the stream of history in order to be able to judge it and transcend it. In his speech Camus was expressing the ruling principle of his life: the inalienable right to spiritual freedom. His thoughts on this question are summarized in the speech as well as in the interview he gave at almost the same time: The Wager of Our Generation. The writer, according to Camus, should be committed, while keeping at a sufficient distance to avoid being engulfed in history. He must save certain values from history—not his own, Camus specifies, but values belonging to all men, these very values professed by Camus from his earlier days as a writer: life (and happiness), honor, and liberty.

> To begin with, I feel a solidarity with the common man. Tomorrow the world may burst into fragments. In that threat hanging over our heads, there is a lesson of truth. As we face such a future, hierarchies, titles, honors are reduced to what they are in reality: a passing puff of smoke. And the only certainty left to us is that of naked suffering, common to all, intermingling its roots with those of a stubborn hope.
> In the battles of our time I have always been on the side of the obstinate, on the side of those who have never despaired of a certain honor.[5]

According to Camus, art has no other aim than to increase the portion of freedom and responsibility that exists in each man and in the world:

> There are works of art that tend to make man conform and to convert him to some external rule. Others tend to subject him to whatever is worst in him, to terror and hatred. Such works are valueless to me.[6]

In his carefully prepared speech for the Nobel Prize, Camus

---

5. Published in *Demain*, October 24, 1957, and reproduced in *Resistance, Rebellion and Death*, pp. 239–40.
6. *Ibid.*, pp. 240–41.

not only reiterated the ideas that made Benda unpopular twenty-five years before, but also specified that the writer's "difficult duty" is to stand at some distance from parties and from makers of history, thereby opposing masters and conquerors.

Commenting on the task of his generation, which lived through "over 20 years of history run mad," he observes:

> Probably every generation sees itself as charged with re-making the world. Mine, however, knows that it will not remake the world. But its task is perhaps even greater, for it consists in keeping the world from destroying itself. As the heir of a corrupt history that blends blighted revolutions, misguided techniques, dead gods, and worn out ideologies, in which second-rate powers can destroy everything today, but are unable to win anyone over, in which intelligence has stooped to becoming the servant of hatred and oppression, that generation, starting from nothing but its own negations, has had to re-establish both within and without itself a little of what constitutes the dignity of life and death.[7]

In this mistrust of history, Camus can be compared to Pierre-Henri Simon (*L'Esprit et L'Histoire*), who definitely locates values outside history; Camus also brings to mind a more humorous contemporary novelist, Romain Gary, who plainly stated, at the end of his war service in the Royal Air Force, "la civilisation, c'est ce que l'histoire nous laisse quand on n'a reussi à la foutre dehors" (civilization is what history leaves us after one has succeeded kicking it out). (*Les Couleurs du jour*)

2. Faith for Modern Man: The Existential Dialogue

The mission Camus assigns to the artist of rescuing human values from the stream of history raises anew the unsolved problem of the foundation of his thought. For one who does not believe in transcendence, what is there for mankind apart from history? Although Camus does not end in mysticism like many

---

7. *Ibid.,* p. 241.

of his nineteenth-century predecessors (Victor Hugo, Lamartine, Michelet), he makes rational humanism burst at the seams in every direction, for his problems and aspirations are religious, even though his solutions are not.

Camus struggled bravely with the problems of evil, suffering, and nothingness. They remained unresolved. "Why do even children have to suffer," he once asked the Catholic writer François Mauriac? The Rebel found no satisfactory answer and went on searching for the dignity of man without metaphysical help. But where does the urge to rebel come from? Why does man simply not accept his fate? Is not revolt itself a transcendent value? What prompts Socrates to drink the hemlock, and Jesus to endure His death on the cross?

Camus never considered the possibility of a limited God, as conceived by some of the Gnostics he studied in his youth; he did not think it possible, like Jacob Boehme and, in our time, Berdyaev, that Nothingness or the Abyss could be part of the divine. Nor could he accept the Greek idea of a divine architect who conceived a cosmos acceptable to the mind out of a primordial chaos; nor, like Henri Bergson, the existence in nature of a trend akin to human consciousness. Camus was left with the absurd universe. Of all metaphysical possibilities offered by contemporary thinkers, he chose the most desperate—either by some tragic confusion of religious thought with masochistic submission, or as a result of his passion for lucidity. Nevertheless, Sisyphus did not despair. The message that permeates the entire work and thought of Camus is that a dialogue between man and man, completed by his nuptials with nature, can transcend despair.

> What balances the absurd is the community of men fighting against it. And if we choose to serve that community, we choose to serve the dialogue carried to the absurd against any policy of falsehood or of silence.[8]

This theme is central in Camus's work. Damnation came to

---

8. *Notebooks*, 2: 126.

Caligula, and Martha in *Cross Purposes,* from the impossibility of
entering into dialogue. Salvation, from *The Plague* onwards, comes
from the ability to establish contact.

What are the main obstacles to this opening of the heart? What
takes away from man this straw of hope and makes his absurd
existence even more meaningless and unbearable? Are the mor-
tifying forces that make a meaningful dialogue impossible peculiar
to our time? From all quarters of the philosophic world comes the
same positive answer: the Marxists speak of the reification of
man. For Marcuse man is a deluded commodity in the consumers'
society. Among the psychoanalysts, Erich Fromm sees modern
man as a marketing personality, Karen Horney as "a shallow
personality" who does not even feel his alienation. In Heidegger's
profound analysis, man is drowned in things, takes refuge in the
anonymous *Man,* the "IT" of things, and the anonymity of "empty
chatter."[9]

Next to Heidegger, it was probably Jaspers who expressed
Camus's intuitions most exactly. According to Jaspers, modern
man transforms everything into objects, including his fellow man
and himself.

Heidegger and Jaspers call us back to our inner being, away
from shallowness and the greed for money, and above all power.
For the modern mass man, in Heidegger's phrase: "das Sein des
Seienden ist Wille zur Macht" (The being of Being is will to
power).[10]

There is one modern thinker who does succeed where Camus
hesitated and was unable to accept. Martin Buber, foremost
philosopher of the opening of man to his being via man and God,
makes the fundamental distinction between the "I-Thou" and
the "I-It" relationship. This fundamental insight, as Buber often
reiterated, cannot be fully verbalized or articulated. But the two
categories refer to all human relationships, with the visible and

---

9. "Das Gerede," in Martin Heidegger's *Sein und Zeit* (Halle:
Niemayer, 1927), p. 169.
10. See Martin Heidegger, *Holzwege* (Frankfurt: V. Klostermann,
1950).

the invisible. The "I-IT" yearns after the gratification of desires; it is self-centered, wants pleasure, gain, and power—appropriation in the true Sartrian fashion.[11] But for Sartre there is no escape.[12] Buber on the other hand does offer us the "I-THOU," "the eternal life," the "encounter." In this spontaneous confrontation a "new presence" is born, "we let ourselves be" (the exact analogy of Heidegger's *Gelassenheit* or the "Opening ourselves to Being.") In Buber's dialogue we are transformed by experiencing a "revelation" of the "Presence of God." Camus did experience this "encounter" in his relationship with nature and by communicating with his suffering fellowmen.

Like Martin Buber, Camus was terrified by the ever-growing depersonalization of modern man, "a progressive augmentation of the world of IT."[13] The phenomenon is, of course, most advanced in totalitarian states, but the ever-growing bureaucratization threatens all societies alike. The Byzantine pressure of the bureaucracy, however, is not the primary cause of the sickness, but only a symptom of the decline, the decadence, of our age.

> We live in a world of abstraction, of bureaus and machines, of absolute ideas and of unsubtle, unyielding messianisms. We are being smothered by people who believe themselves to be absolutely in the right, whether because of their machines or their ideas. And for all who cannot live except in dialogue and friendship with men, this silence is the end of the world.[14]

For Camus and Buber a truly humane society does not consist in the mere augmentation of pleasure and comfort.[15] What it does mean is an open, genuine human relationship with one's fellowman. Surprisingly, Camus once stated that "he would not mind

---

11. Martin Buber, *I and Thou,* p. 96.
12. Jean-Paul Sartre, *Being and Nothingness,* trans. Hazel Barnes (New York: Phil. Library, 1956).
13. Martin Buber, *I and Thou* (Edinborough: T. and T. Clark, 1937), p. 33.
14. *Actuelles I,* p. 14.
15. Camus never identified himself with the pleasure-plain philosophy of the English utilitarians or with modern pragmatism.

being called religious in Buber's sense," and Buber himself re-
ciprocated by saying, ."I would not call Camus an atheist. He
was one of the men who are destroying the old images. You
know how I feel about them."[16]

Camus did affirm and reaffirm the "Dialogical Presence" as the
only salvation for modern alienated man. This "openness and
solidarity" is the true affirmation of man's dignity. According to
Buber it is a permanent rebellion against the world of the IT.
The THOU, this contact of the suffering creature with another
spirit and with the divine, bears witness to the spark of God in
man, to the mystery of consciousness and of free will. At this
juncture Prometheus and the mystical Jewish Godhead become
one. Such was Buber's message to a world rushing into catastrophe.
Camus's Rebel, however, extends the call to man only, not to
God.

3. Rebirth of the Rebel

Albert Camus's philosophy of life, enriched by the philosophies
of his great contemporaries, appears as a coherent whole, entirely
acceptable to twentieth-century criteria and needs.

The current image of the twentieth century, as bereaved through
the "death of God" and helpless against the impact of its technological development, is a myth, the result of fatalistic half-
truths. "Beware of the terrible oversimplifiers," was Jakob Burckhardt's warning.

The twentieth century did succeed in offering a body of beliefs
acceptable both to its metaphysical and political aspirations, in
no way inferior to the great syntheses of the past. However, the
tragic irony of our age is that our civilization might be coming to
a premature end because of the lack, not of a viable set of values,
but of the will to enforce them. Camus remains to us the exponent
of this creed and the witness of this failure.

One of the most amazing phenomena of our time, not fully

16. Maurice Friedman, *The Problematic Rebel, An Image of Modern Man* (New York: Random House, 1963), pp. 442 n, 487 n.

appreciated by the comfortable consumers' societies, including its "idealistic dissenters," is the rebirth of the true rebel in totalitarian countries.

It is remarkable that Camus's works have been a source of inspiration to another political thinker from a country where freedom was drastically curtailed.

In contrast to Camus, Milovan Djilas held power; for years he was at the very center of power in a Communist state. But he resigned from his post as Vice President of Yugoslavia; he let himself be expelled from the Central Committee of the Yugoslav Party; he suffered imprisonment and years of solitary confinement—all in the name of truth and his desire to unmask the power structures of a Communist society, which he himself had helped to form and create.[17]

In his remarkable book *The New Class,* published in America in 1957, and his *Anatomy of a Moral,* which came out in English one year before Camus's death, Djilas expresses his disillusionment with the realities of Communism wherever it has acceded to power. The "New Class" establishes itself, according to Djilas, as a byzantine, bureaucratic, and monopolistic caste over the entire society, and, in the name of the working class, a new exploiting layer of Communist rulers holds all the reins of power, only more despotic, more pernicious to freedom and to dignity than the old class of capitalists.

This, however, was only the first stage of Djilas's departure from Marxism-Leninism. The second, an even more important part of his thought, appeared in book form more than ten years later.[18] Djilas's *The Unperfect Society* is a revolutionary treatise of political philosophy, not yet fully appreciated in the United States. (The number of critiques in learned journals is very meager

---

17. It is known that Djilas frequently expressed his admiration for Martin Luther and his ringing sentence at the Diet of Worms: "Here I stand and can do no other."

18. Milovan Djilas, *The Unperfect Society: Beyond the New Class,* translated by Dorian Cooke (New York: Harcourt, Brace and World, Inc., 1969).

or not quite to the point, one of the exceptions being that of Ghila Ionescu.)[19]

From the point of view of the development of Camus's political ideas during the last few years of his life, it may be regarded as a misfortune that he had lived in almost complete political isolation, theoretical and practical. Had Djilas's *The New Class* been translated into French soon after it had been smuggled out to America, Camus might have felt supported and justified in many of the ideas he had been trying to express since the publication of *The Rebel*.

Camus did not read Djilas, but the Yugoslav writer did read Camus. There are two references to him in *The Unperfect Society* (pages 35 and 67). Djilas, like Camus, remains faithful to the original ideal of genuine revolt:

> And if I sometimes felt at my wit's end, torn by doubts in my "faith" and beset by notions of the existence of some higher law which sets everything in motion, including my personal destiny, I reacted at once against such "culpable" weaknesses and lack of faith. I reveled in the fiendish notion that, if the existence of God should become incontrovertible, I would rebel against his omniscience and immutable order, in the same way that I had reveled in my heretical infection of the party's despotic, inhuman, and contrived unity. Revolt against "higher powers" was to me a sign of man's creative life force no less categorical than his propensity to bow to the inevitable. At that time I had not come across Camus's well-known aphorisms: "Man is the only creature who refuses to be what he is" and "I rebel, therefore we exist"; but if I had, I would certainly have included them in my prison notes as an epitome of my own feelings and thoughts."[20]

The kinship between Djilas's thought and that of Camus is already evident in the introduction to *The Unperfect Society*. The issue is once more Utopia, chiliasm. Djilas explains the odd title of his book, and why he did not choose the word *Im*perfect Society:

19. *Political Quarterly* (June 1959), pp. 208 ff.
20. *The Unperfect Society,* pp. 208 ff.

Society cannot be perfect. Men must hold both ideas and ideals, but they should not regard these as being wholly realizable. We need to comprehend the nature of utopianism. Utopianism, once it achieves power, becomes dogmatic, and it quite readily can create human suffering in the name and in the cause of its own scientism and idealism. To speak of society as imperfect may seem to imply that it *can* be perfect, which in truth it cannot. The task for contemporary man is to accept the reality that society is unperfect, but also to understand that humanist, humanitarian dreams and visions are necessary in order to reform society, in order to improve and advance it.[21]

Both Camus and Djilas point out the insufficiency of the economic interpretation of history, both violently oppose the bureaucracy of Communist societies, which they regard as inevitable once regimes establish themselves as monopolistic party oligarchies. Both object to the utopianism and chiliasm of the Communists' promise, and both are frantically looking for means to avoid the Communist barrack system, which has nothing in common with the original message of socialism, and is but a totalitarian disfigurement of a byzantine society.

By the time he wrote *The New Class,* Djilas was already aware of the inadequacies of post-Marxist dogmas, which he criticized by Marxist methods:

the society that has arisen as the result of Communist revolutions, or as a result of the military actions of the Soviet Union, is torn by the same sort of contradictions as are other societies.[22]

Other similarities between Camus's and Djilas's thoughts are astonishing. Both condemn the Jacobin spirit of Communism in the name of happiness:

The world is satiated with dogmas, but people are hungry for life.[23]

---

21. *Ibid.,* pp. 4, 5.
22. *Ibid.,* p. 8.
23. *Ibid.,* p. 57.

Both authors condemn the new Caesars who established themselves in the center of power after breaking the promise to bring dignity and brotherhood to man. And, finally, both are searching for a remedy, preventive and post-operative, to avoid this predicament. The Yugoslav finds a partial remedy in the workers' councils, Camus in the trade-union movement.

Djilas undertakes a psychological investigation into the past of his own thoughts and faiths. He asks himself why the God has failed, and discovers to what extent he had been a victim of dogma. He examines Marxism-Leninism and finds its utopian claims highly dangerous, because it justifies means by ends, confuses ideas with realities, and sacrifices men to mankind. He questions the usefulness of Leninism in present-day conditions and finds it irrelevant. Djilas extends his criticism to Marx himself:

> Marx, in fact, has suffered the same fate as other great thinkers. Having arrived at a truth—man's economic dependence—he turned that truth into *the* truth about man. Being aware of the static nature of every formulation, he avoided making formulations. Nevertheless, with his antecedent conviction that his own views were irrefutably scientific, and his work exclusively so, he presented his social-research findings, drawn from history and European society (particularly from the English society of the first half and middle of the nineteenth century) as a discovery of laws that operate "with the inexorability of some natural process."[24]

Rejecting this dogmatism, he reverts to long-forgotten humanistic values—anticlerical, so to speak—and denounces as regressive the collective control of individual consciences.

> The evidence is that society itself passes into stagnation and illiberality once the conscience of its individual members —religion, in other words—comes under the control of monopolistic ideologies.

24. *Ibid.,* p. 138.

The concepts Communism, capitalism, even socialism—insofar as it does not mean freer personalities, greater rights for social groups, and a more equitable distribution of goods than obtains at present—all belong to earlier ages. And the reason people in the East and in the West still come across these concepts, and why, by all accounts, they will have to contend with them for a long time to come, is to be found in the fact that ideas are like vampires; ideas are capable of living after the death of the generations and social conditions in and by which they were inspired. Today such vampire ideas persist in the spiritual delirium and putrefaction of contemporary social groups that are in decline.

Nations, people, the human race are living now in a new world, though their thoughts remain in the old: therein lie humanity's hopes as well as humanity's misfortunes.[25]

The spark of Prometheus does not die out.

In a world in which there is more empty chatter than ever before but very little dialogue, Albert Camus, as witness of the decline of the West, would today pay homage to the new rebels against totalitarianism. In Solzhenitsyn's *The First Circle* and in his *Cancer Ward,* the slaves of modern tyranny, whose families are hounded, continue, in their prisons, to love life, and also justice, truth, freedom, and mercy. In the camps and dungeons, and in the underground press, the dialogue continues.

This was Camus's message: the virus of the Plague is in all of us, but so is the spark of Prometheus. And such is the enigma of man: a creature caught in "the heavy burden of fatality"[26] but endowed with the trembling flame of his consciousness and metaphysical freedom.

25. *Ibid.,* pp. 39, 19.
26. Friedrich Hölderlin, *The Death of Empedocles,* as quoted by Camus in the epigraph to *The Rebel.*

Bibliography

Novels, Plays, Essays, Articles, and Prefaces by Camus

NOVELS

L'Étranger. Gallimard, 1942 (*The Stranger.* New York: Vintage Books, 1954).

La Peste. Gallimard, 1947 (*The Plague.* New York: A. Knopf, 1949).

La Chute. Gallimard, 1956 (*The Fall.* New York: A. Knopf, 1957).

L'Exil et le Royaume. Gallimard, 1957 (*Exile and the Kingdom.* New York: A. Knopf, 1958).

PLAYS

Le Malentendu et Caligula. Paris: Gallimard, 1944.

L'État de Siège. Paris: Gallimard, 1948.

Les Justes. Paris: Gallimard, 1950.

Caligula and Three Other Plays. New York: A. Knopf, 1960.

ESSAYS

L'Envers et l'Endroit. Alger: Charlot, 1937.

Noces. Alger: Charlot, 1938.

Le Mythe de Sisyphe. Les Essais XII, Paris: Gallimard, 1942.

The Myth of Sisyphus and Other Essays. Translated by Justin O'Brien. New York: A. Knopf, 1955.

Lettres à un Ami allemand. Paris: Gallimard, 1948.

Actuelles, Chroniques 1944–1948; *Actuelles II,* Chroniques 1948–1953; *Actuelles III,* Chronique algérienne 1939–1958. Paris: Gallimard, 1950, 1953, 1958.

Notebooks (Carnets). 1935–1942. Translated by Philip Thody. New York: Alfred A. Knopf, 1963.

L'Homme révolté. Gallimard, 1951. (*The Rebel.* New York: Vintage Books, 1956).

Lyrical and Critical Essays, Edited by P. Thody. New York: A. Knopf, 1968.

Resistance, Rebellion and Death. New York: A. Knopf, 1961.

L'Été, Les Essais LXVIII. 21st ed. Paris: Gallimard, 1954.

Speech of Acceptance upon the Award of the Nobel Prize for Literature. Translated by Justin O'Brien. New York: Alfred A. Knopf, 1958.

With Arthur Koestler:

Réflexions sur la peine capitale: Introduction et étude de Jean Bloch-Michel. Paris: Calmann-Levy, 1957.

ARTICLES AND PREFACES

"La Nausée." *Alger-Républican* (October 1938).

"Remarques sur la Révolte." *L'Existence; Essais par A. Camus et al.* Paris: Gallimard, 1945.

"Réflexions sur le Christianisme." *La Vie Intellectuelle* (1 December 1946).

"Le Meurtre et l'absurde." *Empédocle,* no. 1 (1949).

"Nietzsche et le nihilisme." *Les Temps Modernes* (August 1951).

A. Rosmer. *Moscou sous Lénine: Les Origines du communisme.* Paris: Editions de Flore, Pierre Horay, 1953.

"Hope and Absurdity." *The Kafka Problem.* Edited by Angel Flores. New York: New Directions (1946).

"Réponse à l'appel des écrivains hongrois." *Franc-Tireur.* no. 3623 (10-11 November 1956), pp. 1, 3.

"Le Socialisme des potences." *Demain,* no. 63 (21-27 February 1957), pp. 10–11. Translated as "Parties and Truth." *Encounter* 8 (April 1957): 3–5.

"Le Parti de la liberté." *Monde Nouveau-Paru* 3-5, nos. 110-11 (April-May 1957): 1–9.

"Letter of Reply to Peter L. Caracciolo." *Encounter* 8 (June 1957): 68.

"Le Pari de notre génération." *Demain,* no. 98 (24-30 October 1957), pp. 11–13.

"Hommage à un journaliste exilé." *La Revue Prolétarienne,* no. 442 (November 1957), pp. 2–4.

"Camus nous parle." *Le Figaro Littéraire,* no. 682 (16 May 1959), pp. 1, 4.

Books on Camus

Brée, Germaine. *Camus.* New Brunswick, N.J.: Rutgers University Press, 1959.

————, ed. *Camus: A Collection of Critical Essays.* Englewood Cliffs, N.J.: Prentice-Hall, 1962.

Lyrical and Critical Essays. Edited with notes by Philip Thody. Translated by Ellen C. Kennedy. New York: A. Knopf, 1968.

Camus, Albert: *Resistance, Rebellion and Death.* Translated by Justin O'Brien. Alfred A. Knopf: New York, 1961.

Grenier, Jean, ed. "Remarques sur la Révolte." *L'Existence.* Paris: Gallimard, 1945, pp. 9–23.

Luppé, Robert de. *Albert Camus.* Paris: Presses Universitaires, 1951.

Maquet, Albert. *Albert Camus ou l'invincible été.* Paris: Editions Debresse, 1955.

Parker, Emmet. *Albert Camus; The Artist in the Arena.* Milwaukee: The University of Wisconsin Press, 1965.

Quilliot, Roger. *La Mer et les prisons: Essai sur Albert Camus.* Paris: Gallimard, 1956.

————, et al., eds. *Théâtre, Récits, Nouvelles* N.R.F. Bibliothèque de la Pléiade. Paris: Editions Gallimard, 1962.

————, et al., eds. *Albert Camus.* Essais. N.R.F. Bibliothèque de la Pléiade. Paris: Editions Gallimard, 1965.

Simon, Pierre-Henri. *L'Homme en Procès: Malraux—Sartre—Camus—Saint Exupéry.* Neuchâtel, Switzerland: Les Editions de la Baconnière à Boudry, 1950, pp. 11–12.

Articles on Camus

Albérès, R. M. "Albert Camus et le mythe de Prométhée." *La Révolte des écrivains d'aujourd'hui.* Paris: Editions Correa, 1949, pp. 65–81.

————. "Is There a New Ethic in Fiction?" *Yale French Studies,* 4, no. 8 (1951).

Astorg, Bertrand d'. "De la Peste et d'un nouvel humanisme." *Aspects de la littérature européenne depuis 1945.* Paris: Editions du Seuil, 1952, pp. 191–200.

Ayer, A. J. "Novelist-Philosophers, VIII—Albert Camus." *Horizon* 75 (March 1946).

Barrett, William. "The Myth of Sisyphus and Other Essays by Albert Camus." Book Review Section, *The New York Times* (18 September 1955).

Bataille, Georges. "La Morale du Malheur: 'La Peste.' " *Critique* (June-July 1947).

———. "L'Affaire de l'Homme Révolté." *Critique,* no. 67 (December 1952), pp. 1077–81.

Berl, Emmanuel. "Lettre à Albert Camus." *La Table Ronde,* nos. 103-4 (July-August 1956) pp. 301–6.

Bespaloff, Rachel. "Le monde du condamné à mort." *Esprit* 163 (January 1950).

Bieber, Konrad. "The Rebellion of a Humanist." *The Yale Review* 43 (March 1954): 473–75.

Boisdeffre, Pierre de. "Métamorphose de la littérature de Proust à Sartre." Paris: Editions Alsatia, 1952, 2: 287; Albert Camus, "Notebooks," 1942–1951. Translated by Justin O'Brien. New York: Alfred A. Knopf, 1965, p. 113 (entry of September 1945).

———. "Albert Camus ou l'expérience tragique." *Etudes* (December 1950), pp. 303–25.

Brée, Germaine. "Introduction to Albert Camus." *French Studies* 4 (January 1950): 27–37.

———. "Albert Camus and *The Plague.*" *Yale French Studies,* no. 8 (1951), pp. 93–100.

Breton, André, and Patri, Aimé. "Dialogue entre A. Breton et A. Patri à propos de l'Homme révolté d'Albert Camus." *Arts,* no. 333 (16 November 1951), pp. 1, 3.

Daix, Pierre. "Albert Camus: Prix Nobel." *Les Lettres Françaises,* no. 693 (24–30 October 1957), pp. 1, 5.

Doubrovsky, Serge. "Camus en Amérique." *La Nouvelle Revue Française* 98 (1 February 1961): 292–96.

Durand, Anne. *Le Cas Albert Camus.* Paris: Editions Fischbacher, 1961.

Guérard, Albert J. "Albert Camus." *Foreground* 1 (Winter 1946).

Hanna, Thomas. *The Thought and Art of Albert Camus.* Chicago: Henry Regnery Company, 1958.

Jeanson, Francis. "Albert Camus ou l'âme revoltée." *Les Temps Modernes* (May 1952), pp. 2070–90.

Lausner, Kermit. "Albert Camus." *The Kenyon Review* 14, no. 4 (Autumn 1952): 562–78.

Mauriac, Claude. "L'Homme révolté, d'Albert Camus." *La Table ronde,* no. 48 (December 1951), pp. 98–109.

Mohrt, Michel. "Ethic and Poetry in the Work of Camus." *Yale French Studies* 1, no. 1 (Spring-Summer, 1948).

Mounier, Emmanuel. "Albert Camus, ou l'Appel des Humiliés." *L'Espoir des Désespérés.* Paris: Gallimard, 1944.

Peyre, Henri. "The Resistance and Literary Revival in France." *Yale Review* 35, no. 1 (Sept. 1945): 84–92.

Rousseaux, André. "Albert Camus et la philosophie du bonheur." *Littérature du XXème siècle.* Paris: Albin Michel, 1949.

Sartre, Jean-Paul. "Explication de l'Étranger." *Situations* 1 (February 1943). Paris: Gallimard, 1947.

————. "Albert Camus." *France-Observateur,* no. 505 (7 January 1960), p. 17.

Spiegelberg, Herbert. "French Existentialism: Its Social Philosophies." *Kenyon Review* 16, no. 3 (Summer 1954): 446–63.

Stockwell, H. C. R. "Albert Camus." *The Cambridge Journal* 7, no. 11 (August 1954): 690–704.

Thody, Philip. *Albert Camus: A Study of his Work.* London: Hamish Hamilton, 1957.

Thoorens, Leon. *A la Rencontre d'Albert Camus.* Liège: La Sixaine, 1946.

Truc, Gonzague. "La Querelle Sartre-Camus." *Hommes et Mondes,* no. 76 (November 1952), pp. 370–75.

Select Bibliography

The following books have been used in preparing the analysis of Camus's philosophical and political thought.

Arendt, Hannah. *The Human Condition.* Garden City, N.Y.: Doubleday Anchor Books, 1959.

————. *The Origins of Totalitarianism.* New York: Harcourt, Brace and Company, 1951.

Aron, Raymond. "The Philosophy of History." In *Chambers Encyclopedia* 7: 147–59.

————. *The Opium of the Intellectuals.* Translated by Terence Kilmartin. Garden City, N.Y.: Doubleday, 1957.

Barzun, Jacques. *The House of Intellect.* New York: Harper, 1959.

Beauvoir, Simone de. *Les Mandarins.* Paris: Gallimard, 1954.

————. *The Ethics of Ambiguity.* New York: Philosophical Library, 1948.

Berlin, Isaiah. *Historical Inevitability.* London, New York: Oxford University Press, 1954.

Bieber, Konrad. *L'Allemagne vue par les écrivains de la résistance française.* Geneva: Droz, 1954.

Blanchot, Maurice. "La Confession dédaigneuse." *La Nouvelle Revue Française,* no. 48 (December 1956), pp. 1050–56.

————. "Réflexions sur le nihilisme." *NRF,* no. 17 (May 1954), pp. 850–59.

Bollnow, Otto. "Existenzialismus und Ethik." *Die Sammlung* 4 (Jahrgang) (1949): 321–35.

Buber, Martin. *Paths in Utopia.* Translated by R. F. C. Hull. New York: Macmillan Company, 1950.

————. *I and Thou.* Edinborough: T. & T. Clark, 1937. (*Path in Utopia.*)

Bukharin, N. I. *Marxism and Modern Thought; What Is the Soviet Union and Where Is It Going?* Translated by Ralph Fox. New York: Harcourt, Brace and Company, 1935.

Burckhardt, Jacob. "On Fortune and Misfortune in History." In *Force and Freedom.* Edited by James H. Nichols. New York: Pantheon Books, Inc. 1943.

Champigny, Robert. "Existentialism in the Modern French Novel." *Thought* 31, no. 122 (Autumn 1956): 194–204.

Collinet, Michel: *La Tragédie du marxisme; du manifeste communiste à la stratégie totalitaire; essai critique.* Paris: Calmann-Lévy, 1948.

Crossman, Richard, ed. *The God That Failed.* New York: Bantam Books, 1952.

Duhrssen, Alfred. "Some French Hegelians." *Review of Metaphysics* 7, no. 2 (December 1953): 323–37.

Geyl, Pieter. *Debates with Historians.* New York: Meridian Books, Inc., 1958.

Guardini, Romano. *The End of the Modern World; A Search for*

Orientation. Translated by L. Thernan and H. Burre. New York: Sheed and Ward, 1956.

Hartmann, Nicolai. *Das Problem des geistigen Seins.* 2 Auflage. Berlin: Walter de Gruyter and Company, 1949.

Hegel, G. W. F. *Lectures on the Philosophy of History.* Translated by J. Sibree. New York: Dover Publications, Inc., 1956.

Heidegger, Martin. *Holzwege.* Frankfurt: V. Klostermann, 1950.

Hodges, H. A. *Wilheim Dilthey.* Introduction by H. A. Hodges. London: K. Paul, Trench, Trubner, and Co. Ltd., 1944.

Hook, Sidney. *From Hegel to Marx; Studies in the Intellectual Development of Karl Marx.* New York: Reynal and Hitchcock, 1936.

Hughes, Serge. *The Fall and Rise of Modern Italy.* New York: Macmillan, 1967.

Jaspers, Karl. "The Unity of History." In *The Origin and Goal of History.* New Haven: Yale University Press, 1953.

Juenger, Ernst. *Der Arbeiter; Herrschaft und Gestalt.* Hamburg: Hanseatische Verlagsanstalt, 1932.

Kautsky, Karl. *Die Materialistische Geschichtsauffassung.* Berlin: J. H. W. Dietz, 1929.

Lenin, V. I. "What Is To Be Done?" In *Selected Works.* New York: International Publishers, 1943, 2: 27ff.

———. "State and Revolution." In *Selected Works.* New York: International Publishers, 1943, 7: 5ff.

Lessing, Theodor. *Geschichte als Sinngebung des Sinnlosen.* Munich: C. H. Beck, 1921.

Löwith, Karl. *Meaning in History.* Chicago: The University of Chicago Press, 1949.

———. "Nietzsche's Doctrine of Eternal Recurrence." *Journal of the History of Ideas* (June 1945).

———. "Heidegger: Problem and Background of Existentialism." *Social Research* (September 1948).

Luethy, Herbert. *France Against Herself.* Translated by Eric Mosbacher. New York: F. H. Praeger, Inc., 1955.

Magny, Claude-Edmonde. "The Objective Depiction of Absurdity." In *The Kafka Problem,* edited by Angel Flores. New York: New Directions Press, 1946.

Malraux, André. *La Condition Humaine.* Paris: Gallimard, 1946.

———. *Les Noyers de l'Altenburg.* Paris: Gallimard, 1948.

Marcel, Gabriel. *Les Hommes contre l'Humain*. Paris: La Colombe, 1959.

Masaryk, T. G. *The Ideals of Humanity; Lectures Delivered in 1898 at the University of Prague*. Translated by W. Preston Warren. London: G. Allen and Unwin Ltd., 1938.

Merleau-Ponty, Maurice. *Humanisme et Terreur; Essai sur le Problème Communiste*. Paris: Gallimard, 1947.

Michel, Henri. *Histoire de la Résistance*. Paris: Presses Universitaires de France, 1950.

————. *Les Idées Politiques et Sociales de la Résistance*. Paris: Presses Universitaires de France, 1954.

Monnerot, Jules. *Sociologie du Communisme*. Paris: Gallimard, 1949.

Nadeau, Maurice. *Histoire du Surréalisme*. Paris: Editions du Seuil, 1946.

Neumann, Franz L. *Behemoth; the Structure and Practice of National Socialism 1933–1944*. Toronto, New York: Oxford University Press, 1944.

Niebuhr, Reinhold. *Faith and History; A Comparison of Christian and Modern Views of History*. New York: C. Scribner's Sons, 1949.

Nietzsche, Friedrich. *Taschenausgabe*. Vol. 11. Leipzig: C. G. Neumann-Verlag, 1906.

Pascal, Blaise. *Entretien avec Monsieur de Sacy sur Epictète et Montaigne, Pensées et Opuscules*. Edited by Braunschweig. Paris: Hachette-Classiques Français, n.d.

Peroutka, Ferdinand. *Democratic Manifesto*. New York: Voyages Press, 1959.

Pierce, Roy. *Contemporary French Political Thought*. London, New York: Oxford University Press, 1966.

Popper, Karl. *The Open Society and Its Enemies*. Princeton, N.J.: Princeton University Press, 1950.

Rauschning, Hermann. *The Revolution of Nihilism; Warning to the West*. New York: Alliance Book Company, Longmans, Green and Co., 1939.

Russell, Bertrand. *Mysticism and Logic, and Other Essays*. London: George Allen and Unwin Ltd., 1917.

Scheler, Max. *The Nature of Sympathy*. Translated by Peter Heath.

Introduction by W. Stark. London: Routledge and K. Paul, 1954.

Schlick, Moritz. *Problems of Ethics.* New York: Prentice Hall, Inc., 1939.

Spengler, Oswald. *Untergang des Abendlandes,* vol. 2. Munich: C. H. Beck Verlag, 1921.

Tillich, Paul. "Existential Philosophy." *Journal of the History of Ideas* 2 (January 1944): 44–70.

———. *The Interpretation of History.* New York: C. Scribner's Sons, 1936.

———. *The Courage to Be.* New Haven: Yale University Press, 1952.

———. *Politische Bedeutung der Utopie im Leben der Voelker.* Berlin: Geber Weiss, 1957.

Tison-Braun, Micheline. *La Crise de l'Humanisme.* Vol. 2. Librairie Nizet, Paris, 1967.

Troeltsch, Ernst D. *Der Historismus und seine Probleme; in Gesammelte Schriften.* Vol. 3. Berlin: J. C. B. Mohr, 1922.

Trotsky, Leon D. *The Revolution Betrayed; What is the Soviet Union and Where Is It Going?* New York: Pioneer Publishers, 1945.

Toynbee, Arnold. *A Study of History;* Abridgment of Vols. I-X by D. C. Somervell. New York, London: Oxford University Press, 1947 and 1957.

Wahl, Jean. *Esquisse pour une Histoire de l'Existentialisme.* Paris: L'Arche, 1949.

Weber, Max. *From Max Weber: Essays in Sociology.* Translated, edited and with an introduction by H. H. Gerth and C. Wright Mills. New York: Oxford University Press, 1958.

Wilhote, Fred H., Jr. *Beyond Nihilism.* Louisiana State University Press, Baton Rouge, 1968.

Wolheim, Richard. "The Political Philosophy of Existentialism." The Cambridge Journal 7, no. 1 (October 1953): 3–19.

Index